Oakland Community College
Orchard Ridge Campus Library
27055 Orchard Lake Road
Farmington Hills, MI 48018

D1252382

DATE DUE

Oakland Community College
Orchard Ridge Library
27055 Orchard Lake Road
Farmington Hills, MI 48334

DEMCO

A History of Household Government in America

Carole Shammas

University of Virginia Press
CHARLOTTESVILLE AND LONDON

University of Virginia Press
© 2002 by the Rector and Visitors of the University of Virginia
All rights reserved
Printed in the United States of America on acid-free paper

First published 2002

1 3 5 7 9 8 6 4 2

Frontispiece: William Hogarth, *William Stroude Family.*
Courtesy of Tate Gallery, London / Art Resource, New York

LIBRARY OF CONGRESS CATALOGING-IN-PUBLICATION DATA

Shammas, Carole.
    A history of household government in America /
Carole Shammas.
        p.   cm.
Includes bibliographical references and index.
    ISBN 0-8139-2125-2 (hard : alk. paper) —
ISBN 0-8139-2126-0 (pbk. : alk. paper)
    1. Family—United States—History.
    2. Households—United States—History.
    3. Domestic relations—United States—History.
    4. Sex role—United States—History.   I. Title.
    HQ536 .S4814 2002
    306.85'0973—dc21

2002006062

For Darryl Holter

CONTENTS

ILLUSTRATIONS

TABLES

PREFACE AND
ACKNOWLEDGMENTS

THIS BOOK IS A HISTORY OF HOUSEHOLD GOVERNMENT IN THE UNITED States. I write *household* rather than *family*, because I am not interested strictly in those persons related to one another by genes or marriage but in a broader group held together today by coresidency and earlier by dependents' relationship with the head.[1]

While many societies in the past and present have relied on household government for the supervision and disciplining of their populations, the relevance of this history to the general political history of the nation has not been appreciated. That generalization certainly applies to the United States. The household is the crucial institution linking the history of the British American colonies with the history of the early republic. Most inhabitants of early America had no direct access to the state; the household head mediated between his dependents, whether children, wife, servants, slaves, or wards and formal governmental bodies. It is impossible to incorporate gender, race, and class into a coherent political narrative for the seventeenth and eighteenth centuries without considering household authority and dependency. The laws governing the operation of coverture, minors and orphans, masters and servants, and slavery are the mass politics during most of the early American period.

Much more central to the definition of a modern United States in the middle of nineteenth century than industrialization or urbanization is the disintegration in the powers of the household head: the increasing ability of wives, children, and labor to exit legally from their relationship with the head and the placing of limitations on his control of their property and labor. The nation did not have a majority of its population living in urban places until 1920. Industrialization was a revolution for a very small number of businesses by mid-century, with changes in technology and the organization of labor and capital occurring incrementally over the 1800s and well into the 1900s. In contrast, a flood of legislation in a forty-year period between 1840 and 1880 forever changed the relationships between head and dependents, eliminating statuses definitely viewed as nonmodern. The functions of the state were also altered. Whereas in many other countries the secular authorities had to wrest control of social welfare matters from ecclesiastical officials and institutions, in the United States the welfare state initially developed in response to issues of household management.

In 1980, the United States Census Bureau replaced the term *head of household* with the designation *householder,* a status any person can assume by grabbing the form out of the mailbox first and placing his or her name on the top line. In a formal sense, the position no longer exists in America, though the label *dependent* is still around. With an uncertain future, it seems household government should acquire a past.

This book had its beginnings in an essay I wrote in 1994 for a forum cosponsored by the Omohundro Institute for Early American History and Culture and the Huntington Library. I thank those institutions and most particularly Ronald Hoffman and Roy Ritchie for that opportunity. On that occasion, I benefited greatly by the comments of Michael McGiffert, then editor of the *William and Mary Quarterly,* Patricia Seed, Richard White, and, as always, Daniel Scott Smith. Parts of chapter 2 later appeared in the *Quarterly* as "Anglo-American Household Government in Comparative Perspective" (3rd ser., 52 [1995]: 104–44, and response, 163–66), and I appreciate their allowing me to include them in this book.

Portions of the manuscript were presented to the History Seminar at the University of Minnesota; the Andrew Mellon Seminar at Johns Hopkins University; the Early American History Seminar at the Huntington Library; and, on three different occasions, to my colleagues in the College of Letters, Arts, and Sciences at the University of Southern California. I derived a good sense of the weaknesses in the argument from those encounters. The College and its dean, Joseph Aoun, have provided research support through the John R. Hubbard Chair and other funds as well as a congenial work environment. For research assistance, I am greatly indebted to Lynn Sacco—then USC history graduate student and former lawyer, now Ph.D.—for the magnificent job she did in compiling early American and nineteenth-century laws on family dependents and in finding obscure but valuable secondary sources. Hisako Matsuo, Kate Fawver, and Shirli Brautbar also assisted with the research, as did Andrea Gronwald, who, in addition, helped in preparing the manuscript for the press. Stephanie Schnorbus created the index. I very much appreciated the fine copyediting work of Susan Brady. Margo Anderson, Lois Banner, Holly Brewer, Judy Coffin, Philip Ethington, Philip Morgan, Peter Onuf, and Sharon Salinger all furnished advice or references in their areas of expertise. Thanks as well to Richard Holway and the University of Virginia Press. Despite the depressing subject matter, Darryl Holter loyally read and commented on the entire manuscript.

A HISTORY OF
HOUSEHOLD GOVERNMENT
IN AMERICA

1

THE HOUSEHOLD GETS A WAR
AND A HISTORY

IN JANUARY 1864, IN THE MIDST OF THE CIVIL WAR, HARVARD UNDER-graduate John Fiske wrote to his fiancée about how he rang in the New Year.

Thursday evening I began reading Henry Sumner Maine's *Ancient Law* and read it all New Year's, finishing it at exactly midnight. No novel that I ever read enchained me more. . . . Years of study are richly rewarded when they enable one to experience such an intellectual ecstasy as I felt New Year's Day![1]

"I have passed through an era," he added dramatically, "and entered upon a new Epoch of my life!" Decades later, Fiske, who went on to become a popular historian and lecturer, continued to regard *Ancient Law* as one of the "really Great books," among the few that "have quite changed the aspect of the questions with which they deal." "Maine's lucid exposition of early ideas regarding contract, property, and family relationship," he explained, "obliges us to look at all the phenomena of society from an altered standpoint."[2] Although we do not know how his fiancée reacted—she may have thought his passion somewhat misdirected—others apparently shared Fiske's opinion, as publishers on both sides of the Atlantic frequently issued reprints and new editions of *Ancient Law* for the remainder of the nineteenth century. It has been characterized as "the only legal best-seller of that or perhaps any other century."[3]

Why it achieved best-seller status, though, does not emerge immediately from either the title or Henry Maine's rather dry opening description. "The chief object" of the book, he declared, is "to indicate some of the earliest ideas of mankind, as they are reflected in Ancient Law, and to point out the relation of those ideas to modern thought." More specifically, Maine, a British law professor and occasional journalist, took laws and texts of societies with which many educated Victorian-era readers had some passing familiarity—the Old Testament, Homer, the civil law, the English common law, the Enlightenment philosophy of Locke and Rousseau—mixed them in with some that were of current interest in imperial circles, such as the Hindu legal code of India, and wove them into a history of human development that went right up to "progressive societies" of his own day.[4]

To Maine, the written record of the cultures he examined revealed a clear pattern of development in which changes in the family and household played a crucial role. The still popular view, derived from eighteenth-century philosophers, that societies had their beginnings in social contracts made by individuals out of enlightened self-interest could not be supported by the evidence from ancient societies or even from contemporary Hindu-speaking cultures that had been relatively untouched by the individualism of western Europe. Rather, Maine felt that the earliest laws baldly exposed the intense patriarchal nature of the earliest governments, indicating their familial origins. In the most ancient societies, he contended, "the eldest male parent—the eldest ascendant—is absolutely supreme in his household. His dominion extends to life and death, and is as unqualified over his children and their houses as over his slaves."[5] The early state was no more than an aggregation of these families into a house, or gens, and from a gens into a tribe. People identified not with a territorial unit, but with their tribe, which they thought of as being of one "blood," even if the association had been achieved through adoption or enslavement. In this context, family and household were interchangeable words and were so used, as all those owing obedience to a particular household head were part of the "family." Family government was *the* government.

As societies evolved—for example, Rome in the imperial period—the authority of the household head shrank. The civil magistrates took over the job of trying and punishing dependents for serious crimes, and dependents obtained some ability to counter patriarchal power. While the feudal period, according to Maine, temporarily brought back some of the more despotic features of household government, the trend in western Europe since that time had moved more and more in the direction of freedom from patriarchal control. Societal change, he wrote,

has been distinguished by the gradual dissolution of family dependency, and the growth of individual obligation in its place. The Individual is steadily substituted for the Family, as the unit of which civil laws take account. . . . Nor is it difficult to see what is the tie between man and man which replaces by degrees those forms of reciprocity in rights and duties which have their origin in the Family. It is Contract.[6]

Ancient Law offered a political history of the household.[7] Today we would say Maine "historicized" family rule. He traced changes in the authority of the household head over time and among different legal cultures. The concept of household government has had a long history, although the terminology to describe the institution has varied. Aristotle's *Politics* commences with a discussion of the dependent relationships involved in *oikonomike* (household rule).[8] European countries whose legal codes followed Roman law wrote of the *patria potestas* (paternal power). Use of that term is not normally seen among the English. Robert Filmer, the defender of the royal prerogative, entitled his book simply *Patriarcha*. When early modern common law authorities such as Mathew Hale and William Blackstone categorized the laws regarding persons, they borrowed from the Greek tradition by referring to the rights and duties of master and servant, husband and wife, parent and child, and guardian and ward as all being under "relations oeconomical," by which they meant relations of the household. They drew a distinction between those relations and the "political," or "public," relations of kings, magistrates, and subjects, although both involved governance and formed part of the civil order.[9] After liberal theorists of commerce and wealth appropriated the term *economic* to refer to the production and distribution of goods and services, the writers of late eighteenth- and nineteenth-century United States legal treatises switched to the Latin root for household, *domus,* and grouped household dependencies under the term *domestic relations.*[10] In early modern religious and political documents designed for a more general audience, the term *family government* cropped up most often. *Family,* however, did not mean relatives, as it does today;. instead it referred to those who were under the authority of the household head and usually resident with him. This uderstanding of the term *family*—in which servants and slaves are considered part of the family—today is more often expressed by the term *household.*[11] Whatever the term used, these writers treated household organization as fixed. Maine, on the other hand, treated the institution as inevitably evolving, with the powers of the household head disintegrating over time. To him, patriarchal household government was a stage, not a constant.

The discrepancy between popular Victorian-era conceptions of appropriate family behavior and the inappropriate domestic behavior indicated in laws and texts of societies otherwise held up as models for emulation had grown very great. Maine's patriarchal theory provided an interpretation that explained this discrepancy. For these readers, *Ancient Law* could make sense of those puzzling family interactions encountered in the Bible that hardly seemed very Christian. One can well imagine a reader of the time thinking, "So this is why it was all right for Abraham and Jacob to sleep with their wives' maids, why Abraham had the authority to make a burnt offering of his son, and why Jacob's prospective father-in-law, Laban, forced Jacob to take both of his daughters, Leah and Rachel, as wives." It could also explain all those tedious *begats*, tracing father and son relationships through dozens of generations.

Patria potestas in Roman law also received a context. Victorians had been encouraged to rid their own customary law codes of irrationalities by adopting provisions from the highly touted Roman legal tradition, but that tradition originally included a father's right to take the life of his children, to force a wife on his son or a husband on his daughter or order them to divorce, and to transfer or sell dependents to another family. The discovery of similar types of patriarchal power in Hindu law suggested the universality not of the institution, but of this stage in human development. Maine's theory of "status to contract" allowed one to go from that stage all the way to the Victorian family as depicted in that era's sentimental novels and prints of comfortable domestic interiors.

Whether writers were working independently on the origins of human social and political units or were inspired by *Ancient Law* to contribute to the subject, a slew of books on the subject came out on the heels of Maine's book.[12] Clearly, great minds of the era were running in the same channel. Some authors, like the French historian N. D. Fustel de Coulanges, came to similar conclusions.[13] Many, however, questioned Maine's chronology of household development. They did not criticize what came to be his most famous contribution, his theory of the transition from a status-based to a more modern contract-based society. Rather they attacked him for assuming that human society began as a patriarchy. Scouring ancient writings, myths, artifacts of European and Middle Eastern cultures, and later travelers' accounts of "primitive" societies in the Americas, Africa, and Asia, writer after writer refuted this notion by providing examples of societies in which men were not in control or were not responsible for women and children. Instead investigators pointed to evidence that families began as "promiscuous" groupings and then transformed themselves into matrifocal (mother-centered) households. Patriarchy came at a later stage.

The most notorious of these mother-power advocates was Swiss-born Johann Jakob Bachofen, who published his book in the same year that *Ancient Law* appeared. Like Maine and many of those who came to write on the subject, Bachofen was an expert in Roman law, but unlike Maine, he relied heavily on evidence from ancient mythology, religion, and art to support his theory, according to which patriarchal household authority had suppressed an earlier matriarchal order. He contended that traces of this matriarchal order could be seen in such things as the Lycians' naming their children after their mothers and in the feminine characteristics of Egyptian statuary. Women had initiated civilized society in order to put an end to the violent and lustful behavior of men in a sexually promiscuous society, only to be subsequently overthrown by a higher-level patriarchal order that was more civilized but lacked certain spiritual qualities.[14]

The work of American Lewis Morgan on northeastern American Indians exerted much more influence over the subsequent direction of research. This intellectually inclined lawyer from Rochester, New York, has been credited with "inventing kinship."[15] Morgan first became interested in Indian lineage questions when he helped in the formation of an upstate New York fraternal club that appropriated the tribal names and confederate organization of the Iroquois. With a characteristic seriousness of purpose, he undertook a thoroughgoing review of all written materials on the group as well as making contact with Indians living in the area. Morgan's first book on the Iroquois, which he wrote in 1851 to "encourage a kinder feeling towards the Indian," contained a chapter on the lineage system and its role in holding together society.[16]

The Iroquois, Morgan noted, like the Jews of the Old Testament, had a tribal order, "the most simple organization of society." But unlike the Jews, the Iroquois traced descent following the female line. Men rose to leadership in a tribe through their mothers' lineage, not their fathers'. Sons and daughters inherited status and property rights from their mother. Furthermore, all distinctions between lineal descendants and collateral kin collapse, as children of all sisters were considered brothers and sisters to one another.

The implications of these differences, however, Morgan did not develop in detail until a few years later, after he found that many other Indian tribes also favored this system, and after the publication of Maine's work.[17] Morgan argued that the kinship patterns of Indian groups provided insight into "the history and experience of our own remote ancestors when in corresponding conditions."[18] In other words, the developmental stages of human society could be traced anthropologically by studying the customs of groups that had not yet entered the stage of civilization. The Iroquois and their matrilineal system typified the stage of barbarism, the stage between savagery and civilization through which all societies must pass. Clearly in this type of family system, the authority of a household head was very different from what the historic record suggests about European family governance. Indeed, even the household unit itself seemed unimportant compared to the greater kin group.

John Ferguson McLennan, a Scottish lawyer, also took on Maine for assuming that the patriarchal family was the primordial social unit. The key to unraveling the mystery of family origins, in McLennan's opinion, was a peculiar ritual—the enactment of bridal capture in marriage ceremonies—that he encountered in accounts of disparate ancient societies. In his 1865 book *Primitive Marriage,* he hypothesized that this ritual reflected what had been an actual practice at an earlier time. A shortage of women explained the need for these captures. That shortage also would have necessitated polyandry, and polyandry meant that matrilineal descent would have had to precede patrilineal. To McLennan, we owe the terms *endogamy* and *exogamy,* and so he vies with Morgan for the title "inventor of kinship."[19]

Soon the origins of patriarchy became a subject about which few self-respecting scholars could refrain from theorizing.[20] These debates have been chronicled by a number of historians.[21] Sometimes it is assumed that evolutionary theories of society simply sprang into being after the publication of Darwin's *Origin of Species.* But a closer examination of the dates when people like Maine, Bachofen, and Morgan began their ruminations indicates that these writers' speculations preceded the 1859 publication date of Darwin's book.[22] Darwin may have helped create an audience for these theorists' work—Maine's admirer Fiske, for example, had read Darwin's *Origin of Species* with similar enthusiasm a couple of years before tackling *Ancient Law*—but Darwin's research cannot explain their own.[23]

Others trying to explain the emergence of the debate point to scientific discoveries such as the dating of fossils that undercut the biblical chronology and resulted in the declining use of the Judaic-Christian text as a source for understanding changes in humans and in society.[24] At the same time, thanks to imperialism, more and more cultures not mentioned in the Scriptures and exhibiting decidedly non-Christianlike behavior surfaced in travel literature.[25]

While both of these factors certainly became important in pushing intellectuals to develop a new paradigm for studying society, both had been around a long time. Most eighteenth-century Enlightenment figures had little affection for literal interpretations of the Bible, so why didn't this debate break out then? Travel literature detailing the family life— or, by western European standards, the lack thereof—among peoples in Asia, Africa, and the Americas go back to the sixteenth century. Proto-ethnologists in the Society of Jesus carefully recorded the deviations in kinship and marriage practices they observed among Indian groups in the early eighteenth century.[26] Why didn't anyone try to reconcile the obvious contradictions in household forms earlier?

In fact, efforts to formulate an evolutionary account of patriarchal authority can be found in the late eighteenth century—one hundred years before Maine published his book—among what J. G. A. Pocock has termed the "enlightened narratives."[27] Adam Smith, delivering a series of lectures on jurisprudence at Glasgow University in the 1760s, sketched out a history of household authority in which household heads in "rude nations" exerted greater power over wives, children, and servants than did their counterparts in civilizations from Rome to eighteenth-century Britain, where men experienced a declining ability to divorce easily, leave children to die, and hold slaves. Yet Smith stopped short of fitting household government neatly into his theory of stages of society, perhaps because polygamy, infanticide, and slavery continued to exist in so many areas of the world that could not be dismissed as "rude." Interestingly, Smith associated freedom and equality among family members with a strong monarch and a Christian clergy. Weak civil government encouraged household domination as did, in his view, a republican polity, due to the fact that the ruling class owned slaves.[28] "We are apt," he wrote, "to imagine that slavery is entirely abolished at this time, without considering that this is the case in only a small part of Europe." After pointing out that it prevailed in Asia, Africa, Muscovy, and "the greatest part of America," he predicted that "it is indeed almost impossible that it should ever be . . . abolished. In a republican government it will scarcely ever happen. . . . The persons who make all the laws in that country are persons who have slaves themselves."[29]

Adam Smith's pupil and then colleague at Glasgow, John Millar, however, had less difficulty in identifying an evolutionary pattern. The first edition of John Millar's *Observations Concerning the Distinction of Ranks in Society* came out in 1771, and an expanded version soon followed in 1773. Millar, who held a professorship at Glasgow University until his death in 1801, was—like almost all of the nineteenth-century writers on household government—a specialist in civil law. He used similar sources and anticipated their major arguments. Millar considered the family as the origin of society: "When the members of a family become too numerous to be all maintained and lodged in the same house, some of them are under the necessity of leaving it. . . . Thus the original society is gradually enlarged into a village or tribe."[30] He believed the condition of women, children, and servants gradually improved as societies progressed in stages from rude and barbarous times, to pastoral, then to agricultural, finally becoming commercial societies with thriving "arts and manufactures." Millar began his narrative with women, presumably because he regarded the development of marriage as being essential to civilization and better treatment for all dependents of the household head. How marriage improved women's lives is complicated by his discussion of the premarriage stage when—according to the accounts of ancient Greek, American Indian, and East Indian cultures—the mother was the principal person in the family and had the primary connection to the children. Aside from this digression, to which I will return at the end of this book, Millar's story is basically one of progress.

He traces the improvement in the treatment of children and servants (both described in a way that suggests males, not females), including their right to hold property, not to be sold as slaves, and to marry. Women, having gained the protection of marriage, first cloistered themselves from the generality of men; later, with further improvements in society, they felt safe enough to enter more freely into public life. Millar does warn that under certain circumstances affluence produced dissolute behavior, and he worried that in a "commercial age . . . the members of a family will be raised to greater independence than is consistent with good order, and with a proper domestic subordination."[31] In the 1806 edition, coming after the period of the French Revolution and the rise of Napoleon, Millar dwelled more on Roman examples that demonstrated the role of luxurious living in promoting prostitution and easy divorce. He viewed these developments as posing a threat to the continued rise in female status.[32] But this edition also drew attention to positive actions in Britain and North America to eliminate slavery.[33] Throughout the various versions of the book, his point remained that the more economically developed the nation, the weaker the patriarchal authority of husband, father, and master.

Although Millar made arguments that were destined to become widely accepted, no one picked up on his work in the late eighteenth century or thereafter. It disappeared, and even with the mid-nineteenth-century burst of interest in the evolution of the household, only his fellow Scot McLennan belatedly looked up his volume and cited it.[34]

Probably the biggest difference between Millar's world and that of a century later is that by then theorists and the reading public had been bombarded by decades of controversies concerning the relationships between the household head and his dependents. Not only could the folly of modeling state relations on household ones—the controversy that had engaged Filmer and Locke centuries earlier—be demonstrated, but the very future of governance at the household level could be questioned. The international antislavery movement, the movements in the English-speaking world and much of western Europe to allow divorce and to grant women child custody and property rights, and the push for public schooling for children previously considered to be under the disposition of fathers and masters alerted even the least socially aware that something was afoot. The figure of the master took on a sinister, deviant cast, and the husband and the father could be charged with operating in his interest rather than his wife's and his child's. International movements concerning the rights of household dependents were in effect movements to reduce the patriarchal authority of the head in all of his various roles. So if patriarchal prerogatives could evolve into some other form of family governance, it stood to reason that they had once evolved from something else.

Those who initially launched the investigation into the evolution of the family—Maine, Morgan, Bachofen, McLennan—could hardly be described as a radical group in terms of household politics. Personally, they settled into quite conventional, if not staunchly conservative, domestic arrangements, and none took a prominent public role in the cause of slave, servant, female, or child emancipation. Mid-nineteenth-century activists in these causes more often relied on arguments derived from natural rights, republican, or liberal Protestant ideology. The evolutionary theories of family development advanced by this first group of theorists may have been a way to explain and thus manage the change that seemed to be going on around them. The framework they imposed was a way of demonstrating that society was evolving, not dissolving into anarchy.

For example, Maine, writing in 1861—far from a time of consensus about the rights of dependents—seemed so pleased at having identified the withering away of patriarchy and the triumph of individualism that he tended to ignore the formidable institutional arrangements that continued to stand in the way of dependents going their own way. One rather unreflective contemporary reader remarked that Maine's interpretation described "a revolution of one thousand years of constant progress, without a violent shock throughout!"[35] Later in life, as he grew much more appreciative of hierarchy, Maine corrected his error, but not in *Ancient Law*. In one passage, Maine claimed that "in Western Europe . . . the status of the Slave has disappeared." While technically correct, in the colonies of western European countries slavery had expanded for three hundred years and had a sizable group of defenders. It also had provoked an international movement organized to end the practice. As Maine's book was coming off the press, the United States commenced a bloody war over the issue. In the same year, John Stuart Mill began writing his famous philosophical essay on inequality between the sexes, *The Subjection of Women*. Women's rights advocates had launched a campaign to remove married women from the arbitrary authority of husbands in not only England and the United States but elsewhere in Europe as well, including France and Germany. All undoubtedly would have found rather disingenuous Maine's assertion that "the status of the Female under Tutelage, if the tutelage be understood of persons other than her husband, has also ceased to exist," given the power of the exception and the clamor against the passage of legislation favoring women's legal independence.[36]

Although Bachofen, Morgan, and McLennan attacked Maine's patriarchal theory for ignoring an earlier stage of matrilineal-based societies, they also placed patriarchal societies in a more advanced stage in the evolutionary process. Family units of large lineage groups that were reckoned through the mother and emphasized the mother-child bond fell into the "primitive" category and thus could hardly be seen as a viable alternative in the civilized world. None of these social scientists predicted a *future* of matrifocal family units. To them, things were progressing, step by step, in the right direction.

Yet it does not seem that in the society of the time household heads and their dependents moved happily and conflict-free into autonomous individuality. Scholars could give patriarchal authority a past, but neither they nor anyone else knew its future. In the mid-nineteenth-century England of Henry Maine—and even more so in the United States—one's legal position still depended to a large extent on a person's position in the household. The notion that such dependency was necessary for the continued prosperity of society had supporters as powerful or more powerful than those who argued in the name of the individual. While today the rationale for maintaining bound servitude, child labor, bastardy, coverture, and marriage without possibility of exit save death may seem less than compelling, contemporary defenders marshaled a long pedigree of precedents and traditions as justification for the way that they thought family relations should be restored or reinvigorated.

What Maine and his colleagues were trying to explain away was really a household civil war, and nowhere was its presence more obvious than in the United States. The best-known part of it—the fight over the enslaved dependents of southern and western household heads—turned into a real war in 1861. The enormity of the Civil War—the deaths, the devastation, the constitutional crisis—has until recently obscured the relationship of that struggle to the other battles, more civil perhaps but nonetheless of major consequence, being waged against the authority of the household head. Over the last few years, a number of studies have appeared that link the struggle between slave and master with the conflict over household authority in general.[37]

In the North, slavery had been abolished, indentured servitude had disappeared, and all types of servitude itself had come to be viewed as degrading.[38] Abolitionists took things a step further and connected the moral reformation of the human race to the eradication of the master's control over slaves. Perhaps the most disturbing charge made by these abolitionists—and the one that gained them the most attention—was their assertion that the archaic patriarchal power of the slave master led to dreadful consequences for the families of both whites and blacks. Victorians enjoyed railing against the uncivilized behavior of non-Christian societies. Hindu and Moslem cultures were objects of scorn for their poor treatment of women, as evidenced by their practices of polygamy and concubinage and by their keeping of harems. American women were supposedly protected from that kind of treatment, but—as the abolitionists pointed out—slaveholders could have harems without fear of legal action. Frederick Douglass, a former slave who became an important political figure in the antebellum and postbellum United States, began his moving *Narrative of an American Slave* with the disclosure that his and his mother's master was also probably his father. Page after page of description of his master's arbitrary and cruel behavior follow, made all the worse to his readers because the perpetrator was also his progenitor. To use Maine's terms, the continued reliance on status rather than contract relationships between free people poisoned household relations.[39]

Most of the white population in the southern United States still supported slavery on the grounds that African Americans could not manage their own households and needed the slave master to take care of them. Prints of happy slaves much better off with their plantation master than were the free factory workers slaving away in the North or Great Britain underscored the point. In one print entitled *America* (1841), the slave thanks "massa" for taking care of him, and "massa," speaking to his white family, explains that "these poor creatures are a sacred legacy from my ancestors" and magnanimously vows that "while a dollar is left me, nothing shall be spared to increase their comfort."[40]

In their efforts to justify chattel slavery, some white southerners glorified the exercise of strong patriarchal authority generally. George Fitzhugh, the most frequently quoted apologist for slavery, argued that a good part of the world operated happily under family government where "slaves, wives and children . . . do not come directly in contact with the institutions and rulers of the State." Yet he also could spew forth elements of the Victorian domestic feminism that logically emanated from a separate spheres ideology. "Woman is better than man," he wrote in 1861. "She is of more delicate and refined fibre, more sensitive, more alive to impressions from without, more sympathetic, more benevolent; better, therefore, by nature."[41] Why, in a Christian society, men should rule when women were morally superior is the kind of internal contradiction that characterized the reasoning of these latter-day patriarchs.

The United States also was the site of the first full-fledged uprising of female dependents. A group of women's rights advocates gathered at Seneca Falls in upstate New York in 1848. They used the text of the Declaration of Independence to make their point, replacing George III with "man," and the colonists with "women." Organization of state associations and lobbying followed. Though they and their supporters fought on the floor of state legislatures and not on battlefields, they framed women's struggle for legal recognition in a human rights context similar to the one employed by the antislavery forces. There were a few like Margaret Fuller, the Boston intellectual, who would maintain that if they wanted, "women should be sea captains!" but the primary objectives of the first feminists were not equal opportunities in the job market or in the political arena. Rather their goal was the empowerment of women in households, and this was a tricky issue.

The major function served by the separate spheres ideology constructed over the course of the nineteenth century was to justify the granting of citizenship rights to men—whether they were household heads or not—while denying them to women, on the basis that females had won enhanced moral authority in the home. When men were fools, drunkards, or wastrels, though, women had a hard time keeping the domestic sphere in orbit. Still, the household could not have two heads. Only the man could represent the family to the outside world. Moreover, how could women with no education or experience in commerce manage their own property, make wills, go to court? State legislatures, which had the authority over most family issues, argued over bills that limited the control husbands had over the property and earnings of their wives. They debated acts giving judges the right to strip fathers of custody of their children if that change in custody appeared to be in the best interest of the child. They also squabbled over changes to divorce laws, some ultimately allowing cruelty as a ground for dissolution of a marriage. Such laws, the first anywhere in Europe or the Americas, removed the legal protection husbands had for physical correction of their spouses as well as making it easier for women to exit a marriage.[42]

Suspicion of the motives of women's rights advocates ran high. If women became involved in the public sphere, who would care for the five to six children born to the average woman in the mid-nineteenth century, and who would assume the other domestic responsibilities? Was that the agenda of the "Amazons," as the press called women like those at Seneca Falls—to subjugate men and bring the propagation of the human race to a halt? Those joining the Mormon movement argued for a return to biblical-style patriarchy as a better way to ensure the happiness and welfare of household dependents. Utopian socialists thought communal upbringing the panacea.

As a final affront to the household patriarch, reformers began to speak up for children's rights as well. Besides the efforts in northern state legislatures to deprive abusive men of their right to the custody, guardianship, and apprenticing of their children, a free public school movement spread throughout the United States during the antebellum period. Many felt, however, that a father's right to control the education and labor of his children was threatened by these state laws being passed that set up public schools at taxpayers' expense and, even more, by bills being introduced that mandated the minimum number of days children must attend. Traditionally, the household head decided when children—whether sons, daughters, apprentices, or servants—received education and when they worked. Large families depended on the work or the outside wages of youth. Otherwise, a wife who was supposed to be providing household services (childcare, meals, laundry) had to neglect those duties and spend time in market work. The mid-nineteenth-century movement for public education pitted the economic and political needs of the republic and the social mobility of an older child against the material well-being of the rest of the family, especially mothers and the very young. Consequently, even the greatest nineteenth-century advocate for universal public education in the United States, Horace Mann, feared interfering with the household head's control over the labor of his children.[43] Public schools cropped up all over the United States, though, making it difficult to argue that the decision to educate a child rested with the father.[44]

Within a decade, the theorizing on the family took a sharper, more political tone. Gone was the sunny optimism of Maine's 1861 work and the academic character of the arguments in Bachofen, Morgan, and McLennan about the early mother-centered family. Accepting the concept that a change had occurred, theorists wanted to deal with the implications. Radicals like Friedrich Engels—who wrote the book Karl Marx had intended to compose, *The Origins of the Family, Private Property, and the State* (1884)—gleefully anticipated the end of the family. "The English jurist H. S. Maine thought he had made a tremendous discovery," sniffed Engels, "when he said that our whole progress . . . consisted in the fact that we had passed 'from status to contract,' . . . which, in so far as it is correct, was already in *The Communist Manifesto.*"[45] Engels's new book—which drew attention to the way Lewis Morgan's work supported Marx's point that the accumulation of property had produced the patriarchal family—predicted that the overthrow of capitalism would result in the eventual triumph of free-love relationships and the communal rearing of the young. Some European and North American feminists, often with socialist affiliations, combined an interest in state assistance for women and children with a call for sexual emancipation.[46]

Other theorists, however, grew less rather than more revolutionary on the subject of household evolution and expressed concerns that already things had gone too far. Back in 1850, when he published his first book, *Social Statics,* Herbert Spencer implied that the family had undergone an evolution by arguing that anything short of complete equality for women and children meant marital slavery and filial subservience, both of which belonged to barbarism, not civilization. By 1864, his staunchly egalitarian position obviously embarrassed him, because he wrote in the introduction to the American edition that if he had had time to revise the book, he would "now make qualifications to the chapters on Rights of Women and on Rights of Children."[47] By 1876, Spencer had arguably become the most widely read social theorist in the English language, and for the first time he set out in full his own version of household history. In *Principles of Sociology*, his families evolved from the low level of promiscuity and matrifocal social groups, to polygamy, to the monogamous unit characteristic of his own Victorian society. Spencer no longer worried about the rights of women and children. He fretted about the future of the family. "Is there any limit," he asked, "to disintegration of the family? . . . Are we on our way to a condition like that reached by sundry communistic aggregates in America and elsewhere?" Spencer suspected that "probably the rhythm of change, conforming to its usual law, has carried us from the one extreme a long way towards the other extreme; and a return movement is to be looked for." Women had grown brazen and clamored for inappropriate rights that actually would be unfair to men, while "juvenile freedom" had in some places—"I refer to the United States"—gone too far as well. "Functions of the parents have been too far assumed by the State," he scolded.[48]

Lecturing on the other side of the Atlantic about the new research of Maine, McLennan, and others regarding the primitive family, Henry Adams communicated a similar concern that independence could go too far, as he felt it had in regard to the legal rights of women in certain periods of Roman history. While he did not support the "re-establishment of the family in [its] sterner aspect," he counseled against taking "the independence of women to its logical extreme" and warned that allowing the family "to fall into contempt" would bring a violent reaction.[49] Carl Starcke, a Danish theorist on the primitive family, also felt compelled to comment on this peril. In a book published first in German in 1888, he, like Adams, warned against repeating the errors of the Romans in regard to female property and divorce. In his analysis, he blamed "the movement in favour of the greater independence of women which is now so strong" on unmarried women, who, having no place in the family system, sought a dangerous form of equality.

The unmarried, whether man or woman, are and must always remain the exception, and they must accept whatever is arranged for them. It would be impossible for their sakes to imperil all which the experience of a thousand years has shown to be the best means of promoting the development of those aspects of human life which are the most productive of happiness. The movement for the emancipation of women has not always been mindful of this general law.[50]

A half-century of transatlantic debate on the evolution of the household culminated in 1904 with the publication of *A History of Matrimonial Institutions*, an erudite three-volume study written by an American academic and Progressive, George Elliott Howard.[51] Howard can be grouped with the historical institutionalists, men and women who helped establish the first social science disciplines in the United States during the 1880s and 1890s. At the beginning, this group stressed the centrality of the history of the household in their theories about the creation of modern society.[52] Reform-minded, they moved back and forth among academia, public service, and political activism, and as a result their research often had obvious policy implications. Their interests and those of the Settlement House women—who represented what has come to be known as the female dominion of reform—often overlapped.[53] Rather than offering strong rebuttals to views such as those expressed by Spencer, Starke, and Adams, the historical institutionalists presented alternative explanations and solutions, because they too believed the family was in a state of disintegration and had to be bolstered. While they more and more favored state action to stabilize families in distress, they also emphasized ways to preserve the household as a social and private institution. Most has been written about the high-profile women of the reform movement who described their mission as child saving, but institutionalists like Howard shared these concerns.[54]

Howard's volumes, still useful today, exhaustively reviewed prior studies on the origins of the family, starting with Maine's patriarchal theory. When Howard completed the section on medieval society, however, his geographical focus narrowed to a description of the laws on marriage and divorce in early modern England, the British colonies, and the nineteenth-century United States as background to a hundred-page conclusion on "Problems of Marriage and the Family" in America. Rather than attacking divorce laws for their role in family disintegration, Howard defended them as a means of exit for women and children subject to patriarchal abuse. Instead, Howard identified the longstanding laxity in marriage laws in most of the states in the Union—the young age of consent and the continued existence of common law bonds—as the culprit. His recommendation was to reform marriage laws rather than to close off divorce. To Howard, there was little alternative to the state's assumption of certain powers once wielded by the head of household, because individualism interfered with the fulfilling of family responsibilities. Still, the household had to be preserved, and the best hope for stability lay in a uniform marriage law in the United States, an increase in the age of consent, and an educational program for youth on the subjects of sex and marriage.

A decade later, Columbia Teachers College professor Willystine

Goodsell published *A History of the Family as a Social and Educational Institution*, a book that mimicked Howard's argument. Moving from an examination of the legal arrangements inherent in families in primitive and ancient societies to a discussion of the legal arrangements of the present-day family, Goodsell's study concluded with a long section on the sources of family instability—divorce, desertion, "urban congestion," "commercialization of vice," and low birth rates—as well as an analysis of the solutions proffered by socialists and "moderate" progressives.[55]

Howard and Goodsell were transitional figures, trying to reconcile a scholarship that conceptualized society evolving from a group of household relationships to modern power structures with an emerging taxonomy based on a very different intellectual structure. This structure featured a suspicion of or lack of interest in the old evolutionary framework, a receptivity to dividing the study of humanity into specialized subject areas, and a strong dedication to policy-oriented research.[56]

Only a couple of years after Goodsell's text appeared, a new work came out that made little effort to relate to the older tradition. Arthur W. Calhoun's *A Social History of the American Family: From Colonial Times to the Present* had originated in a long seminar paper for one of the most prominent Progressive institutionalists, E. A. Ross, while Ross taught at the University of Wisconsin, and it had grown to three volumes by the time of its publication in 1917. Calhoun scrapped the whole debate about the family in primitive society, and among the Greeks, the Romans, and so forth. The American family, he wrote, was the product of three factors: "European folkways," traced back no further than the late medieval period; the "economic transition to modern capitalism"; and "the distinctive environment of a virgin continent."[57] European customs of subordination within the household—already weakened by Protestantism—had further degenerated by the time of Independence. This was due not to republican ideology—Calhoun paid no attention to the Revolution—but to the frontier, and then finally to industrialism. The last volume is almost entirely devoted to the problems of the modern family in a time of social revolution. With the frontier gone, the Industrial Revolution undermining the present social order, and the end of class domination in sight, "a new family," Calhoun wrote, "is inevitable," one based on very different economic conditions.[58] Like Goodsell, he took seriously the work of Progressives and socialists—including women such as Elsie Clews Parsons and Charlotte Gilman who wished to experiment with household arrangements—but his framework offered more encouragement to students of the economy and social class than to historians of the household. The use of the term *social* in the title—and here Goodsell's is revealing as well—not only announced a work of policy rather than antiquarian interest but also signaled the resubordination of the household to "economic" forces and its reassignment to the provision of nongovernmental services.

Calhoun's weighty tomes enjoyed a positive reception, but they failed to inspire further work on the history of the American family. Quite to the contrary, the field hibernated for decades. Why? While it is always risky to try to explain why something did not happen, a couple of trends offer some potent suggestions. Institutionalists and the next generation of scholars in the social science departments that the institutionalists created turned more and more to questions centered around the corporate industrial state, an inquiry to which the household now seemed only remotely connected. The decline in the authority of the household head had seemingly separated the household from the state, and the emergence of industrial corporations in which the family was the site for neither labor nor capital completed the severance package. Academia partitioned the study of the family: anthropologists, espousing cultural relativism, got so-called "primitive societies"; sociologists and economists—or more often their feminine partners, social workers and home economists—got the modern family. Whatever fell in between got lost. It especially got lost among historians, because they had no women's auxiliary in the academy.

And then, in the 1920s, the policy angle was losing its urgency. Calhoun wrote at the time of the Bolshevik Revolution and the disarray produced in Europe by World War I. When the middle class turned out to have more resilience than many had thought, and industrialism continued to chug along, a less apocalyptic position—similar to the ones expressed by Maine and others when the debate began—gained new respectability. Marianne Weber had restated this position early in the twentieth century. A German intellectual active in women's rights issues, Max Weber's wife and associate, and a person who experienced firsthand the operation of the double standard in monogamous marriages, she nonetheless favored an interpretation of family development that was more upbeat than the one offered by conservatives, progressives, or socialists. Critical of feminist writers who had seen some paradise lost in the passing of the mother-right horde, she felt that the triumph of the patriarchal family represented a step in the right direction. It fostered separate households and the values of the individual rather than the group. Those values eventually trickled down to dependents and enriched the lives of everyone.[59] Mainstream social science opinion in liberal democracies embraced this version of family development—often labeled modernization theory—more often than any other throughout the first half of the twentieth century.

With the family no longer perceived as being in deep crisis, the last remaining reason to write about its history was withdrawn. Relatively little appeared on the subject in the major works of social theory or history between 1920 and the 1960s.[60] The household had lost its position as the origin of the state, and in modernization theory it had been reduced to a creature of the economy and social class. The emphasis in family studies switched from evolution to staying functional. What later critics would denounce as "therapeutic rhetoric"—which focused on saving marriages and reforming juvenile delinquents—became the prevalent mode of expression, and those employed in relatively low-status, female-dominated helping professions became the principal discussants. The reputation of the early family theorists—from Lewis Morgan to George Elliott Howard—declined in importance as well, seldom receiving serious treatment by historians writing on the origins of American social sciences.[61]

The next and last eruption of academic interest in the household occurred between the mid-1960s and the early 1980s, a period that coincided with generational conflicts, heightened marital instability, a sharp fertility decline, and the second wave of the women's movement. This story has been told many times. As social history triumphed over political history, the family—which had been assigned earlier to the social realm—attracted new attention. Suddenly the actual process by which the family was modernizing—specifically, the adequacy of the extended versus nuclear family construct and its linkage to industrialization—became a very important area of research. Changes in household composition and size attracted the most attention. Books like Peter Laslett's influential *The World We Have Lost* and the demographic community studies done in western Europe and the United States began chipping away at broad assumptions that had been made, usually in the absence of research, about family development. Probably the finest set of quantitative data available in all of American history, the IPUMS census samples, has come out of that preoccupation. Those less quantitatively inclined preferred to examine transformations in the emotional climate of the family. Studying the political and legal structure of household authority over time proved less popular, as the prevailing assumption was that economic factors predetermined household status. As the economy changed, women's work changed, children's educational needs changed, and so on. The work on household structure, which claimed as its prime accomplishment the finding of a basic nuclear family form over the past four centuries, in some ways discouraged further investigation.

The habit of considering family structure only as the result and not the cause of political and economic events and the relegation of it to a private, nongovernmental realm is striking. One still finds in texts on the history of the family assertions such as, "compared to seventeenth-century families, today's families are much more isolated from public life and specialized in functions," with the functions being "the socialization of children and the provision of emotional support and affection."[62] In fact, it could be argued that most household dependents in the seventeenth century were more isolated from public life than their contemporary counterparts, and that specialization has to be related to specific members of the family, not to the family in general, which has no legal functions.

Those intrigued by the power relations between household members split off the task into its constituent parts; some went off into women's history, others into the history of servitude and slavery. By this manner of proceeding, the history of childhood—less robust from the beginning—got strangled in the cradle and has been gasping for life ever since.[63] While putting the elements back together and thinking seriously about what headship and household authority have and have not meant historically is now much more common than it was a decade ago, its impact on how we think about the history of what government does and does not do is still marginal.[64]

Only in that brief interlude during the third quarter of the nineteenth century could it be said that the family's past occupied a central place in social science theory. The first debates on the history of the family were sparked by the tumult around household relations in the mid-nineteenth century, and I argue that those relations took a decisive legal turn at that point. The efforts to change the status of legal dependents in the household is the household's civil war. The story cannot begin there, however. Servitude, slavery, coverture, and the wardship of minors date back to institutional arrangements made in the colonial period. During the first two and a half centuries of Atlantic settlement, the household constituted the primary unit of governance for the vast majority of inhabitants—married women, children, servants, and slaves. They fell subject to the authority of husband, father, or master, and in almost all households a white male head performed these roles. Dependents were allowed to have little *direct* relationship with the rest of the state during the term of their dependency, and they did not have the legal right to sever ties with the household head.

In chapter 2, I ponder the distinctive nature of the household system established by the Atlantic migrants to America in the seventeenth century. While western European nations during the early modern period busily worked to solidify the position of the household head, the colonists in America went far beyond those activities of monarchs and parliaments in expanding the head's jurisdiction. This characterization of the early American household is not the usual one put forward, but it does, I think, explain certain aspects of the colonial political order, particularly why governmental institutions remained so underdeveloped and why slavery became the principal method of incorporating groups such as American Indians and Africans who had very different household systems from the European colonists.

In chapter 3, I speculate on how well the colonial household head could actually rule his dependents given the political developments of the later eighteenth century, specifically the American Revolution and the attack on hierarchical relationships implied by republicanism. Some clues are provided by dipping into what historians have discovered about the households of the Founding Fathers. Doubt is cast on the transformative power of the American Revolution as far as household authority is concerned, which then raises the question: If not the Revolution, then what, beyond the rampant republicanism of the founders' generation, caused the quite powerful American household head to become such an early victim of household egalitarianism? Decades of research have pummeled beyond recognition the stories of European patriarchs journeying to a new land and being progressively weakened by the freedoms their dependents won because of land availability, high sex ratios (more men than women), intense Protestantism, and/or the rise of market relations— all explanations offered at one time or another to account for familial change.[65] The only suspect that has not yet been rounded up is a facet of the family system itself, the extremely weak and truncated lineage forms in colonial Anglo-America and beyond. I follow that line of inquiry in chapter 4 by checking the evidence for one of the household head's supposed powers, the management of his offspring's marriage. Although they do not portray the household head as a tyrant dictating marriage to his son or daughter, most histories do assume that an important difference between early American and modern marriages was the explicit financial deals struck between the bride's and groom's families. Yet I have found evidence about such arrangements peculiarly illusive, which points up a strange vulnerability in the powers of the early American patriarch that seems directly connected to his downfall in the mid-nineteenth century.

Chapter 5 concerns that downfall, what I call the household civil war; the none-too-subtle play on words is intended. Enthusiasm for the asylum by everyone except the inmates and the vogue in communal living presage a period of breathtaking legal change at the state level and a violent civil war nationally over the legal rights of husbands, fathers, and masters. The period of greatest legal turmoil over power in the household—from the 1840s to 1880—coincides with the Victorian era, an age generally depicted in art and literature as being infused with domesticity, affectionate family relationships, and men's and women's satisfaction with their separate spheres. Why that representation emerges at a time of such dissatisfaction with the politics of the household is the puzzle.

In chapter 6, I scrutinize the status of the household after the "war" and into the twentieth century. Of particular interest here is the relationship between the decline in the authority of the household head and the ragged beginnings of the so-called "welfare state." Given the head's weak legal position, one might expect a great alteration in social relations and living arrangements. Why did the brave new worlds of institutional residence and communal living experiments in the end come to little, and why did social welfare advocates return largely to the household as a base for relief payments and for foster care? The peculiar church-state relationship in the United States, the dependence on private charities, and the rivalries among religious denominations are key.

Chapter 7 concludes the book with a reconsideration of the debate that raged in the mid-nineteenth century over the matriarchal origins of the family in light of the late-twentieth-century trends in household composition. While, as Bachofen, Morgan, McLennan, and Marx hypothesized, Indian matrilineal societies soon lost ground to patrilineal households invading from Europe, the presence of matrifocal rather than male-headed or two-parent households has continued in the United States as elsewhere right up to the present day. This "troublesome alternative"—judged primordial or pathological or unstable by every generation of social scientist—has in fact shown remarkable resilience. What is not said in these debates is that the debates themselves exist because children are the last household dependents, and that policy decisions since the beginning of the twentieth century show a firm commitment to keeping children as dependents, not of an institution, but in households under the rule of birth parents, birth parent, adopted parent, or foster parent. Household government is not completely dead.

2

THE EXPANSION OF
HOUSEHOLD GOVERNMENT IN
THE COLONIAL PERIOD

WHY THE UNITED STATES BECAME THE SITE FOR SOME OF THE EARLI-
est and fiercest battles over the powers of the household head as master,
husband, and father is not easily understood without going back to the
colonial period, when the Atlantic migrants not only put into place a English version of household law but began expanding the powers of the
head over his dependents. While a variety of cultural groups with a variety of approaches toward household government inhabited the territory
that ultimately became the United States, the hegemony of the British
Crown over the area east of the Mississippi placed English law in a privileged position during the colonial period, a position it continued to hold
after the formation of the nation. Even today some of the central tenets
of family law in the United States—monogamy and testamentary freedom, for example—derive from principles enunciated centuries earlier as
part of the Christian Church's canon law and the statutes and common
law of England.

By design, the English household head relieved the state of many
governing functions. According to the common law, he could administer
"moderate" physical correction to keep his dependents in line.[1] It was the
household head who decided the guardianship and the educational needs,
if any, of his children. He determined when an injury to them, his wife,
his servants, or their property required court action. In most circumstances, there were no viable legal means for wives to divorce, for children
to be adopted, or for servants to quit before the term of their service had
ended. In exchange for this authority, he was responsible for his dependents' support.

On the bright side for dependents, the common law and the canon
law did put limits on patriarchal authority. The head in early modern

England as in the rest of western Europe exercised no power over life or limb. He could not take as many wives into his household as he pleased, force a son or daughter to marry, or sell his servants. Over time, the medieval monarchies and the Christian Church, for their own reasons, had worked to limit such prerogatives of patriarchs.[2] So from this perspective, the powers of English household heads and their counterparts on the continent were relatively weak compared, for example, to what the laws granted Mesopotamian or Roman patriarchs.[3]

During the early modern period, many monarchs—both Catholic and Protestant—found it in their interest to bolster the powers of the household head over his dependents.[4] It has been argued that the English system of household governance, particularly, stressed the power of the individual head. Lawrence Stone, probably the most influential twentieth-century historian of the early modern English family, maintained that the individual household head of the sixteenth and seventeenth century exercised greater authority than did his late medieval forebears, largely because of the Reformation and new measures taken by the monarchy and Parliament to weaken aristocratic power. Many critics during the past twenty years have taken issue with Stone's formulations, although what they have found least convincing is not his depiction of the legal system producing the "restricted, patriarchal nuclear family" of the sixteenth and seventeenth centuries, but the way he uses legal relations to make assumptions about the emotional climate in the family.[5] In the long run, the Reformation and Puritanism empowered the household head, Stone contended, by reducing the intervention of priests and church courts on behalf of dependents. The Tudor-Stuart secular state did its part by diminishing the role of manorial and feudal custom in the economic and social existence of that class of householder who previously had had to fulfill the obligations of a bondsman, villein, or liveried retainer.[6] Some of these measures, however, occurred elsewhere as well.

What really seems distinctive about English developments were Tudor-Stuart inheritance statutes that dramatically increased the powers of the individual household head vis-à-vis the greater lineage, his wife, and his children.[7] Prior to the enactment of these laws, customary rules prevented heads from alienating all of their property from the lineage. The 1540 Statute of Wills and later supplementary acts, however, allowed the testator nearly complete freedom to devise realty and bequeath personalty and relieved him from many of the customary restrictions over disposition of wealth. He could disown his children and leave his wife

1 William Hogarth, *William Wollaston Family* (1730).
COURTESY OF ANONYMOUS LOAN TO NEW WALK MUSEUM, LEICESTER CITY MUSEUM SERVICE / BRIDGEMAN ART LIBRARY, NEW YORK

with no more than a lifetime interest in one third of the income from whatever real estate he owned (her dower).[8] The law did require him to have a justice of the peace examine his wife before he arranged the sale of his or her land, to verify her consent to the transaction. Wifely refusals, though, appear to have been very rare and occurred mainly among those who had separated or were on the verge of separating.

Over time, the common law courts further narrowed the circumstances under which widows could demand dower rights in landed property.[9] Furthermore, the statutory obligation to support children fell only on parents and grandparents, not on collateral kin. Likewise, adult children only had responsibility for support of their parents. To say that the lineage system was truncated does not mean that strong social, political, and economic ties did not exist among collateral kin.[10] The point is that the law did not compel or support such ties in the way that it did in other places or in earlier times. This freedom came at a price for the household

2 Arthur Devis, *Robert James Family* (1751).
COURTESY OF TATE GALLERY, LONDON/ART RESOURCE, NEW YORK

head, however, especially if he died or became disabled. He could not rely on any lineage apparatus, powerful relatives, or family councils to enforce his will.

To celebrate the household and headship, early modern aristocrats, gentlemen, and burghers began commissioning conversation pieces, which were informal group portraits of family members celebrating an event or showcasing their domicile, either townhouse or country estate. Most common among the Dutch and Flemish in the seventeenth century, the form gained popularity in England and Scotland early in the eighteenth, and artists found a new source of wealth beyond the single portrait. For example, William Hogarth—best known today for his satiric treatment of aristocratic and nouveau riche family pretensions in paintings such as *Marriage à la Mode*—earned his early money portraying the domestic lifestyles of the rich and famous in a much more respectful light, as in his portrait of the Suffolk merchant William Wollas-

3 William Hogarth, *William Stroude Family* (ca. 1738).
COURTESY OF TATE GALLERY, LONDON/ART RESOURCE, NEW YORK

ton, his wife, relatives, and friends taking tea and playing cards in his London house (fig. 1). Figure 2 provides an example of an even more common type of conversation piece: East India official Robert James and his wife and daughters are portrayed with his house and estate in the background. Figure 3, another painting by Hogarth, *The Stroude Family* (1738), depicts a more informal group with the head seated.

Regardless of his pose, the head of the family was the focus of the conversation piece during this era. William Wollaston stands in a central position presenting the scene. With James, the central and the tallest figure, it is his wife, his children, and his estate that are on display. London magnate William Stroude is sitting off center, but the painting he commissioned is nevertheless designed to draw attention to his authority. The curtain in the top left corner has been drawn aside to reveal an impressive room in which are depicted his former tutor and later archbishop of Dublin, Arthur Smyth; his servant pouring tea; his wife, Lady Ann Cecil; and his relative Colonel Stroude, along with assorted pets. The portrait painter of a single subject supplied a likeness; the conversation piece artist worked on a smaller canvas and provided an identity for the family. He filled the canvas with objects and persons belonging to the head, who presided over the assemblage.[11]

No comparable visual record memorializing a mid-century colonial household exists, although we have evidence that at least one British American while abroad tried to commission such a painting. Benjamin Franklin in London in 1758 had hoped to have a "family piece"—another name for the conversation piece—painted, using miniatures of his wife and daughter to give the artist a sense of their likenesses. He found, however, the "limner very unwilling to undertake anything of the kind." One suspects the unwilling painter was the source of Franklin's erroneous statement that "[conversation pieces] . . . are quite out of Fashion."[12] In fact, they were enjoying their greatest popularity at mid-century.

Creating conversation pieces for colonists clearly posed problems. Paintings produced by skilled artists cost a lot of money: colonists paid as much for a full-length portrait as for a carriage. A rich American would first commission his own portrait, and then perhaps another for his wife. The wife sometimes shared the space with a young child or two, or the children appeared in their own painting. The very few family groups captured on canvas are more like collections of individual formal portraits, with everyone posed stiffly in front of a stock pastoral backdrop with the requisite drapery and pillars. The Isaac Winslow family of Boston in 1755 is depicted in figure 4. Winslow, who had already sat for an individual portrait several years earlier, here presents his family with a stylized gesture and a patriarchal stance like those of his British counterparts. Indeed the pose probably was derived from a British print.[13] The number of portraits Winslow commissioned indicates that the colonies possessed at least a few potential customers for conversation pieces. The stiffness of the figures, however, suggests a second problem in the portraiture market, the lack of artists in the colonies skilled in group portraiture.[14] Third, the absence in the picture of an elegant interior or stately home and gardens—the personalized contexts increasingly found in British conversation pieces—points up the colonial dilemma of what to present in these fashionable pictures as a backdrop to the household. Should they depict completely fictionalized interiors and landscapes or provincially decorated parlors, asymmetrical wooden structures, and rice fields with slaves

4 Joseph Blackburn, *Isaac Winslow Family* (1755).
COURTESY OF MUSEUM OF FINE ARTS, BOSTON

dressed not as postillions but as farm workers and dockside labor?[15] The combination of these problems of demand, supply, and content apparently defeated all efforts of colonial household heads to leave an impressive visual legacy of their household rule.

The absence in British America of a titled aristocracy and of visual images of large elite families in luxurious settings may contribute to the illusion that household hierarchies had more to do with the Old World than the New. Yet in Europe men and widows from the laboring classes often had their own, albeit poor, households, while in colonial America, the people in those strata were frequently swept into the households of others, magically erasing wealth inequality and poverty and concentrating the power of household heads into fewer hands.[16] As hierarchy and authoritarian structures are associated more often with the Old World than the New, these findings are counterintuitive and merit some discussion, particularly as not everyone agrees about how to interpret the status of women, children, and those in servitude in the colonies.[17] The traditional assumption about the transference of hierarchical arrangements within the household from the Old World to the New is that rather than expanding, household arrangements became less hierarchical due to environmental factors. While some of the more extravagant claims about the ability of the frontier to weaken patriarchal authority have been rejected, rapid population growth, land availability, and labor shortages are generally regarded as allowing for a more egalitarian household in America by the eighteenth century.[18]

It is hard to argue with the picture of the archetypal early American family that exists in most textbooks, because in certain respects it is as near to a modal household as one can get for the mainland colonies. The common depiction is of a household located in a rural northern community. The head of household is a British Protestant dissenter farmer with a British Protestant dissenter housewife; five to seven children; a local farm girl servant, if the wife's children are young; and either an indentured immigrant male to help in the field or a white, Indian (prior to 1720), or black (post-1750) farmhand hired for the year. Together they all produced—on a plot of 120 acres of improved and unimproved land owned by the farmer—wheat, corn, livestock, and livestock products for their own needs and for the market within and outside the region, as well as household services for one another. In Britain, freeholds of this size and type were not generally available.[19]

I react to this archetypal family in the same way as to the revelation from a present-day politician that most firms in the United States are small businesses and that small businesses therefore determine the economic future of the nation. It is true that as beans are counted by the Commerce Department, most businesses are small. A quick resort to the latest *Statistical Abstracts,* however, tells a different story about their economic importance. According to data from 1997, two-thirds of firms have fewer than ten employees, but these firms generate only 12 percent of private employment and 9 percent of the payroll. In comparison, firms with more than five hundred employees—comprising a mere 0.3 percent of all firms—employ 48 percent of the private sector labor force and dispense more than 50 percent of the wages.[20]

Similarly, when the story about egalitarian households is built around northern yeomen farmers and their adult sons, it is easy to forget that 80 percent of the population in the thirteen colonies was comprised of *legal* dependents. Even if one considers only those over twenty-one, more than half still fell into the dependent category. If one were to include all of British America—particularly the sugar islanders who provided most of the broader markets for said yeomen and the Indian nations outside of British settlements—the picture would be even bleaker.

American agriculture undoubtedly depended upon a great deal of affection, cooeration, and positive feelings among household members, but it also involved a considerable amount of legal subordination inside and outside of those households.

What is especially surprising is that seemingly aristocratic Britain had lower ratios of dependence. Table 1 compares the proportion of the population of England and Wales with that in the thirteen Anglo-American colonies who were legal dependents in the latter part of the eighteenth century: 68 percent in England and Wales in 1755 versus 80 percent in the colonies in 1774. High fertility in the area soon to become the United States partially explains why dependency was rampant, but many minors were slaves or indentured servants. If one eliminates minors from consideration, however, and focuses just on the adult population, the thirteen colonies again soar ahead, 54 percent to 40 percent. That 54 percent, moreover, did not include a lot of people who might be considered economically dependent: for example, widowed mothers living with their adult children; adult children living with parents; or other unattached adults. Nor did it include freemen whose household heads had certain powers over them.[21] They are not being counted as dependents because they had the right to depart.

Among legal dependents, wives constituted the biggest category. American white women were less likely than English women to be heads of household and more likely to be married and under the household government of their husbands throughout the colonial period. Twenty percent of early modern English households had female heads, while less than 10 percent of colonial households did.[22] Men migrated across the Atlantic more readily than females, producing high sex ratios (more men than women), which meant that most women married and widows remarried at high rates. High sex ratios brought down the proportion of legal dependents, but the high marriage rate brought it back up.

At the same time, colonial wives from propertied families had fewer devices than did English wives to protect and control the wealth they brought to their marriages, so their husbands had more economic power over them. According to the common law of England, a married woman had to relinquish her personal property (all nonrealty) to her husband at marriage, and he could do as he pleased with it. He also obtained control of any realty she owned and could do anything he pleased with it, short of selling it. He retained for life these privileges—under the custom of curtesy—even if she died. Her lineal heirs had to wait for his death. The lack of protection of a wife's lineage property led the English courts to develop a separate branch of law known as equity. Equity jurisprudence in the early modern period provided a means to safeguard wealth through the making of prenuptial marriage settlements. These settlements created separate estates supervised by trustees. Judging by the modest yet steady levels of litigation in chancery, English women and their families did

TABLE I

Legal Dependents in Relation to the Total Population,
Later Eighteenth Century (in thousands of persons)

	England and Wales, 1755		*13 Colonies, 1774*
Minors (under 21)	2,978		1,343
children and hired servants			1,034
indentured			27*
enslaved			282
Wives†	1,088		292
Adult Servants/Slaves	217		258
hired women		73‡	16*
indentured women			3*
hired men		129	17*
indentured men		15	24*
enslaved women			107
enslaved men			91
Total Legal Dependents	4,283		1,893
Total Population	6,260		2,354
% Legal Dependents	68.4		80.4
Adult Population	3,281		1,011
% Legal Dependents	39.8		54.4

Sources: Peter H. Lindert, "English Occupations, 1670–1811," *Journal of Economic History* 40: (1980): 702–4; Alice Hanson Jones, *American Colonial Wealth* (New York, 1977), 1787.

*Age and sex breakdown of hired and indentured servants based upon "The Population of Maryland 1755," *Gentleman's Magazine* 34 (1764); David Galenson, *White Servitude in Colonial America* (Cambridge, 1981), 25–27.

†Based on assumption that in England, wives comprised 60 percent of adult free female population and in the colonies, 75 percent. For statistics on both places, see Daniel Scott Smith, "Female Householding in Late-Eighteenth-Century America: A Proto-Classical Overview" (paper presented at the "Lois Green Carr: The Chesapeake and Beyond" conference, University of Maryland, May 23, 1992), table 2.

‡Free adult female servants in England estimated at 4 percent of total adult females to correspond with figures Lindert cites before and after 1755.

make use of these tools,[23] though opinions differ as to how effective they were in protecting women and giving them some autonomy in property matters.[24]

It is clear that during the early modern period both strict family settlements and chancery proceedings to enforce separate estates and marriage settlements were activities limited to the wealthy and did little to lessen the authority of the vast majority of individual household heads. Of the more general population, perhaps 1 to 2 percent of women made some sort of provision for a separate estate, and another 2 to 3 percent had their husbands set aside before marriage or during marriage some amount to ensure they would not be left destitute.[25] On the other hand, when one considers the proportion of total personal wealth affected, these devices were not trivial. In the colonies the slow implementation of equity jurisprudence meant that propertied married women had little legal recourse if they or their male relatives wished to shelter their wealth from a predatory husband. The dissenter colonies refused to recognize marriage settlements because of their historical associations with "despotic" Tudor-Stuart courts and their potential for undermining marital unity. Most of the other colonies eventually set up some form of chancery courts dispensing equity law, but marriage settlements continued to cover an inconsequential amount of wealth.[26]

What explains most of the difference in table 1 is that 26 percent of the total *adult* population in the colonies was comprised of servants and slaves, compared to 7 percent in England and Wales. The adoption of chattel slavery produced the greatest increase in dependency in colonial America. By the time of the American war for independence, Africans transported across the Atlantic, their descendants, and those of "mixed" racial ancestry constituted 20 percent of the mainland population of the British colonies and about 90 percent of the population of the British West Indies. They comprised majorities in the American possessions of the French, the Dutch, and the Portuguese. In the thirteen colonies, 96 percent of African Americans were chattel slaves—permanent members of the household of their masters—and no household they set up, whether the conjugally based patrilineal type preferred by Anglo society or any other form, had legal standing.[27] Neither the marriage legislation nor the laws on bastardy and fornication so enthusiastically endorsed by colonial authorities had relevance for the enslaved population. The powers given to men as husbands and fathers did not apply. Nor, according to some colonial laws, could any "Negro, Mulatto, or Indian," free or enslaved, be a master to a white indentured servant.[28] There is some evidence that the African cultural groups transported to the Americas had concepts of family government as different from the Anglo concepts as the customs of many Native American societies. Lineage powers and the mother-child tie may have had a privileged position unknown to Anglo-Americans.[29] Whatever the preferences of African cultural groups in familial organization, British colonial society gave no legal recognition to them.

The authority of household heads also expanded because of changes made by colonials in the laws governing servitude. The English basically confined bound servitude to the apprenticeship of minors. One form was a privileged status that required a father to pay a sum of money to a master of a trade in order that his son might learn the "mystery" of that trade and be able as an adult to practice it. The other form, called *parish apprenticeship,* placed indigent children in households where they worked without wages until they came of age.[30] The colonists made frequent use of parish apprenticeship to relieve their welfare problems, and perhaps because of the greater demand for labor, they were able to indenture children at much younger ages than were the English. Whereas records on the apprenticeship of the poor in eighteenth-century England show few children bound out before age eight, with a median age of from eleven to twelve, the colonists in both the North and the South apprenticed children from age four or five, with lower medians and means. For apprenticeship of the poor, the average age in Rhode Island was seven and in Virginia, it was eight; the median age in Boston was nine. The majority of children had at least one parent. If they were bastards or mulattos, they were more likely to be bound out at an earlier age than if they were children of married whites.[31]

A Maryland census taken on the eve of the American Revolution reveals how many children lived under the governance of someone other than a parent or relative.[32] Among those between the ages of five and fourteen, the census shows 35 percent in a household not headed by their parent, grandparent, or sibling. Slavery, of course, accounted for much of this situation, but even among the free population, 15 percent of the boys and 11 percent of the girls lived with those outside their families of origin. In contrast, less than 3 percent had been taken in by siblings or grandparents.

English authorities did not bind out adults for service within England. In British America, however, adults did serve without wages for terms of four to five years and also without any promise of training for a trade. In England, service for adults as well as youth consisted of one-year terms for pay. The legal distinction between "free," or hired, and "unfree," or indentured, white labor has come under close scrutiny as of late.[33] What has struck most historians is how "unfree" the English provisions for "free" labor were. Robert Steinfeld has even gone so far as to argue that "the colonial law of indentured servitude, too, only differed modestly in its fundamentals from the law that governed early modern English service," though he does believe that in practice the institution was harsher.[34] Given the fact that legally indentured servants were chattel of their masters and could be sold or transferred and that adults could be forced to serve without pay, Steinfeld's position seems too extreme. Why, in colonial America, the worker bore the cost of transportation to the colonies—while in most other times and places it fell to the employer who needed labor or to the government who wished to encourage immigration or emigration—has never been adequately explained. Colonial masters had much greater powers over the labor and discipline of indentured servants than over hired servants. Behavior that brought no penalty or at worst a firing for hired servants in England resulted in whippings and extended service for those indentured in America. The primary advantage over slavery was the limit on service and the access to action by the county justices of the peace in cases of violation of the indenture or of extreme brutality.

By stressing the disadvantageous position of indentured servants, I am not refuting Steinfeld's main point: being a hired servant also brought legal dependency. Those with a term of service of one year or less had to serve out their term or risk criminal action.[35] The servant who quit also had no claim on unpaid wages that he or she had earned to that point, and courts did not always recognize the claims that a servant made for compensation in cases where the master violated the contract by physical abuse or refusal to maintain the servant and treat his or her illness. After completion of service, a servant needed to obtain a testimonial from the master in order to travel and take another position. The master, not the servant, could sue in court for injuries the latter suffered at work or, in the case of a female servant, due to seduction.

Hired servants, indentured servants, and slaves suffering illness or disability due to injury or old age had to be maintained by their masters during their term of service, which meant, in the case of slaves, for life. As these members of the population performed the most strenuous physical labor, they were most at risk to be injured. With such a high proportion of the working population falling into the servant category, public responsibility for the incapacitated, the so-called "deserving" poor, was reduced.

Almost all the northern colonies also used involuntary servitude as an option for creditors, particularly those owed debts by persons without dependents. In Pennsylvania, single persons under fifty-three could be bound for up to seven years, while married defaulters could be forced to labor for five.[36] However one chooses to look at involuntary servitude, whether as a practice preferable to imprisonment or as a tactic to wring the last ounce of work out of petty debtors, it did increase the domain of the household head.[37]

Another reason colonial bound servitude grew is that governments used it as a substitute for houses of correction. A Virginia indentured servant assaulting a master or a North Carolina servant marrying without a master's consent each served an additional year. In North Carolina, running away brought extra service equal to double the time absent; in Virginia, it brought extra service equal to the cost of retrieval and lost time. Any disorderly conduct also meant extra time. Women servants in Virginia who became pregnant served an extra year if the father was Euro-American and two extra years if he was African American. The mulatto child or the child of a convict woman, moreover, faced servitude to the master up to the ages of twenty-eight and twenty-one, respectively. In almost every colony, female indentured servants had their service extended for the offense of bastardy. While servants could complain about mistreatment to any justice of the peace, the enthusiasm for such a suit in a place like North Carolina might evaporate upon learning that an unsuccessful complaint brought additional service equivalent to double the time spent on the prosecution, and a successful one meant ultimately that the servant would be sold, with the master getting the proceeds.[38] Unlike the situation in England, where masters received few material benefits from reporting the infractions of their servants, colonial masters desperate for workers had the incentive of squeezing additional time out of their labor force.

Even in colonies not usually associated with the trade in indentured servants, the authorities used bound servitude in households to take care of both their disciplinary and their welfare problems. In Massachusetts, selectmen or overseers of the poor could bind out an unmarried woman for up to five years for the expenses incurred in lying-in or in support for her child. English practice was for the parish to absorb the cost of lying-in as a case of "casual impotence," while the maximum penalty for putting the parish to the expense of supporting a child to age seven was one year in the house of correction. Massachusetts selectmen even had the authority to bind into service people with an estate whom the selectmen found to be idle and dissolute, giving the produce of their labor to family or kindred.

The colonies only slowly constructed institutional buildings. Despite the fact that the Crown had issued instructions to build poorhouses and workhouses in every province, few such institutions were established outside of the major port cities. The administrative units responsible for the poor—townships in northern colonies and parishes in the South—tried from time to time to build a house for welfare purposes, but invariably they had trouble running the establishments or found them too expensive and reverted back to using private households. The experience related in the vestry records of St. Paul's Parish, Hanover County, Virginia, is illustrative. Virginia parishes were nearly as large as counties. Whereas in England the parish covered no more than ten square miles, in Virginia it could stretch to more than five hundred. As early as 1707, the overseers of St. Paul's paid two men to construct an almshouse, but no mention is made of it being used. Not until 1764 do the minutes record a new attempt to set up an institution, this time in conjunction with a neighboring parish. By 1767, the two parishes had completed the house and began sending the poor there. An overseer and slaves staffed the poorhouse. During the Revolution, the parish had trouble getting help and supplies. The vestry record for December 1781 reads: "Resolved, the few who are now on the Parish be let out to the lowest Bidder and the Land and Plantation on which the Parish House stands to be rented to the highest bidder."[39]

Overseers of the poor paid each household head who agreed to care for elderly, disabled, or ill persons. The able-bodied, like the children described above, were bound out to masters. Generally, more affluent households took in these "impotent" poor, but the frequent turnover—overseers usually moved paupers annually—indicates that not many household heads relished the task. In a minority of cases, poor household heads got assistance to care for their own disabled or ill family members. These arrangements were probably the most controversial, as officials clearly worried about being importuned by every household head with a chronically ill dependent. Overseers would pay household heads boarding the poor more per person than they would offer as a pension to persons who wished to stay in their own home. If a household head needed full support for his family, then the household was broken up and members were boarded and bound out to various families. Out-relief consisted of supplementary benefits—tax exemptions, medical care payments, articles of clothing, or food items—that would restore households to viability. In neither the mother country nor the colonies did overseers cheerfully dole out relief, but the former had a broader definition of those it would support. In England, the justice of the peace manuals refer to the poor as those who "are old and decrepit, unable to work, poor widows, and fatherless children, and tenants driven to poverty . . . by mischance."[40] In colonial Massachusetts, the wording of such manuals became more narrow. It directed officials to support only "impotent and distracted persons," meaning that young children and unwed mothers were much more likely to be bound out. For this reason and for the reasons discussed above, the welfare system channeled the poor into large, more affluent private households governed invariably by male heads. Welfare cases and disciplinary cases joined slaves, servants,wives under coverture, and underage sons and daughters to swell the ranks of dependents in the colonies and contribute to the more patriarchal appearance of colonial households.

Using only a little imagination, it is possible to envisage in colonial America a quite different household system developing, one that would not concentrate so much authority in the individual household head. For one thing, all the Native American cultures with which settlers came into contact allocated familial authority in a radically different way than they did. In the early years of colonization, when the Indian population in most areas exceeded that of the newcomers and so few English women migrated, one might expect that Indian concepts of household organization might alter or transform English practices. An initial revulsion might be followed with accommodation.

Certainly the revulsion can be documented. The English, like the Spanish in the South and Southwest and the French in Canada and the Great Lakes, found Indian household practices among the most baffling and disturbing of all the differences between the invaders and the native inhabitants. Whatever separated these Europeans from one another in regard to family organization paled in comparison to the differences they perceived between themselves and the Indians. And from what can be gathered about many Indian cultures after contact and conquest, the native inhabitants found European notions of household government equally strange.

Early modern European explorers, missionaries, and settlers frequently commented on certain features of Indian family organization, and the same issues surfaced irrespective of whether the observer was English, Spanish, or French and whether the Indian group being discussed was the Algonquian or the Iroquois—the two most common woodland groups on the eastern seaboard and near the Great Lakes—the Sioux in southeastern and central North America, or the Pueblo in what later became the southwestern United States. James Axtell has collected many of these complaints in his anthology *The Indian Peoples of Eastern America*.[41] In the 1630s, the French priest Sagard wrote of Huron women doing "more work than the men. . . . [T]hey have the care of the cooking and the household, of sowing and gathering corn, grinding flour, preparing hemp and tree-bark, and providing the necessary wood." He is echoing Champlain: "They had almost the whole care of the house and the work . . . and besides are required to follow and accompany their husbands from place to place . . . where they serve as mules to carry the baggage." Englishman William Wood characterized Algonquian women of southern New England as more "laborious than their lazie husbands." The male Micmac in Maine got similarly bad press. Among the Delaware and Miami—according to the late-eighteenth-century Moravian missionary David Zeisberger—"in the management of household affairs the husband leaves everything to his wife." Father Lafitau alleged that Iroquois "men, who are so idle in their villages, make their indolence a mark of honour."[42] Similar observations appear in other recent histories of early American Indian groups. The heavy outdoor work of seventeenth-century Powhatan Indian women drew the censure of Virginia Company settlers. According to observer George Alsop, among the Susquehannock of Pennsylvania, "the women are the Butchers, Cooks, and tillers of he ground . . . the men think it below the honour of a Masculine to Stoop to anything but that which their Gun, or Bow and Arrows can Command."

Whites clearly disapproved of the division of labor among the Creeks of Georgia and Alabama, because a 1790 treaty specified that healthy Creek men would no longer be allowed to avoid agricultural labor and engage in "leisure" activities such as hunting, fishing, and ball playing while Creek women chopped wood and toted water. Quaker missionaries and later the United States government worked hard to make farmers out of Seneca men, just as a couple of centuries earlier the Franciscans of New Mexico had sought to straighten out the Pueblo Indians by having the men be in charge of the construction of housing while women did the weaving.[43]

Historians have pointed out the misconceptions that lay behind many of these comments and actions. In his book on the Indian peoples of eastern America, James Axtell goes to considerable length to argue against western European society's biases. He discusses the exhausting and dangerous nature of the hunt, the absence of European observers in the winter when much of this hunting took place, and the tendency of Europeans to think of hunting and fishing as leisure activities rather than as primary economic functions. On the other hand, he suggests that most of the daily chores of women "were reasonably light and performed around the household." So basically, in Axtell's view, the economic contributions of each sex were equal.[44]

More seems to have been involved in European assessments of gender inequities, however, than differing concepts of work. What in fact was the logic behind the insistence of Europeans that men handle the fieldwork and perform certain kinds of household tasks? It is difficult to believe that Europeans worried too much about Indian women doing hard labor. European males had little problem putting indentured and slave women, whatever their ethnicity, in the fields. In fact some commentators didn't think Indian women worked hard enough either and implied that they were none too rigorous in their cleaning and housekeeping.[45] Rather, European discomfiture with Indian gender roles seems to center around the commitment and contribution the adult male made to his household, by which they meant the unit containing the husband's wife and children. Indian men did not take charge of their households in the way that European men did.

Most of the cultures encountered by these Europeans were matrilineal, not patrilineal. Descent was reckoned and identity obtained from one's maternal relatives. Some Indian cultures that followed patrilineal descent rules still kept to matrilocality in residence: a husband and the children he had by his wife lived in the village or that section of their common village where his wife's family lived. And even where no matrilineal or matrilocal tradition prevailed, the house and household utensils often were considered female property. Richard White, in discussing the Great Lakes Algonquin, points out one of the effects of these kinship and descent patterns. "Depending on her tribal identity," he writes, "an Algonquian woman often had a more durable and significant relationship with her mother, father, brothers, sisters, or grandparents, or with other, unrelated women than with her husband or husbands."[46] Another effect, anthropologists and historians tell us, was that a married Indian man, even if he only had one wife at a time—and this seems to have been the case for most Indian men regardless of tribe—had obligations to more than one household: that of his wife and children and the household or households associated with his mother's line.[47] These obligations could take the form of the man giving the proceeds from his labors, returning to his natal household for ceremonies, or assuming the duties of clan leader and permanently residing with the matrilineage. Advancement in the clan, village, and tribe depended upon his relations with his mother's relatives, not with those associated with his conjugal unit. In this respect, women's allegiances were less split, because they resided with or near the matrilineage, which also gave them and their children their identity. The woman was, as an early-eighteenth-century Jesuit put it, the "mistress" and the "heiress" of her cabin.[48] If she carried her household on her back when the tribe moved, it might be because she had the rights to it. If she worked the fields, she might be doing so because they were the fields of her lineage.

This perception of male remoteness and limited commitment to the conjugal household unit also lurks behind other complaints commonly lodged against Indian family life in the early modern period—the failure to discipline children, female sexual promiscuity, and easy divorce. In the contemporary accounts, mothers not only tended the children but also had the principal authority over them. Much to the despair of European observers, only Christianized Indian mothers engaged in physical punishment of their young. The father was of little assistance. As one account related, he had affection for his "naughty" children but took little role in shaping them into responsible adults. The training and education of sons often fell to the men of the matrilineage, not to the father.[49] Because of the sexual freedom of unmarried women and easy divorce, husbands— European observers feared—may not even have fathered their consorts' children. Marriages ended by mutual consent, and the parties each went off with someone else. So the household authority of the male was— as these commentators portray it—greatly limited by the fact that his children could ignore him, that he could not police the sexuality of the women in the household, and that his wife could walk out or, more likely, send him packing.[50]

Europeans could not understand how stable societies could be fashioned from such unstable household units. To one early-eighteenth-century analyst, the "isolation and numerical weakness of the race" could be attributed to this household system. "For the women, although naturally prolific, cannot, on account of their occupation in these labors, either bring forth fully developed offspring, or properly nourish them after they have been brought forth." To another, the system smacked of the "brute beast"; yet another claimed that "owing to the instability of family relationships, children are often neglected," even though the Indians loved them a great deal. Many commentators wrote of the frequent resort to abortion among mothers who carried their offspring and nursed them for a longer period than was common among western Europeans.[51] The Indian family became the first in a series of household systems that clashed with Euro-American ideas about household government. Systems in which authority is dispersed — often lodged partially in lineage groups rather than being exercised solely within the domestic unit — or in which the family is centered around the mother-child tie rather than the conjugal tie tend to be judged nonviable. One suspects that the English found this reliance on lineage particularly curious, given the weakness of their own extended kinship connections.

Disapproval of Indian household government, however, should probably not be considered the decisive factor in the colonists' failure to adapt their family structures in response to those of the Indian cultures they encountered. The Spaniards disapproved of Indian household government too, yet that did not stop the development of a mestizo culture in their colonies. In fact, the family system of Indians had some attractive features, especially for European men who faced high sex ratios in their own settlements. Early Virginia had a sex ratio of seven men to every woman. Even in the better-balanced colonies of New England, the ratio stood at one-and-a-half men for every woman. Over time the ratios tended toward equality, but not on the Anglo frontier, where Indian settlements were of course most likely to be found.[52] Moreover, men — especially those drawn to life in the wilderness — might consider not only the sexual availability of unmarried Indian women but the contacts they provided with the Indian settlements, their economic self-sufficiency as wives, and the easy divorce provisions to be very appealing attributes. Some Anglo women also chose the Indian way of life. The stories of captured girls — Eunice Williams from Deerfield and Mary Jemison, an Irish immigrant living in Pennsylvania — have been the subjects of books and articles in recent years.[53] So what on the macro level might seem undesirable to missionaries and colonial leaders might on the micro level seem more attractive to male and even some female settlers. The genetic composition of the majority of residents of the Americas today stands as monument to the ability of these factors to overcome perceptions of cultural difference.

Interracial couples, however, had to face considerable legal opposition in the British colonies. In Virginia, the records indicate only two legally sanctioned intermarriages after the wedding of John Rolfe and Pocahontas in 1614. In 1691, the House of Burgesses passed an act banning marriages between "white people and Negroes, Mulattoes and Indians."[54] In 1741, North Carolina's legislature made it an offense punishable by a fifty-pound fine for any white man or woman to marry an "Indian, Negro, Mustee, or Mulatto Man or Woman, or any Person of mixt Blood, to the Third Generation, bond or free."[55] Nor, claims one modern investigator, does the historical record indicate any legal colonial marriages between a New England male and an Indian woman in the seventeenth century. In Connecticut in 1642, those who fled the settlements to "take up their abode with the Indians in a profane course of life" faced three years of imprisonment and possible fines and corporal punishment. In 1680, the synod of Congregational churches decreed that Christians could not marry "Infidels." Given the extremely weak New England missionary efforts, this injunction, in effect, prevented most interracial couples being married under English law.[56]

Of course, a lot of British men and women never bothered with all the legal niceties involved in marriage either, a subject I take up later in this book. In regions not dominated by one religious sect, coupling was not patrolled very closely in the colonial period. When sex ratios were also high in such regions, it seems quite likely that Anglo-Indian unions were hardly rare events. Nor apparently were African American and Indian conjugal relationships especially rare, judging by the descriptions of the physical characteristics of Indians on nineteenth-century eastern seaboard reservations.[57] Discriminatory marriage laws did have an important effect, however. When a man and woman of European descent cohabited for a long period of time, the supposition—unless challenged publicly by an interested party—was that they were married and their children were legitimate. No such presumption would or could be made for a mixed race couple.

Most Indian societies, it appears, did not initially oppose intermarriage. They were accustomed to exogamous unions made for purposes of alliance. In matrilineal Indian societies, though, the care and education of children was the domain of the mother, and in most interracial marriages the mother was Indian. One Anglo official in the late eighteenth century complained that a white man marrying an Indian woman of the Creek Nation, "so far from bettering his condition becomes a Slave of her family."[58] Nevertheless, in areas where Indians and whites traded with one another, there were many such households. While successive waves of British and African migration—combined with the demographic disasters suffered by Native American populations—hampered the spread of the Native American form of household government, the impact of English legal hostility to their family system and ethnogenesis should not be underestimated.[59] Later, male Indian leaders also became more hostile toward mixing with Euro-Americans in British colonies, seeing such unions as a threat to the continuance of Indian nations.[60] Children of mixed unions had to identify with one culture or another. No new cultural category evolved, and inclusion of Indian household norms within colonial traditions of household government did not take place, although obviously beyond the line of European settlement and in small pockets within it various forms of Indian lineage structure prevailed.

In Hispanic America, neither the Catholic Church nor the secular authorities exhibited such zeal in stopping interracial unions. The conquests had produced immediate mixed marriages, some very celebrated where a conquistador had married an Indian princess. Of course it was always thought best to be able to trace one's lineage back to "pure" Spanish Catholic roots. The Reconquest of Spain and the Inquisition suggest a home society not particularly enamored with diversity. Gradually a complicated status system based on degrees of racial mixture evolved that, perhaps unintentionally, laid the groundwork for a mestizo cultural identity.[61] What is uncertain is the degree to which this recognition of mixture made more acceptable deviations from Spanish practice, such as the high rate of female-headed households observed in many Latin American countries by the nineteenth century,[62] or other manifestations of less conjugally oriented family living among mestizo and Indian populations.

The most obvious contribution of Indian household organization to political culture came later in the nineteenth century, when the social theorists discussed in chapter 1 classified the matrilineal aspect of some Indian societies as a primitive, preproperty form of family organization. The matrilineal and corporate lineage characteristics of Indian cultures acquired a doomed, world-we-have-lost character among social theorists, although intellectuals and radicals have continually referred back to them in order to critique prevailing forms of Anglo-American household government.[63]

When population studies revealed the high sex ratios and the high mortality rates of plantation communities in the seventeenth century, scholars investigated the consequences for traditional household authority. The inability of fathers—because of shortened life expectancy—to supervise the careers and marriages of their children; the need for husbands to make comparatively generous provisions of dower for much-in-demand wives; the opportunity that healthy widows and affluent women had to direct family affairs in the absence of appropriate male heirs; and the problems that masters experienced in keeping their bound servants from becoming a civil threat have all been identified as being part of seventeenth-century household history in the region and in plantation societies elsewhere.[64]

In the South, the demographic peculiarities that weakened patriarchal control—high mortality and high sex ratios—began lessening in the later seventeenth century, taking with them some of the power that adult women and minors might have derived from the situation.[65] Even more important, the tendency to throw the remnants of economically unviable households into wealthier households kept patriarchal household government strong whatever the fate of particular family heads.

In the dissenter colonies of New England and Pennsylvania—where all but the earliest settlers enjoyed longer life expectancy than in England and where the sex ratios were more balanced than in plantation colonies—the threat to household authority emanated from a different source, one that previous research has not necessarily seen as a threat. Puritan clerics raised to a new importance family government and the authority of its head. When the religiously inspired flocks set about erecting a godly society in the New World, however, household heads did not escape the surveillance accorded every inhabitant of these Bible commonwealths.[66] The imperatives of community often outranked those of the individual household.

Probably the most dramatic confrontation between the two occurred in Plymouth Colony. As Mary Beth Norton has pointed out, the flip side of the often told story of communalism's collapse among the Pilgrims is a tale of household government reasserting itself.[67] Young men complained about having to "spend their time and strength to work for other men's wives and children without any recompense." There was dissatisfaction that the stronger man, or "man of parts," received no more provisions than weaker men, as the "aged and graver men [were] to be ranked and equalized in labours and victuals, clothes etc. with the meaner and younger sort." And the forcing of men's wives to "do service" for other men, preparing their food and washing their clothes, also aroused discontent. All of these complaints arose from the colony's violation of the principle that service and the rewards of that service should be organized and distributed within the established household framework.

Young men expected to work either for their father or for a master who offered wages. The mature "man of parts" was accustomed to heading a household where he supervised the resources and the labor of young people and adult females. Wives assumed their domestic services extended only to household members. Plymouth quickly reinstituted a more orthodox form of household government, and other dissenter settlements in the seventeenth century did not repeat the experiment. Nevertheless, the New England and Pennsylvania colonies set up other mechanisms that circumscribed the powers of the household head in order to pursue community objectives. Some of these mechanisms empowered dependents, giving them more rights. Others—designed to bolster a lax or weak household head—resulted in more stringent policing of dependents. The ultimate goal in both cases was the encouragement of a more godly community, not of individual freedoms.

Household dependents gained power in several ways. The prohibition on any physical chastisement of a wife in Massachusetts Bay and the allowance of absolute divorce (divorce with remarriage by the innocent party) throughout New England reduced the legal authority of husbands. In all these colonies, petitions from women exceeded those from men, indicating the utility of this form of redress for women under coverture.[68] Much earlier than elsewhere in the colonies or in England, Puritan law required parents and masters to teach their children and servants to read, and these provisions were actively enforced.[69] New England and Pennsylvania intestacy laws also encouraged more equal distribution of estates among children by reducing the eldest son's share of realty to a double portion rather than the entire parcel he would have received under the common law's more dynastically oriented custom.

The effects of these measures that enhanced the rights of dependents vis-à-vis the household head were clearly limited. After all, divorces affected very few New England households in the seventeenth century. Authorities granted about one a year, on the average.[70] Doubts have been raised as to how frequently town officers actually prosecuted wife beating, because cases were so rare.[71] The kind of education provisions specified in New England laws did not require fathers and masters to devote many good working years to schooling their young dependents. Fathers could write wills and undo the more egalitarian intestacy provisions.

What affected more seventeenth-century households, though, was the policing of negligent heads: governmental intervention into household affairs to assure that family order was being maintained. Ironically, the assumption by the Puritan authorities of the patriarchal duties of the household head often placed greater restrictions on the actions of dependents and punished the dependents' transgressions more severely than would have been done under traditional household government. Massachusetts authorities put into operation a tithingman system to ensure that inhabitants did not flaunt provisions mandating good household government. Under this system, the tithingman watched over from ten to twelve families in a neighborhood and reported not only stubborn and disorderly children but also unruly servants, Sabbath breakers, drinkers, and people roaming the streets at night.[72] These officers joined an already impressive array of church elders and local civil officials—magistrates, sheriffs, constables, the watch, grand jurymen, overseers of the poor, and selectmen—whose duties included checking up on the morals and manners of the inhabitants.[73]

In early Pennsylvania, also a dissenter colony, the mechanisms for ensuring household order among the godly took the form of the Quaker meeting, which had its women's and men's units. Quaker meetings in America discouraged masters from owning slaves, disciplined husbands and fathers for abuse of wife and children, punished fornication by ordering the seducer to marry the seduced, overruled parents trying to stop a marriage, forced those marrying non-Quakers to leave the meeting, and ordered families to move to escape sinful influences.[74]

By all accounts, this support staff for family government provided by the New England Congregationalists and Pennsylvania's Quakers had its desired effect. The research on infractions relates mainly to New England, and there, during the seventeenth century, lived a law-abiding bunch. In the area of sexual offenses, it has been shown that the inhabitants exhibited very low rates of fornication and bastardy compared to elsewhere in the British colonies and in England during this period.[75] This was the case even though the population at risk was large, due to the interest of dissenters in making men as well as women bear responsibility for illegal sexual intercourse.[76] Not that women, as a group, necessarily benefited by the increased policing either. Once the authorities began mucking about in household affairs and labeling as crime things such as premarital pregnancy and living outside family government, dependents—a status into which almost all females fell—were at a heightened risk to be reported for those rare infractions they did commit.[77] So the most common crime prosecuted in New England county courts during the colonial period was fornication, an offense that almost always involved a female defendant, though not always a male.[78] Fornication was such a common crime in this region because it included not just the single women who became pregnant but also the married couples who had children before they had been married for nine months.

The spread of Puritanism in England encouraged these kinds of prosecutions in the period 1585–1640, but only selected parishes undertook to punish married offenders.[79] In Puritan New England, however, prosecution was more universal and long-lasting. As fornication became more common in the later seventeenth century, the proportion of criminal offences attributed to women grew, so that by the 1690s, nearly a third of offenders in Massachusetts and New Hampshire were women, while in Connecticut it was around 20 percent.[80] One also finds the percentage of New England females being defendants in serious crime during the seventeenth century rising to historically high levels, because the society investigated closely deaths of infants, witchcraft accusations, and charges of spousal infidelity. Due to infanticide, witchcraft, and adultery charges, women made up 33 percent of the Massachusetts felony defendants in the 1670s, 39 percent in the 1680s, and 60 percent in the 1690s (the latter figure does not include the special Salem court proceedings). In contrast, rates for the United States in the third quarter of the twentieth century ranged from 9 to 19 percent.[81]

Would not household heads welcome this assistance by the state in the maintenance of orderly dependents? Undoubtedly, under certain circumstances, the activities of Puritan congregations, tithingmen, selectmen, and the Quaker meeting served the purposes of masters, husbands, or fathers. Masters clearly appreciated knowing when their servants were skulking around the neighborhood rather than doing their jobs. Husbands would want to be apprised of their wives' adulterous behavior and could take advantage of the New England divorce laws to free themselves of their unfaithful spouses. Having children know that the punishment for fornication and bastardy would be public and painful—either physically or financially—discouraged young men and women from taking complete charge of their sexual lives and thus served the matchmaking interests of parents. On the other hand, what father was genuinely pleased when he had to appear in court with his daughter to pay a fornication fine, knowing such a fine would put a dent into his pocketbook and weaken her prospects for making an advantageous marriage? Even less welcome to a household head would be the tireless efforts of a local official to substantiate a female servant's charge that he, the household head, was the father of her bastard child or a male servant's accusation of sodomy. Similarly, an accusation that his wife was a witch would hardly improve the reputation of either himself or his household in the community. In Pennsylvania, the Quaker meeting's insistence on marriage within the fold and between seducers and seduced might conflict with dynastic interests of the household head. Masters, trying to assemble a stable labor force, might resent Quaker disapproval of slavery. Household heads who exercised their right to administer "moderate" physical chastisement to their wives or children might object to the interference of a committee of Friends who had a different definition of the word *moderate*. In short, whe state authorities took on duties that might be characterized as patriarchal, their actions and their interests often diverged from those of patriarchal household heads, lessening rather than bolstering the latter's authority.

In the northern dissenter colonies, time also brought a diminution in the degree of community interference suffered by household heads. For example, by the mid-eighteenth century, the authorities in most towns stopped prosecuting married couples for fornication and reduced the severity of punishment for the crime among the unmarried. The incidence of nonmarital sexuality came to resemble more closely that of other Anglo-American communities.[82] While historians of Quakerism do not indicate any falling off in the supervisory role of the meetings, the proportion of the middle colonies' population subject to their control diminished steadily. Unlike Europe and Latin America, none of the Anglo-American colonies developed church courts or religious bureaucracies to enforce morality and place a check on the household head.

Seventeenth-century English colonists had inherited a system of household government that bestowed an unusual amount of power on the individual household head. It featured a weak lineage, a church that relied on the paterfamilias for religious instruction, and a monarchy and aristocracy less and less able to reach into the household for services and goods. The English landed classes may have had some fears about the degree of individualism wrought by the testamentary freedom innovations of the Tudor-Stuart period, because in the eighteenth century members of that group more and more directed attorneys to draw up instruments known as "strict family settlements" to protect the patrilineage. Under these arrangements, heirs received only lifetime use of an estate and in effect lost their ability to alienate the bulk of the wealth they inherited. Instead, as much of the estate as possible descended to one male heir without completely disinheriting daughters, younger sons, and widows.

Individual household heads lost a certain flexibility and personal power, but the eldest male heir usually gained greater lifetime resources, because these settlements often gave less than dower to widows and shrank the portions of heiresses.[83] The basic idea, though, was to ensure that the patrilineage survived a wastrel or an imprudent household head.

Nothing comparable emerged in the thirteen colonies. Virginia's use of entail comes closest, but it was utilized much less comprehensively than the strict family settlement, unevenly protected in the courts, and enjoyed little popularity outside of the Chesapeake.[84] Nor, as mentioned above, did marriage settlements that hemmed in grooms enjoy much popularity in America. The colonial leadership was interested in expanding the power of the household head, not in finding ways to temper it, and for this authoritarian tendency, we may have to blame those two freedom cognates—land availability and religious diversity.

High land-labor ratios enhanced the powers of masters and raised the costs of public institutions that competed with household heads for authority. One of the oldest themes in the history of the United States is the emancipating effect of land availability on the population. It is usually considered to be a threat to the household head's control over his dependents. The problem is that the effects of land availability are not straightforward. True, it correlates closely with a lowered age at marriage and high fertility, implying freedom for children.[85] Yet unoccupied land is not always available land. Only in certain times and places could Anglo-American youth fully exploit the natural resources of the continent and migrate freely.[86] Setting up a separate household without assistance from the older generation usually meant great hardship. But the biggest problem with the equation of land with personal freedom is that in America land's plentiful presence so obviously led to bound servitude. To secure a workforce for the production of profitable crops, colonists adopted systems of indentured labor and then chattel slavery, whereby masters gained much greater rights over servants than they had in the Old World.

High land-labor ratios also were a factor in Anglo-Americans' predilection for using the household rather than public institutions to handle social and economic problems. The mutual benefits the white free community and masters derived from throwing potential welfare cases into household-based bound servitude seems one reason. The expense of serving a spread-out community is a second.

Increasing religious diversity—another freedom cognate—had a dampening effect on public institutions as well, because it prevented colonial populations from adopting the European model whereby the established church developed legal, educational, and welfare institutions to intervene in household government. To different degrees, these phenomena affected both southern and northern populations. Initially dissenter colonies made a relatively heavy investment in public welfare goods—meetinghouses, colleges, schools. One might have projected a nascent welfare state evolving, a proto-Sweden, that would continue to police and usurp the authority of household heads. While it seems that colonies like Massachusetts continued to exceed the social spending levels of most other provinces, it does not seem that the community-building momentum was maintained. What happened? For one thing, as the Salem witchcraft episode illustrated, surveillance to ensure that the household head was keeping his dependents in line could be quite disruptive and divisive even within the community of true believers. The constituency for establishing public institutions to ensure standards of morality, education, and welfare dwindled as the population grew more religiously diverse and more suspicious of the dominant denomination.

3

THE AMERICAN REVOLUTION
AND THE HOUSEHOLD

WHY HAS THE AMERICAN REVOLUTION NEVER CAPTURED THE INTER-
est and imagination of the reading and viewing public to the same extent
as the War between the States or the French Revolution? Even as great a
proponent of the transformative nature of the war for independence as
Gordon Wood admits in the introduction to his *Radicalism of the American Revolution* that a problem exists. The war, he insists, was radical in the
degree of social change it produced and in the way it changed the course
of subsequent history. "In destroying monarchy and establishing republics they were changing their society. . . . By the early years of the nineteenth century the Revolution had created a society fundamentally different from the colonial society of the eighteenth century."[1] Still, he has
to concede that the general perception is of a much more conservative event. To Wood it is an image problem. The Founding Fathers, he
feels, do not fit the stereotype of the revolutionary. George Washington,
Thomas Jefferson, and John Adams, in contrast to Robespierre, Lenin, or
Mao Ze-dong,

seem too stuffy, too solemn, too cautious, too much the gentlemen. We cannot
quite conceive of revolutionaries in powdered hair and knee breeches. . . . They
made speeches, not bombs; they wrote learned pamphlets, not manifestos. They
were not abstract theorists and they were not social levelers.[2]

But is that the answer? Stuffiness and hair powder? How about some
of Benjamin Franklin's outfits? Speeches not bombs? What about the
Boston Tea Party, tarring and feathering, and the guerrilla warfare waged
by the Americans before and after declaring independence? Learned
pamphlets, not manifestos? *Common Sense*? Not abstract thinkers? Well,
Robespierre, Lenin, and Mao were quite focused too. Not social levelers?

Isn't social leveling what both friend and foe thought eighteenth- and nineteenth-century republicanism was all about: removing layers of state licensed privilege—kings, aristocrats, and bishops—from the body politic?

The difficulty, I would argue, stems from another source. *Radical* and *conservative* are terms that mean little unless compared to something concrete. If one compares the United States to western European nations, Wood appears to be right: the United States was a radical departure both politically and socially. It had no monarch; it had no titled nobility with special privileges; and it had no spiritual lords and national church. From the 1780s to the Civil War, the steady stream of Europeans who came to observe and then write about the great republican experiment stands as a testimony to the radical nature of the United States in contemporary world terms. Before the storming of the Bastille, the visitors came to observe a republic in action.[3] After the Restoration of the Bourbons, they came to study how the Americans had achieved a broad consensus on the desirability of a republican form of government, while that remained the impossible dream in nearly all of Europe.

If one's point of comparison changes to the thirteen colonies, however, the case for radicalism is much weaker. The United States, transforming itself into a nation from a group of colonies, created administrative, military, and financial institutions that were not there previously. But the view that by the early years of the nineteenth century the Revolution had created a society fundamentally different from colonial society in the sense that "social relationships" or "the way people were connected to one another" had undergone fundamental change is much more difficult to demonstrate.[4]

Over the past generation, most interpretations of colonial politics—from Bernard Bailyn's *Origins of American Politics* (1968) to Jack Greene's recent essays in *Understanding the American Revolution*—have stressed the way pre-Revolutionary British America already differed from the Old World.[5] One major reason why the American Revolution has so frequently been seen as a nonradical event in the United States is that the uprooting of monarchy, aristocracy, and an established church brought limited trauma. These institutions had not become entrenched in the colonies the way they were in European society. None of the Hanoverian kings had been to British America. Sending George packing, in fact, involved no packing and no messy execution as with Charles or Louis. The number of royal officials displaced by the overthrow of monarchy was small, and almost everyone left the country during or immediately after the war rather than staying around to plan a restoration. The tendency of the Crown to use colonial offices to pay off patronage debts to Britons rather than to solidify ties with America's elite worked to the benefit of the Revolutionaries.

The American equivalent of a titled aristocracy were the proprietors, a handful of individuals, most of whom—like their king—lived in Great Britain. These men, along with an important segment of Loyalists, were immensely wealthy. A considerable amount of property changed hands as a result of the war. Studies of the wealth distribution circa 1800, however, indicate that the level of concentration had not been altered, even though the names of the wealthy had changed.[6]

Nor did the loss of the Church of England as the established church in British America make the kind of difference it would have in the Old World. The Anglican Church never had a firm hold on the hearts, minds, and pocketbooks of the colonial populace. Most of those going to the northern half of the mainland and the southern backcountry could be described as dissenters, sectarians, or Lutherans. Maryland had been founded by Catholics. Massachusetts Bay awarded privileged status to Congregationalism. The Anglicans had made little effort to convert the Indians and even less to bringing African immigrants into the fold. The growth in numbers of congregations did not keep pace with the growth in the population. The failure to establish a bishopric in America made it difficult to build an ecclesiastical organization in the colonies, as aspirants to the pulpit had to journey to London to be ordained. In the mid-eighteenth century, the Anglican Church lost support on the rationalist end due to the Enlightenment and on the enthusiast end due to the Great Awakening, or revivalism. By 1775, fewer than one in five congregations in the thirteen colonies were of the Church of England, and precious few of those enjoyed the kind of financial support associated with parishes in the Old World.[7] No impressive church bureaucracy had been swept away by the American Revolution.

The other major reason, I would argue, that many Americans find the Revolution not so revolutionary is that the quarter century or so after 1776 involved less change in social relations than one might expect from such a major upheaval in the governing structure. If some dramatic change of this sort had occurred as a direct result of the war, it would necessarily have occurred in the relationships among those in what was the major institutional unit in the thirteen colonies, the household. How much did the Revolution curtail or alter the expansion in household authority discussed in the previous chapter? If the Revolution had indeed been a revolution in social relations, what changes did it effect in that sphere—in the power exerted by husbands over wives, fathers over children, and masters over servants and slaves?

In recent years, about the only genuine fireworks generated by the Revolution involve this issue. One side asks how it can be a true revolution without its having provided citizenship rights for women and slaves and more equal opportunity for youth? The other side shakes its collective head sadly and accuses the doubters of confusing the twentieth century with the eighteenth.[8] Perhaps perfect equality did not come, they concede, but even in this realm, movement occurred. Enlightened paternalism toward dependents replaced patriarchal rule as intellectual currents associated with the Age of Reason made household heads more reasonable. This development had a chicken-and-the-egg relationship with the American Revolution, both antedating the war and gaining momentum from it.[9]

Historians have enlisted visual aids in making this argument, pointing to the rise of an affective family in conversation pieces and family portraits produced in the late eighteenth and early nineteenth centuries.[10] Art historians of early America also note a change occurring around 1760, although they are more circumspect about its significance.[11] Similar trends can be found in western European and specifically British painting, and some art historians claim that at this point one finds the rise of the "companionate family" among elites.[12] Conversation pieces produced from the 1760s into the 1780s are the kind of pictures to which these scholars refer. Johan Zoffany painted many of this type in Britain, and both Charles Willson Peale and John Singleton Copley did the same in America. Figure 5, titled *The Thomas Bradshaw Family*, shows a British politician's household painted by Zoffany in 1769. Peale's work is represented in figure 6 by *The John Cadwalader Family* (1772) and Copley's by both figure 7, *Sir William Pepperrell and Family* (1778), and figure 8, *Thomas Mifflin and His Wife, Sarah Morris Mifflin* (1773).

In all of these paintings, the head—we might call him "Mr. Sensitive"—appears much more engaged with his family. And not only does the household head seem softer in such works, but the wife seems more esteemed and the children more beloved; everyone appears more intimate with one another than in the standard conversation piece that dominated family portraiture earlier in the eighteenth century and still survived into this period (see figures 1–4 in chapter 2).

5 Johan Zoffany, *Thomas Bradshaw Family* (1769).
COURTESY OF TATE GALLERY, LONDON/ART RESOURCE, NEW YORK

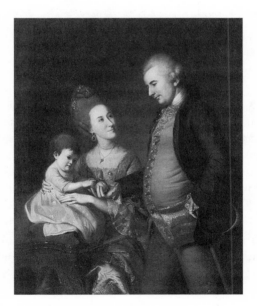

6 Charles Willson Peale, *John Cadwalader Family* (1772).
COURTESY OF PHILADELPHIA MUSEUM OF ART

7 John Singleton Copley, *Sir William Pepperrell and Family* (1778).
COURTESY OF NORTH CAROLINA MUSEUM OF ART, RALEIGH

More often, though, historians asserting that the Revolution transformed household relations base their arguments on textual evidence
rather than images. They cite four developments: the abolition of primogeniture and entail, the passage of divorce legislation, the decline of indentured servitude, and the emancipation of slaves in the North.

Ten of the thirteen colonies in rewriting their laws after the Revolution changed their intestacy statutes to award sons and daughters equal
shares of their parents' estates, rather than giving preference to the eldest
son through primogeniture or double share. In addition, Virginia, notorious for not only entailing land and slaves but for outlawing the ordinary
court procedures used elsewhere for overriding these actions, abolished
the practice altogether. Entail had grown to be a thorn in the side of debt-
ridden tobacco planters eager to sell land they no longer needed or could
afford to develop. It turns out that Thomas Jefferson—who led the charge

8 John Singleton Copley, *Thomas Mifflin and His Wife, Sarah Morris Mifflin* (1773).
COURTESY OF PHILADELPHIA MUSEUM OF ART

against primogeniture and entail—had himself run into problems when in 1774 he sought to remove (bar) the entail on land his wife had inherited from her grandfather.[13]

The abolition of primogeniture, generally, and the end to entail in Virginia certainly would count as an attack on patrilineal arrangements. The powers of lineage in the thirteen colonies—compared to the situation in most other places—had been pathetic enough. These actions taken as the states codified their laws put about the last nail in the lineage coffin. They do not, however, count as an attack on the authority of the household head. A propertied head could always override any intestacy arrangement, including the provision for primogeniture, by simply writing a will.

The abolition of entail, though, actually expanded the power of the head at the expense of his patrilineage and of those who married his daughters. With entail, a testator not only flexed his patriarchal muscle but reduced the power of his successors in the job, because the successors lost the ability to devise entailed property. Fathers, when they gave land to daughters, frequently devised it for life only. Virginia fathers had the added protection of knowing that any life interest made through an entail not only would safeguard the property through one generation but also would make it very difficult to alienate from the lineage in succeeding generations. Jefferson understood how entail encroached upon the power of the household head very well and used it as an argument in his abolition bill. His words sound remarkably unrevolutionary: "[Entail] sometimes does injury to the morals of youth, by rendering them independent of and disobedient to their parents." Though Jefferson wanted to ease the way for the young yeoman hoping to set up his own household, and thus he opposed primogeniture; he also argued for more legal restrictions on marriages of minors because children so often ignored the wishes of their parents.[14] If the American Revolutionaries had been, like the French, interested in dramatically cutting back the power of father, they would have limited a father's testamentary powers. In Jacobin France, equal partition of the estate was not just the default for a father who had neglected to write a will; it was a requirement. As a result, the French wrote more petitions on inheritance reform than on any other aspect of the civil law during the 1790s. Outrage about the loss of paternal power over offspring ultimately led to a restoration of many fatherly prerogatives in the Napoleonic Code.[15]

Comparison of colonial and early national wills shows little change in fathers' attitudes toward the proportion of their estates sons and daughters should inherit. In the colonial period—when primogeniture or double shares for eldest sons prevailed in intestacy statutes—fathers used wills to equalize portions among sons and to shrink daughters' portions. After the Revolution—when intestacy laws equalized portions among children—fathers did less adjusting of sons' portions and continued to give daughters less than intestacy when they had sons. The big shift to equality for daughters comes in the later nineteenth century, not after the Revolution.[16]

In regard to husband-wife relations, most states also provided for absolute divorce in their post-Revolutionary codes, joining the New England provinces that, since the seventeenth century, had permitted dissolution of marriage in extreme circumstances. Close examination of the grounds allowed in these new codes and the kinds of cases that the courts or legislatures acted upon favorably reveals that the legislation served essentially the same purposes that the Puritan acts had performed.[17] Divorce on the grounds of desertion offered women left in the lurch by their husbands a means to claim wages and property to support themselves and their families or to remarry. Divorce on the grounds of adultery permitted men to unload unfaithful wives who bore or were at risk to bear other men's children. The "recognition that there were circumstances justifying absolute divorce constituted an important break with past English practice," if not with New England's.[18] But, as laudable and undoubtedly needed as these statutes were, in neither case could one claim they curtailed the power of the household head or gave dependent wives the right to walk out on their husbands. In the first case, the head made his decision: he walked, and the wife and the state were left to clean up the mess. In the second case, the legislation gave new powers to the household head that had been taken from him by the monogamy preoccupied Christian Church.

The British radical Thomas Paine, separated from his spouse, wrote admiringly of both men and women being able to end loveless marriages. During the French Revolution, couples had the right to divorce by mutual consent, and women could go to family courts with their grievances and obtain divorces.[19] In contrast, Thomas Jefferson's pre-Revolutionary notes supporting divorce legislation—sometimes used to indicate his progressive views on the subject—were occasioned by a quite traditional case that in any Christian nation aside from a colony would have been handled as an annulment. Jefferson's male client feared that his wife—with whom the client had allegedly never had sexual relations—would demand funds for a separate maintenance.[20]

In looking for decisive changes in master-servant relations produced by the Revolution, historians have also drawn attention to the sharp decline in the proportion of persons entering the country as indentured servants.[21] With bound servitude, whether by indenture or slave sale, we enter into that area of household governance that expanded the most during the colonial period. The indentured came primarily from Great Britain, Ireland, and the German states either voluntarily or as part of the convict trade. The heyday for the trade in English indentured servants was the seventeenth century, when economic depression, civil war, and overpopulation created a crisis situation. Once the economy improved, fewer signed up for transportation. By the mid-eighteenth century, Germans and Scots-Irish contributed more indentured servants than the English.

The primary way that English landed in America was as convicts that the British government paid merchants to send overseas. After the war, it is generally agreed, bound servitude of European immigrants declined, but as Robert Steinfeld observes in his recent study of master-servant law, "no broad-based movement to abolish indentured servitude ever developed."[22] In fact, the growth in the indenturing of African Americans as a way to lessen the blow of slave emancipation for owners in northern states may have made up for any declines.

Nor did the immigrant trade end abruptly. In certain years—until the 1820s, when it became rare—indentured servants continued to comprise a third or more of those migrating from certain countries. That this disintegration of the trade occurred because the new republic rejected the indenture system, however, seems unlikely. It is true that the United States did not encourage the dumping of convicts. The British redirected that trade to Australia. The postwar depression in the 1780s and 1790s also would have dampened demand. Indeed, the early republic period is one of the low points for free European immigration as well, because wars continually interrupted trade right up to the end of the era. Still, when servants were offered, even at higher prices, there were buyers, and that has made historians look at supply problems. The only group for whom we have good numbers on the proportion who entered as servants are the Germans who came through what was the major port at the time, Philadelphia. In nonwar years, anywhere from 30 to 55 percent of these migrants registered as servants upon landing.

The servant trade ended abruptly in the 1820s, though, as conditions at home improved and other destinations—some of which subsidized migration—grew in favor with emigrants and merchants. British merchants, stung by the commercial problems that emerged out of the American Revolution, might also have shunned the servant trade, a trade that had been connected with a staple or—in the case of convicts—with a government subsidy that no longer existed for them. As the supply of indentured servants became less and less certain, employers grew accustomed to free labor arrangements or to the indenturing of free blacks, courtesy of the gradual emancipation legislation in northern states.[23] By the 1830s, passage fares had plummeted, and merchants no longer found European servants a good investment. Federal laws against indenturing adult Americans and immigrants did not actually get passed until after the Civil War, and the indenturing of indigent children lasted much longer.[24]

Of all the areas where it has been argued the Revolution changed household relations, the clearest case would seem to be in regard to chattel slavery. The enslavement of Indians and then Africans expanded the household authority of white household heads far beyond the powers claimed in western Europe. The boom in first one plantation crop and then another, the rise of the British and British Americans as the premier slave traders in the world, and the improving mortality rates of African creoles meant that the slave population continued to increase its proportion of the total population in the thirteen colonies.

Even before the Revolution, the problems of increasing the slave population in a community—the cost of policing, fear of rebellion, and the cost of welfare for aged or ill slaves set free by masters who did not want to maintain them—made British and white colonials question the wisdom of continued importation. New York and later Virginia levied higher import taxes to discourage the trade, and Virginia and Connecticut forbade manumissions as a means to get masters to accept their responsibilities. To what degree was the nonslaveowning taxpayer supposed to finance the policing of runaways, who had a whole lifetime rather than four to five years to make a break? The British judiciaries in the early 1770s declared that English and Scottish law offered no support for slavery. Quakers in England and Pennsylvania first expelled members trading in slaves and then those who owned them. Some slaves during the war emancipated themselves by joining the British or received manumission by serving in the Continental forces. As states set up their new governments, those with 1 percent or less of their population of African descent (Vermont and Massachusetts) abolished slavery; others, like New Hampshire, left the law so uncertain, that it was unclear whether slavery would be supported in the courts. Slavery was banned in the Northwest territories. Northern states where the slave population in 1780 represented 10 percent or less of the whole—Rhode Island, Connecticut, New York, New Jersey, and Pennsylvania—opted instead for gradual abolition.[25] Delaware—where slaves represented one in five residents—and all Southern states except North Carolina passed manumission statutes allowing owners to emancipate their slaves.[26]

One might assume by these activities that the proportion of free African Americans steadily climbed in the decades that followed, but that was not the case. Only modest growth occurred in the proportion of the African American population that was free between 1790, when it stood at 8 percent, and 1810, when it reached almost 14 percent. Thereafter, in the fifty years leading up to the Civil War, the percentage of free men and women experienced no further rise at all. So what happened?

In the North, emancipation proceeded, albeit slowly. Connecticut freed the last slaves in New England by the 1848 Abolition Act. In the mid-Atlantic, eighteen slaves show up in the 1860 U.S. census for the state of New Jersey, and of course slavery in Delaware remained legal until the Civil War. Robert Fogel and Stanley Engerman labeled the process of gradual abolition "philanthropy at bargain prices" because it amounted to slaves paying masters to gain their freedom.[27] Under the provisions of these gradual abolition laws, slaves born as slaves remained slaves. Their children, born after an act's passage, labored as bound servants until (and here the laws differed slightly from one another) the ages of eighteen to twenty-one for males and eighteen to twenty-eight for females. Owners could and did sell slaves and their children to those in a state that still recognized slavery. Such sales apparently happened with some frequency in New York and New Jersey. Another tactic was to free the children and then hire them back as bound servants with a subsidy provided from the state. Owners could abandon old and sick slaves. Most of the debates around the measures dealing with emancipation quickly descended from lofty discourses on the natural rights of man to the mundane level of the property rights of slaveowners versus the costs to non-slaveowning taxpayers of bearing the welfare costs of freed slaves.[28] In the South, population growth outstripped manumissions whether the manumissions were owner- or slave-instigated. As such an overwhelming proportion of slaves lived south of the Mason-Dixon Line, what the northern states did within their own borders could not make a dent in the numbers. In contrast, the French National Convention abolished slavery in all French territories.

Gary Nash has offered an explanation for why the American Revolution did not end slavery gradually or in any other way.[29] The decade after the Revolution was a window of opportunity. Neither the cotton boom nor the Haitian Revolution had begun. North and South reached compromises on slavery in the western lands and on the slave trade. Yet no one in the Constitutional Convention or later in Congress either put forward any plan underwritten by the federal government for gradual abolition or took up suggestions offered by those from the Upper South, principally Virginia. Southerners' plans invariably included propositions for slaves' transportation back to Africa or to lands west of the Mississippi River in Spanish/French territory. Nash implies that the North did not care enough about the issue to support gradual abolition in the South because it might involve cost sharing or eating up the revenues from western land sales. Even more thorny an issue, though, was the postemancipation problem. For generations, many white southerners had lived in communities with black majorities, but—as slaves—African Americans had been under the control of white household heads. Having blacks in charge of their own households in the South or having them migrate to set up households in the North was not on the white agenda in either region. Neither were whites interested in engineering and paying for a migration under government auspices thousands of miles away.

Republics and natural rights were bad news for patriarchal theories in the long run. There is no doubt about that. Ultimately each aggrieved dependent group—whether wives, children, or those in servitude and slavery—used the documents of the Revolution as authority for their claims to equal citizenship.[30] (The most famous example is the Seneca Falls Declaration of 1848; see p. 12 above.)

In the Revolutionary period, though, most protest occurred on an individual level. There are many discrete examples of slaves, servants, youth, wives, and widows taking rights rhetoric quite personally and raising questions or—when given the opportunity—running off.[31] The barriers to collective action, however, were formidable. By definition, dependents had no standing in the public sphere. Within the household, they were isolated. Even slaves belonging to planters with large holdings often lived in small groups on quarters spread over many miles.

The generation of the Founding Fathers showed real irritation when parallels were drawn between the dependency of the king's colonial subjects and that of household dependents. John Adams's ridiculing of his wife's plea to "Remember the Ladies" and their legal plight when new laws were passed indicates the attitude.[32] In fact, considering the amount of constitution writing that went on, what is most remarkable is the reluctance to rein in the powers of the household head.

The most famous of those who played pivotal roles in the war for independence and the formation of a republic—Benjamin Franklin, who presented the Revolution to the world; George Washington, the prime sculptor of a republican army and the presidency; John Adams, the Revolution's chronicler; Thomas Jefferson, its principal intellectual and the new republic's most successful politician; and the main explicators of the Constitution, James Madison and Alexander Hamilton—all avoided as much as possible discussions about the domestic subjects of the new republic's citizenry. Because western Europeans—both mischievous monarchists such as Samuel Johnson as well as concerned republicans—constantly brought up the one kind of dependent that they did not have and that Americans did, the chattel slave, the founders had to confront that issue.[33] It was not one, however, on which they liked to dwell. Given that this generation of Revolutionaries was far from being tied to old ways for the sake of tradition, had fewer ties to orthodox Christianity than perhaps any generation of American politicians before or since, and consistently made financial sacrifices in order to follow their dream of national political greatness, why did they ultimately draw a line in the sand around the household? It is not that a revolution in this sphere was beyond the ability of late-eighteenth-century republicans to fathom. During the 1790s, the French revolutionaries mandated equal inheritance for all children, divorce on grounds including mutual consent and emotional incompatibility, abolition of slavery and the slave trade, and a number of other acts leading to a much more egalitarian household system.[34]

Jack Greene, in discussing the limits of the American Revolution, has stressed the preoccupation of the revolutionary generation with private rather than public life.[35] Delving into the family histories of the Founding Fathers reveals how these ambitious household heads relied on the resources their dependents provided. Unlike those with king, lord, and bishop, these household relationships affected everyday life for nearly every inhabitant, including its most celebrated. Only with extreme difficulty could people in this society live on their own, and in most cases such a life was associated with poverty or ostracism. Whether head or dependent, one needed a household.

For the founders, making an economically advantageous marriage was essential for creating or sustaining a successful household establishment. Among that group, only James Madison married a woman—the widow Dolley Payne Todd—whose financial contributions appear to have been negligible. To this case I will return later. Aside from Madison, the Founding Fathers married in their late twenties and generally did better by their marriages than by their father's patrimony.

Benjamin Franklin had sixteen siblings in competition for parental resources. His father refused to set him up as a printer, and even as enterprising as the young Franklin was, he had great difficulty finding anyone to underwrite his business. He began a courtship with his landlady's daughter, Deborah Read, but believing that he had support from the Pennsylvania governor, Franklin abruptly left for London to buy a printing press and forgot about the young woman. No money in fact materialized, and he had to return to Philadelphia, still looking for funding. He then tried to underwrite his business through marriage with the relative of a friend. "I let her [the friend] know that I expected as much money with their daughter as would pay off my remaining debt for the printing house." The friend reported back that no such sum could be spared. Franklin then suggested that the parents "mortgage their house." At that point, they told Franklin to get lost. Deborah and her mother's boardinghouse started looking good again, and it is to be noted that Franklin's union with Read and the opening of his business occurred in the same year, 1730. He never formally married her, allegedly because she already was married to a man who deserted her. The exact legal status of the earlier alliance she contracted, however, rivals the confusion surrounding the maternity of Franklin's illegitimate son, William, who came to live with them. One biographer assumes the shrewd Franklin never sought a legal marriage because he feared being held responsible for his predecessor's debts. He had no problem, though, accepting property from her mother. By 1734, Widow Read had devised to Franklin the land on Market Street where he placed his home and shop.[36]

Washington's father died when George—the son of his father's second marriage—was eleven. Although his half brothers treated him well, they had first claim to and management of the patrimony. Upon reaching adulthood, Washington was to receive ten slaves; a 260-acre farm, where his mother resided with him and his siblings; a tract of undeveloped land; and three town lots in the yet-to-be-realized metropolis of Fredericksburg across the Rappahannock from the Washingtons' farm. As Washington's inheritance would hardly propel him to the top of the planter hierarchy, a strategy suitable for a younger son—a naval or military career—was mapped out. Washington followed the prescribed course, performing additional government service employment as a surveyor. Two deaths, however, intervened to make his future considerably brighter: that of his eldest half brother, Lawrence—through which he eventually inherited Mount Vernon—and even more important, that of Daniel Parke Custis, heir to the fortunes of the Ludwell, Parke, and Custis families, who left a personal estate of over £23,000 sterling, including hundreds of slaves and 17,438 acres of real estate in prime Tidewater locations.

A year and a half after Custis's July 1757 death, George Washington had wed his widow and taken control of the entire estate. Usually it was not so easy, because a man of Custis's wealth would normally have a will in which his wife would receive "for widowhood or life" bequests, which were intended to ensure that his personalty and his realty would devolve on his children and that any subsequent husband would have little opportunity to control the decedent's family's wealth. But strangely, Custis died without a will, and his two children were minors. Under intestacy, Martha—the Custis widow—did only get a life interest in land and slaves (which were considered for inheritance purposes as real estate in Virginia), but the share was one-third larger than most bequests to widows, and it did not expire when she remarried. Her one-third share of the other wealth was not for life, but forever. As also happened with intestate as opposed to testate estates, the widow, Martha, administered the estate and had a role in managing the other two shares, those of her young son and daughter.

Enter George. Following a family tradition, Washington went after the Custis widow, proposing marriage by March of 1758. The first American Washington, John the immigrant, in 1657 established himself by marrying a Virginian woman whose father gave him seven hundred acres near Pope's Creek off the Potomac River. In George's case, all of Martha's personal estate (in Virginia that meant all wealth except land and slaves) became his; also her dower lands and slaves (her lifetime intestacy share) fell to him during their marriage. Washington also took over administration of her children's estate. So in a few years, Washington went from being a man who depended largely on government service for his advancement to one who was in charge of thousands of acres of developed land, hundreds of slaves, and accounts with British merchants totaling thousands of pounds sterling. Washington had to work for his money because of the complexity of the various estates involved, but he also would now be considered a leading member of the planter class in British America's oldest and largest colony.[37]

Moving to John Adams, we switch to fortunes of, at best, hundreds of pounds rather than thousands. His father was a Braintree farmer and shoemaker, not one of the glamour trades in the preindustrial world. He sent John, his eldest son, to Harvard to become a minister, but the younger Adams chose the law, a profession looked upon with some suspicion in the sectarian environment of small-town New England. At age twenty-nine, he married a girl ten years his junior, Abigail Smith, who was the daughter of a minister in a neighboring town and his socially prominent wife. It was apparently not love at first sight. Upon their first meeting five years earlier, Adams noted in his diary that both Abigail and her sister were "wits." Adams did not intend a compliment. "Wits" lacked the "tenderness" and "fondness" necessary, in his opinion, in good wives and mothers.[38] At the time, he had his eye on a more malleable creature. Something made Adams change his mind, though, and he soon came to believe that a marriage to this earlier love would have cast him into "absolute poverty" and "obscurity".[39] Besides his education, Adams could only bring a cottage and ten-acre farm to his marriage. Most biographers of the Adams family draw attention to the gap in social status between John and Abigail and see the union as the outcome of John's dogged determination to please his father and improve himself through marriage. Her parents, according to family tradition, greeted the match with dismay but did not try to block it.[40] As soon as they married, Abigail, in her husband's name, began buying land. Ultimately, Abigail inherited from her father a half interest in an eighty-six-acre farm in Medford, an estate amounting to £439 in the 1780s.[41] After this inheritance came to them, Abigail joined her husband on his mission to France; she also continued to make real estate purchases. Later she received a substantial estate from her maternal uncle.[42] For much of his life, Adams worried about money and complained that public service had interfered with the improvement of his family's financial status.

Thomas Jefferson is a particularly interesting case. In an autobiographical statement written toward the end of his life, he reflected on his only marriage.

On the 1st of January, 1772, I was married to Martha Skelton, widow of Bathurst Skelton, and daughter of John Wayles; then twenty-three years old. Mr. Wayles was a lawyer of much practice, to which he was introduced more by his great industry, punctuality & practical readiness, than to eminence in the science of his profession. He was a most agreeable companion, full of pleasantry & good humor, and welcomed in every society. He acquired a handsome fortune, died in May, 1773, leaving three daughters, and the portion which came on that event to Mrs. Jefferson, after the debts should be paid, which were very considerable, was about equal to my own patrimony, and consequently doubled the ease of our circumstances.[43]

In addition to his focus on the attributes of the father rather than those of the bride, Jefferson's characterization of the portion as "about equal to my own patrimony" is also rather curious. Jefferson received through his wife 135 slaves and over 11,000 acres in 1774, following his father-in-law's death. In contrast, his inheritance from his own father, which he claimed in 1764 at age twenty-one, consisted of twenty slaves and an estimated

2,650 acres, plus the residue of the estate after all debts and legacies were paid. However one looks at these two inheritances, it is difficult to characterize Martha's as merely "about equal to" Jefferson's. Later he blamed most of his financial woes on the £3700 debt left by his father-in-law, although how much of the problem stemmed from the way Jefferson dealt with the disruptions of the war and currency devaluation are unclear.

His own father's estate also carried with it obligations. His mother retained the home plantation, included in his portion, and its profits until her death in 1776. The dowries of his six sisters—£200 and one slave (a portion identical to his mother's)—had to come out of the residue left him, essentially 2500 acres of land.[44] These bequests may explain why he was busily selling off real estate in the late 1760s and early 1770s after taking control of his patrimony.[45] The estate might have been sufficient to support his mother, the other children, and Jefferson in a style to which they had become accustomed when all lived together; however, maintaining separate households for a widow and two sons as well as contributing to the households of daughters might have spread the patrimony a bit thin. Seventeen seventy-one proved a particularly anxious year for Jefferson financially, and he indicated fears about being overextended in his letters to British merchants.[46] Coincidentally this is the year he began his courtship of the young widow Martha Wayles Skelton, whose rich father specialized in collecting debts planters owed to British merchants. They married at the beginning of 1772, and Martha inherited her portion in 1774. At that point, Jefferson went on a buying spree of land. The merger, at least initially, catapulted Jefferson into the upper ranks of landowners and slaveowners in his county.

Alexander Hamilton, born in 1755 on the West Indian island of Nevis, was the son of a Scottish merchant and a woman married to someone else. She had left her husband to live with Hamilton's father, who abandoned them both by the time Hamilton reached the age of eleven. Neither parent provided an estate. Under English common law, bastards had no rights of inheritance. Apprenticed to New York merchants with an office in the West Indies, Hamilton eventually traveled to their home base to study law. In listing the virtues he sought in a wife, the future secretary of the treasury candidly admitted, "as to fortune, the larger stock of that the better . . . as I have not much of my own."[47] Hamilton hitched his star to the Revolutionary cause, and in 1780 he snared the amiable daughter of a Patriot general and important New York landlord, Philip Schuyler, although rumor had it that Hamilton preferred her older married sister.

In an age of family firms, marriage represented the primary means of acquiring capital. If one's object were to gain a fortune or preserve one, marriage to a woman whose family resources promised to be of help down the road seemed essential. As far as I could ascertain from biographical information and family papers, it was not the practice among these Americans—unlike their European counterparts—for the bride's family to make a formal agreement to endow their daughter when she wed. Rather, the transfer of a daughter's portion to her husband normally came at the father's death. In that respect, suitors might prefer either girls with rich dead fathers or affluent widows, because one had a better idea of what might be coming. Given the importance of the capital derived from marriage, husbands from the American propertied classes had little incentive to disturb coverture. Fathers had more reason, but nevertheless, they also may have liked the system because it gave them an excuse, if they wanted, to delay transfer of portions until their death.

Nor should one expect the founding husbands to show much enthusiasm for making divorce easier. Rumors of marital infidelity swirled around Franklin, Jefferson, and Hamilton.[48] Hamilton's wife, particularly, had reason to feel aggrieved. Besides the embarrassment brought on by the public disclosure of Hamilton's adulterous affair with Maria Reynolds and his efforts to buy silence, Hamilton's own financial affairs were in disarray when he left government in the 1790s. When the former secretary of the treasury engaged with Aaron Burr in a duel in 1804, his own eldest son had died three years earlier under similar circumstances, all the rest of his children were minors, and his estate was nonexistent. Before the encounter, Hamilton wrote a will. Knowing the financial disaster he was leaving behind, he gave his minor children an equal opportunity to pay off his debts and take care of their mother, his wife. He had hopes, though, that "her own patrimonial resources" would "preserve her from Indigence."[49] How his wife, Elizabeth Schuyler Hamilton, or her family felt about the situation is reflected on her tombstone in the churchyard of lower Manhattan's Trinity Church. Carved many years later, the tombstone identifies her first as "the daughter of Philip Schuyler" and only second as "the wife of Alexander Hamilton."

Granting wives—so important to one's economic status—the right to handle their own money, to exit the relationship, or to demand a separate maintenance when something happened not to their liking (such as infidelity or insolvency) would seem to run counter to the whole purpose of these unions in the first place.

The often-complicated merger of funds involved in the marriage of husband to wife also complicated the relationship of master and slave. Although the founders condemned the practice of slavery, and several joined and led abolition and manumission societies in their states, all of them had at one time or another headed households with African Americans who were being held in one form of bound servitude or another. The hypocrisy of their position has not gone unnoticed. Why they got caught in such hypocrisy, though, remains something of a mystery. On one level their predicament arose from a need to demonstrate social status, and on another it can be traced to a labor shortage in a high fertility society. What distinguished respectable households from those in the laboring classes, both in Europe and America, was the presence of at least one servant to perform menial tasks. The situation is analogous to the plight of today's managerial class who by definition must employ a secretary or administrative assistant. In addition, households with infants and many small children had difficulty functioning without a nursemaid. Finally, for the plantation elite, slaves proved to be their greatest source of wealth, one not easily parted with if the family were to retain its preeminence.

In the South, these servants overwhelmingly consisted of African American slaves. In the North in times of low immigration, the temptation to solve the servant problem by buying slaves or indentured servants, whatever their color, rather than paying premium prices for free white servants proved hard to resist. In plantation areas, it of course went beyond that—slaves were the most valuable property many white households possessed. In both cases, because property in persons was more moveable than land, slaves were a form of wealth frequently attached to women and passed to their husbands at marriage. Similarly, in some states slaves, like land, had dower rights attached. Consequently, when a man died, his widow's fortunes frequently depended upon her lifetime claim to the profits from slave labor.

In the cases of Washington and Jefferson, slaves constituted one of or even their major form of wealth, due to agricultural depression and the instability of financial assets during the period. Each, like his fellow Virginian James Madison, had over one hundred slaves in his household. The fact that the bulk of both men's slaves had come to them through their wives or stepchildren further complicated matters, as did the very restrictive nature of the state manumission law.

Washington, who composed his own will, catalogued the problems involved in extricating himself from slaveholding.

Upon the decease of my wife, it is my Will & desire that all the Slaves which I hold in *my own right,* shall receive their freedom.—To emancipate them during her life, would, tho' earnestly wished by me, be attended with such insuperable difficulties on account of their intermixture by Marriages with the Dower Negroes, as to excite the most painful sensations, if not disagreeable consequences from the latter, while both descriptions are in the occupancy of the same Proprietor; it not being in my power, under the tenure by which the Dower Negroes are held, to manumit them.—And whereas among those who will receive freedom according to this devise, there may be some, who from old age or bodily infirmities, and others who on account of their infancy, that will be unable to support themselves; it is my Will and desire that all who come under the first & second description shall be comfortably cloathed & fed by my heirs while they live;—and that such of the latter description as have no parents living, or if living are unable or unwilling to provide for them, shall be bound by the Court until they shall arrive at the age of twenty five years;—and in cases where no record can be produced, whereby their ages can be ascertained, the judgment of the Court . . . shall be adequate. . . . The Negros thus bound, are . . . to be taught to read & write; and to be brought up to some useful occupation, agreeably to the Laws of the Commonwealth of Virginia, providing for the support of Orphan and other poor Children.—And I do hereby expressly forbid the Sale, or transportation out of the said Commonwealth, of any Slave I may die possessed of.[50]

The slaves Washington held through his wife, the dower slaves, did not belong to her either but had come to her through her husband's family and upon her death would go to her first husband's heirs, her grandchildren. By law, the fate of the dower slaves and their descendants would fall to those heirs and their spouses, who also had a dower, or curtesy, interest in this wealth. While none of these heirs or their spouses may have loved the institution of slavery, they probably did feel attached to their lifestyle, and, unlike George Washington, they did not have concerns about their place in history prodding them on to emancipate.

Even those slaves that Washington held "in my own right" posed problems under the 1782 emancipation law, the most liberal of the versions of manumission provisions passed in Virginia before the Civil War. Fearful that slaveowners would use the law to free themselves of the expense of supporting very young or old, injured, or mentally or physically impaired slaves and thereby transfer the responsibility to the public, the legislature only allowed the unconditional emancipation of prime age male (twenty-one to forty-five years) and female (eighteen to forty-five years) slaves. The rest, even if emancipated, remained the responsibility of the former owner.[51] So Washington, in making the provisions he did, was attempting to comply with the law. In specifying his slaves' education and banning their transportation out, though, he went further than much current opinion held was desirable. Martha Washington died in 1802. The last of Washington's "pensioned" slaves died in 1833, by which time much more restrictive laws regarding emancipation and the rights of freedmen had been put in place.

Jefferson, dying in poor financial condition in the 1820s, faced an even trickier situation. In 1806, Viginia passed a law forbidding freed slaves from staying in the state, and while legislators modified the law in 1816 to allow court petitions overriding exile, the fear of banishment from friends and kin continued to hover over the heads of the emancipated.[52] Also, unlike Washington, Jefferson had legitimate lineal heirs as well as illegitimate enslaved ones, and the husband of his much doted upon white fifty-something daughter Patsy had gone bankrupt. Along with the grandson of his other legitimate daughter, who had died, Patsy received his estate in a trust to protect it against the creditors of her husband, with her having the right to dispose of that property by will. Much of that property was in slaves, though no mention was made of it in the will. Only in the codicil are slaves noted at all, and that is solely to free five servants, three of them from the Hemings family and descendants of John Wayles, Jefferson's father in law, and himself. Jefferson's apparent taking of Sally Hemings — his slave and his first wife's half-sister — as a concubine, while convenient sexually, posed a variety of problems later for both his legitimate heirs and his children by Hemings.[53]

Emancipation did not jeopardize the estates of northerners in the same way. Yet gradual abolition emancipation seemed more problematic to them than one would think. Franklin held slaves in his household most of his life, despite the fact that he wrote in 1750, "we do not like Negro Servants."[54] His dislike at that time seemed to be based on dissatisfaction with their service rather than guilt about slaveholding. As more and more notice was taken of slavery, Franklin found intellectual reasons for his disapproval of slave work habits. Like Adam Smith, he concluded that free labor outperformed slave labor, because slaves derived no benefit from their work. Yet when the Seven Years' War siphoned off indentured servants, Franklin and his wife bought more slaves. The Revolution turned him into a slaveholding antislavery advocate. Presumably all slaves had died or had been transferred to others by the time he became president of the Pennsylvania Abolition Society. In his last will, Franklin left a bequest to his son-in-law that provided for money to free a slave still held in his daughter's household.

Both John and Abigail Adams denounced slavery as unjust and as a corrupting influence on whites. But even though the Massachusetts courts in 1783 had declared slavery incompatible with the state constitution, John Adams declined to support a bill in the legislature that would have clearly abolished slavery, arguing that it was too divisive. Those of African descent employed by Abigail in the house and in the field seem to all have been servants, although their exact status is difficult to discern. For example, there is Phoebe. This slave Abigail's father emancipated in his 1783 will, the same year the courts acted against slavery, "if she should chuse it." But if she did not, then she could go into the household of one of his three daughters. She went into the Adams household, which received the interest from £100 to maintain Phoebe in the case of her sickness or in her old age. Adams claimed that his refusal to use slave labor earlier, when the "practice was not disgraceful," had cost him "thousands of dollars."[55] Yet the frugal Adamses managed to capture some of the savings available from African American labor. Abigail reported with pride in 1776, a month or so before independence, that she had hired a "Negro fellow" for six months at a price that was "much lower than I had any prospect of getting" elsewhere.[56]

Marriage and slavery are also connected in the life of Alexander Hamilton, a charter member of the New York Manumission Society. He became a slaveowner shortly after his marriage to Elizabeth Schuyler. In 1781, we find him writing to George Clinton that he hoped to soon have the funds to pay "the value of the woman Mrs. H. had of Mrs. Clinton."[57] Her ultimate fate is unknown. New Yorkers had a long tradition of using slaves as domestic servants. Given the disparity in their fortunes, Hamilton would have been in a poor position to interfere with his wife's decision even if he disapproved, and there is no proof that he did. In the years of depression and low immigration from Europe, being able to have perpetual rights to a servant had its attractions to rich white women like Elizabeth Schuyler Hamilton in their childbearing years.

Nor can one find in the lives of the founders much reason for them to want to alter the unique English inheritance system that gave them absolute power over what their children did or did not receive. It is particularly unlikely that they would want to change to the more egalitarian system of revolutionary France, where fathers had no choice but to distribute 90 percent of their estate equally among their children. It is not that they displayed great dynastic ambitions of a patrilineal nature. More characteristically, provisions in their wills served as rewards or reprimands to sons and as protective mechanisms for daughters. Franklin punished his son, who had chosen the Loyalist cause during the Revolution. "The part he acted against me in the late war, which is of public notoriety," the old gentleman explained, "will account for my leaving him no more of an estate [that] he endeavored to deprive me of."[58] Washington died childless but favored certain nephews and step-grandsons. Hamilton left debts rather than bequests to his children, but during life he would have been much less free to operate as he did if he had been forced to promise endowments for his children. Both John Adams and Jefferson had son-in-law problems. As much as husbands benefitted by coverture, fathers of daughters found it a problem, particularly when their daughters' husbands had financial or personal difficulties. Any wealth left a married daughter came under her husband's control and from there went into the coffers of his creditors. Abigail Adams's favorite daughter, Nabby, had a husband who from time to time performed a disappearing act, leaving the family destitute. Because all property fell under the management, if not the ownership, of the husband, any parental assistance had to be carefully transmitted. Jefferson's favorite and only surviving offspring, Patsy, was in her fifties when he wrote his last will. To protect her estate from the insolvency of her husband's, he had to create a trust. Mandatory endowment at marriage would have prevented such patriarchal fine-tuning.

Probably more to the point than looking to the Founding Fathers themselves to rein in their own power, would be to focus attention instead upon their dependents. Why didn't they react to the rhetoric of republicanism—life, liberty, and the pursuit of happiness—that through their association with a Founding Father swirled all around them?

Pursuing this line of inquiry leads us back to the household of James Madison, the one famous founder who diverged from the pattern found among the other major leaders. This time, though, rather than viewing the decisions from the perspective of the head of household, my focus will be on Dolley. Born Dolley Payne to a Virginia slaveholding family, her father, a Quaker, manumitted his slaves in 1782 and moved to Philadelphia to set up a starch business. His enterprise failed in 1789, and the Quakers who equated bankruptcy with profligacy expelled him from the meeting. Spiraling downward mobility forced his wife to convert their home into a boardinghouse. A Quaker lawyer, John Todd, rescued the twenty-year-old Dolley from these depressing circumstances at the beginning of 1790 by proposing marriage.[59] They had two children before he and one of the children died in the yellow fever epidemic of 1793. For a number of reasons too complicated to relate here, Dolley ended up the sole heir to his estate, which included his portion from his father, who also had died in the epidemic.

At that point, the vivacious twenty-four-year-old widow had several options. Her fortune was not vast, but unlike most widows of the time, she had complete ownership of it. Her husband attached no "for life only" or "during minority of child" stipulations to the bequests, and he named her executrix. Teamed up with her mother, Dolley could have perhaps had the finest hotel in town. There were other possibilities as well. She struck up an acquaintance with Aaron Burr, a sometime resident of her mother's boardinghouse, and in her newly minted will named him the guardian of her young son. Gore Vidal notwithstanding, it is difficult to believe Burr's interest was merely avuncular. Her Quaker lawyer, Wilkins, also had romantic intentions. So what did she do? Burr introduced her to Madison, eighteen years her senior and some inches her junior.[60] While many in Philadelphia marveled at his intellect, Madison at forty-two had apparently remained a bachelor out of choice—a choice made by the women who had rejected his overtures. After his introduction to Dolley, he immediately proposed. She did a credit check on his character and finances through her lawyer, put the most valuable part of her estate in trust for her son, and then accepted Madison, who needed her social skills much more than her property. Why did she give up the chance for respectable independence as a widowed proprietress or pass up a romance with the much more dashing public figure Aaron Burr—a path similar to the one followed by her French counterpart, Josephine de Beauharnais—in order to link up with a guy of good though not fabulous wealth who had trouble filling his dance card?

In retrospect, it turned out to be a brilliant move. Madison became secretary of state and then president. The story of the part played by Dolley and other women like her in political networking during the period has now been told.[61] Her son grew up to be a hopeless gambler, going through his own estate and a good part of Madison's. Dolley remained intensely loyal and supportive. Whatever financial problems she had at the end of her life, after James Madison's death, would undoubtedly have been much worse—given her devotion to her only child—if she had attempted to become a Philadelphia businesswoman or ended up following the career moves of Aaron Burr. But no one could imagine these things in 1794. What Dolley had experienced at that point, however, was the barrier put in front of a woman living on her own and the difficulties associated with an improvident husband. She had seen her mother suffer from her father's business failure, watched as the Friends threw him out for insolvency, and then had had to fight tooth and nail to get her dead husband's Quaker brother to release her inheritance. He did so only after she agreed to put most of the estate in trust for her son and to raise him as a Quaker. Marrying Madison meant returning to coverture and to the slave system rejected by her parents, yet for Dolley, an ambitious woman, freedom and the tough love of the Friends apparently had even less appeal. Her ability to operate outside the household government framework was so limited that she seemingly jumped at the opportunity to return to dependency.[62]

Circumstances in the lives of slave women and men have some parallels. Why did Phoebe—the slave of Abigail Adams's late father, Reverend William Smith—when offered the choice of manumission or living in the household of one of his daughters, ultimately choose to live with the Adamses? It appears that Phoebe initially went out on her own, but her own marriage and Abigail's decision to leave for Europe to join John resulted in her becoming caretaker of the house. While it is true that Reverend Smith set aside the interest from £100 for the cost of her upkeep, the money was not put in her hands so that she could use it to start a business or buy property. In her situation, a comparatively good one, she still had few options other than domestic service.[63]

It is commonly believed that northeastern towns offered the least restrictive environments for free blacks in the early national period. In the counties and communities of the South where blacks had a majority, legislators and judges made sure that freedom exacted a heavy price. The fear of African Americans no longer under the household government of white families frightened the citizenry. By the time Madison made his last will, in the 1830s, Virginia required freed slaves to leave the state, which meant leaving all their family, friends, and contacts—and, preferably, the United States. Madison freed no slaves, but he offered a substantial donation to the American Colonization Society, whose objective was to resettle freedmen in Africa. Even if a freed man or woman managed to stay in Virginia, the future was hardly bright. Just as a public school movement was gathering steam in the United States, Virginia—in the wake of the Nat Turner revolt—passed a law making it a crime to teach free blacks to read and write. Freedom came to have many of the aspects of slavery.

What kept the American Revolution a respected tradition, where the French Revolution went off into radicalism and disrepute, is that it did not pretend to mess with what were understood to be natural forms of subordination. Chattel slavery had unnaturally expanded the powers of the household head, and those powers had to be slowly retracted. However, in the South—where most of the enslaved population resided—attempts at reversal proved so economically and politically threatening to white households that ultimately slaveowners turned to justifying the expansion.

To so many contemporaries, the French example of overthrowing the authority of the husband, the father, and the master could only bring a bad name to liberty. As John Adams lectured his grown son in 1799, stable government required "a marked subordination of mother and children to the father."[64] Familial relations based on affection rather than hierarchy produced chaos. Before the French considered restoring monarchy, aristocracy, and the church, they acted, under Napoleon, to reverse the measures taken to remove patriarchal authority from the lives of household dependents—reinstating some paternal testamentary power and revoking a daughter's right to dowry; hiking the age of consent to marriage for sons to twenty-five; reviving the power of the father to have a child confined for disciplinary purposes; reasserting that wives had no legal person separate from that of their husbands; and restricting grounds for divorce. In addition, Napoleon reintroduced the slave trade and slavery in the territories. Those working on the civil code wanted to limit grounds for divorce to a wife's adultery, but Napoleon, who had his own personal reasons, intervened. No women's rights advocate, Napoleon had other objectives. Stung by his wife's adultery and her failure to produce an heir, Napoleon kept his eye on the revisions, wanting to make sure that the legal subordination of wife to husband, the right of adoption (just in case it was needed for purposes of succession), and divorce by mutual consent made it into the final draft. Memoirs from the sessions of the Council of State indicate that he sought to keep the broader grounds for divorce because he felt a man would be loathe to humiliate himself and to cast aspersions on the legitimacy of his children by admitting his wife's infidelity. For the time being, then, Napoleon saved divorce by mutual consent, but ultimately the restoration of the Bourbon kings swept away all divorce rights.[65]

The failure of the French experiment in household egalitarianism left would-be reformers in the United States and elsewhere with no place to go. Ideas discredited as anarchical and libertine could not easily be introduced again for another generation. Meanwhile, household heads of the

United States could congratulate themselves on their own successful revolution, one that left the household power structure more or less intact.

So what happened to "Mr. Sensitive," that appealing head of household featured in the conversation pieces discussed in the beginning of this chapter? Probably his progressiveness has been overestimated. The transatlantic nature of this trend in portraiture and the decidedly loyalist sentiments of many of the subjects and painters rule out attributing it to republican egalitarianism. In just the small sample provided here, Cadwalader and Mifflin supported the Revolution. Peale stayed in America, but not so Copley and Pepperrell. The Pepperrell family piece, which now hangs in a North Carolina museum, was actually painted in England by expatriate Copley after Pepperrell had fled with his children. Although his wife appears in glowing good health, the portrait appears to be a posthumous memorial to her and to a happier time, for she had died in America in 1775. Pepperrell attributed her demise to the Boston boycott of British goods, which forced her to eat salt provisions while nursing a newborn.[66]

These pictures and the persona of "Mr. Sensitive" appear to belong to that late-eighteenth-century phenomenon sometimes referred to as the "culture of sensibility." A particular strain of Enlightenment thought sparked this intellectual trend, which encouraged the development of sensitivity toward others, particularly one's inferiors—the poor and the weak, including females and children. Men of fashion were encouraged to cultivate their feminine side by giving to the destitute, eschewing violence toward women, and appreciating the innocence of the young. The application of "Mr. Sensitive" to the head of household suggests some discomfort with the traditional more authoritarian pose usually seen in conversation pieces. This new figure is more caring, less stuffy and self-important. If we look closely, though, we see that in these pictures of the 1760s and 1770s, "Mr. Sensitive," for all his concern for others, did not exactly allow himself to be marginalized in the family piece.[67] He was still the focus of attention. Thomas Bradshaw is at the center of his family painting, towering above his wife, sister, and children. John Cadwalader benevolently offers his offspring a peach, while his wife admiringly looks up at him. Pepperrell looks down at his child, who is reaching up to him while his wife has faraway eyes, as befits a posthumous subject. Even the portrait of the Mifflin couple—absent children and larger family and often cited as an example of Revolutionary, nonpatriarchal relations[68]—sends mixed messages. The wife, née Sarah Morris, is engaged in the

9 Edward Savage, *Washington Family* (1796).
COURTESY OF NATIONAL GALLERY OF ART, WASHINGTON, D.C., ANDREW W. MELLON
COLLECTION; PHOTOGRAPH ©2001 BOARD OF TRUSTEES

patriotic task of handloom work and stares outward while her husband
admires her activities, but Mifflin's satisfied expression and his pointing
with the book toward his wife, who looks warily at the viewer, also puts
this painting in the category of the household head presenting his family.
In place of a child, she has a loom, and she and her industry are a credit
to patriot Mifflin.

"Mr. Sensitive's" run as head of household in conversation pieces did
not last more than a couple of decades. As the French Revolution gained
steam, his persona became non grata, both with reform-minded women
and men, who viewed his sentimental demeanor as self-indulgent show
with no meaningful action, and with conservatives, who considered him
to epitomize the kind of misplaced optimism about human nature that
produced civil disorder.[69] The most famous conversation piece in American history was painted at the end of the century, and it has a very different tone from the "Mr. Sensitive" paintings. In Edward Savage's 1796
portrayal of the family of George Washington (fig. 9), "Mr. Sensitive" has

been replaced by the subdued and authoritative persona of the first president. Unlike the aforementioned paintings, which were created for the pleasure of the persons who commissioned them, their families, and their friends, this portrait had wide public exposure. Other artists produced copies, and printers issued engravings. The analogy between the head of the household and the head-of-state in this work is far from subtle. While monarchs commonly sat for this kind of paintings, this official form of the family piece for an American president appears to be the first and last. Washington wears the somber garb typical of dissenter household heads prior to the Revolution and of republicans afterward. He and Martha are both seated. The seated male has been associated with a new post-Revolutionary affectionate family,[70] but European conversation pieces of the seventeenth and eighteenth centuries also offer examples of this compositional form. There are many ways to give the household head his due. If he is not the tallest in the picture, then he is centered, foregrounded, or made the focus of the subject matter. Here, the map of Washington, D.C., on the table draws attention to Washington's political role. All others in the picture face him—Martha, her Custis grandson and granddaughter, and a liveried servant, believed to be Billy Lee. Lee was Washington's valet, the man whom Washington freed with an annuity in his will. No other well-known family portrait from the thirteen colonies or states contains a servant or slave. As the caption indicates, the painting portrays "The Washington Family," even though George did not share a common ancestor with any of them. This picture captures a unique moment in time. It has the early modern trappings of the individual patriarchal household with attentive dependents and servants that the "Mr. Sensitive" portrayals tried to minimize. Women (Martha and her granddaughter), however, are actors pointing to places on the map, and the republican signposts are obvious. A no-nonsense air infuses this depiction of the early national household head. The painting rejects both ostentatious stately home settings that could cast doubt on one's political virtue and all playful self-representation that could undermine household and civil authority.

4

MARRIAGE AND THE
EARLY AMERICAN HOUSEHOLD

In Search of Parental Control

IF IT IS IMPOSSIBLE TO DOCUMENT AN IMMEDIATE AND DRAMATIC
shrinkage in the powers of the household head due to the republicanism
and liberalism of the American Revolution, what other factors can help
account for his increasing vulnerability during the course of the nineteenth century? In chapter 2, I argued that the power of the individual
household head expanded significantly over the colonial period. That expansion did not come only at the expense of dependents. It also diminished the influence of lineage, a point heretofore left unexplored. At the
same time, the ecclesiastical bureaucracy, active in policing households
in Europe, compiled a much spottier record in British America. Historically, lineage and church could be rivals of the household head, but when
dependents rebelled, lineage and church could also be his allies. The lack
of allies is particularly noticeable in the father's dealings with the marriages of his children. The inability of the American patriarch—despite
his other powers—to control the household-formation impulses of the
younger generation, left the partriarch, I would argue, primed for an
early fall.

A common assumption made about the history of the American family is that parents, or more accurately, fathers, managed the marriage system throughout the colonial period. While historians seldom portray fathers as forcing a spouse on their offspring, these patriarchs are described
as playing a major role in finding suitable mates, checking their financials,
and drawing up the agreements on portions and dowries. This assumption is made about societies in both the South and the North. "Fathers . . .
until at least the mid-eighteenth century used their leverage as owners
of family land and property to supervise and frequently to arrange their

children's marriages," writes one expert on the eighteenth-century planter families of the Chesapeake. Another remarks that "as soon as a couple decided to wed, negotiations between their fathers ensued to ensure that the couple would have a good chance to succeed. . . . These negotiations were the most protracted among the gentry class . . . but yeomen families also insisted that portions and dowries be paid to the new couple." A third writes that "parents and guardians entered into complex negotiations to settle the size of the marriage portion."[1] The historical literature on the New England family contains similar statements, beginning with Edmund Morgan's description over fifty years ago in *The Puritan Family:*

Parental wisdom was to be trusted in the business of choosing a mate . . . they frequently determined what lady he [their son] should address, and they almost always determined what young man should be given the chance to court their daughter. . . . the usual factors affecting parental consent for a marriage were two, religion and wealth.[2]

Morgan went on to describe the bargaining between the fathers of the prospective groom and bride, and in a frequently cited passage, he even estimated the relative size of each family's contribution. He calculated that commonly the bride's family put into the conjugal fund half as much as the groom's.[3] After Morgan's, probably the most consulted study of a New England family life is Philip Greven's book on colonial Andover. Greven stresses direct parental intervention.

The intimate relationship between paternal authority over children and the possession of land is revealed with some clarity in the marriage negotiations of the sons and daughters of New England families. . . . Although relatively few records of such marriage negotiations have survived . . . enough do exist to serve as models for actions which almost certainly were commonplace at most levels of society during the seventeenth century.[4]

Going along with this assumption of parental control in the colonial period is an accompanying belief that parents' supervision weakened by the late eighteenth century, and that by the beginning of the Victorian period, it had been supplanted by the romantic choices of the participants.[5] The crucial piece of research on this transition is still Daniel Scott Smith's 1973 article probing parental power over marriage in Hingham, a township near Boston, from 1680 to 1880.[6] Smith ingeniously devised four indicators of this loss of influence—no difference in marriage age for sons whose fathers died early (before age sixty) than for those who died later; no difference between the wealth of fathers-in-law of eldest sons and those of younger sons; increased percentage of daughters marrying out of birth order; and a reversal in the effect of wealth on the age at which daughters married. The daughters of richer men first married at a younger age than their less affluent neighbors, and then later they married when older than the poorer girls. The rise in daughters' marrying out of birth order (or not marrying at all) and the loss of a clear association between the son's age at marriage and the age of the father's death both occurred in the last half of the eighteenth century. The loss of a birth order advantage in attracting wealthier fathers-in-law and the shift to poorer girls marrying the earliest happened later, in antebellum Hingham.

One might have thought that such interesting work would have sparked a flood of research on the subject of patriarchal control over marriage, but that was not the case. Little systematic research on the changing importance of birth order, father's death, and parental wealth on the timing of marriage and choice of partner appeared in the intervening years.[7] Consequently, it is difficult to know whether the changes in Hingham resulted from marriage becoming participant-run rather than patriarch-run or whether they can be traced to some other economic or social development that might be peculiar to white native-born communities in coastal Massachusetts. Perhaps the lessening of parental supervision worked so well in historians' minds with the idea of the Revolution reducing patriarchal power and the rise of affective relations within the family that no further research seemed necessary.

In terms of the trends identified earlier in this book, parental control over the marriage of sons and daughters would certainly seem to be consistent with other forms of authority that the early American household head exerted over family members. When one undertakes a search, however, documentation for patriarchal management over marriage proves exasperatingly elusive. Demographic evidence—parental mortality, age at marriage and prenuptial conceptions, data on intergenerational transfers of wealth, and laws on marriage—more often suggest the absence, rather than the presence, of management, especially in comparison to other societies in western Europe and the Americas.

In early America, the ability of a father to manage the marriages of his children depended, first of all, upon his longevity. Wills from the mid-seventeenth to the mid-eighteenth century in England and in the northern British colonies reveal that a similar proportion of children, around 40 percent, entered marriage with their portions already determined because their fathers had died (see table 2). In the later eighteenth and early

TABLE 2
Percentage of Children Who Were Minors at Death of Father, 1660s-1775

Year	Place	N	Minors (%)*
England			
1660s	S. Worcestershire	485	39.0
1660s	London East End	174	42.5
1720s	S. Worcestershire	480	30.8
Northern Colonies/States			
1685–1755	Bucks Co., Penn.	1252	38.6
1750s	Wethersfield, Conn.†	141	39.0
1750s	Upland, Conn.†	106	46.2
1770s	Wethersfield, Conn.†	144	23.6
1770s	Upland, Conn.†	99	19.2
1790s	Bucks Co., Penn.†	1398	16.0
1820s	Wethersfield, Conn.†	106	20.8
1820s	Upland, Conn.†	129	27.9
Chesapeake Colonies			
1660s	Virginia-Tidewater	339	69.0
1660–1750	Middlesex Co., Va.†	184	56.2
1720s	Virginia-Tidewater	824	50.7
1700–1775	Prince George's Co., Md.	n.a.	38.5

Sources: Worcestershire Consistory Court, St. Helens, Worcestershire Record Office, Worcester and Prerogative Court of Canterbury, Public Record Office, London, wills from southern Worcestershire parishes, 1669–1670, 1720–1721; London Commissary Court, Guildhall, London, and Prerogative Court of Canterbury, PRO, London, wills from Stepney, Whitechapel, Stratford-Le-Bow, and St. Leonard Bromley; Registrar's Office, Bucks County Courthouse, Doylestown, Penn., wills 1 March 1685–31 December 1755, and wills 1791–1801; Toby Ditz, *Property and Kinship: Inheritance in Early Connecticut 1750–1820* (Princeton, 1986), table B.5, 183; Virginia State Library, Richmond, wills from York, Henrico, Westmoreland, Isle of Wight, and Northumberland counties, 1660–1676, and from York, Henrico, Westmoreland, and Isle of Wight, 1724–1729; Darrett B. Rutman and Anita H. Rutman, *A Place In Time: Explicatus* (New York, 1984), 66, 80 (assuming 46 percent of the 39.2 percent of children with one parent had no father); Allan Kulikoff, *Tobacco and Slaves: The Development of Southern Cultures in the Chesapeake, 1680–1800* (Chapel Hill, 1986), 170.

*85 percent or more of the wills in each of the samples above were probated within three years, except in the Bucks County 1790 sample, where 74 percent were filed within that time frame.

†Children of all known parental decedents, not just of testators

nineteenth century, only one in four or one in five children in the northern colonies were in that situation (comparable data for England are not available). In plantation colonies, however, as previous research has shown, much higher levels of mortality existed. In the early Chesapeake, the fathers of from over one-half to up to two-thirds of children could have played little role in the choice of a spouse or in the timing of marriage due to early death. Some evidence suggests that mortality improved over the course of the eighteenth century, but the numbers still would exceed those experienced by English children.

Two other demographic measures also suggest weak patriarchal control. That colonists married younger has been commented upon for centuries.[8] Benjamin Franklin made frequent reference to what he perceived to be a New World/Old World difference, and those ruminations inspired Malthus's work on the dangers of population growth. But how much younger and for how long did this discrepancy exist? Statistics on female age at marriage for over two hundred communities in western Europe from the late sixteenth century to 1820 show averages ranging between 24 and 30—depending on country and time period—with national means in the 25 to 27 interval being the most frequently observed (see appendix 1). If anything, the trend over time with this aggregated data is upward. In the northern colonies of British America, the means drop by four to five years. Before 1750, in data on marriage cohorts in nineteen New England and Mid-Atlantic communities, mean age at marriage for females ranged from 19 to 25, with most falling between 21 and 23. From 1750 to the early nineteenth century, the range was similar—from 18 to 25—again with the majority being between 21 and 23. In the southern plantation colonies, the ages are even lower. The average age at marriage in Chesapeake and Carolina communities among cohorts marrying prior to 1750 ranges from 16 to 22, with most values between 18 and 20. After 1750, the range shrinks to from 19 to 22. What is available on males also shows younger ages, with numbers in the 23 to 25 range.

As Daniel Scott Smith recently pointed out, community studies favor long-established communities and people who do not migrate, characteristics that are associated with older marriage ages.[9] The colonies and early United States enjoyed the highest level of internal migration in its history between the late 1760s and the first third of the nineteenth century. Also, most estimates of age at marriage, like estimates of premarital pregnancy, come from church and town records. The very presence of reliable records indicates a functioning parish or religious community whose marital and sexual behavior may not be typical of the rest of the undocumented and lightly policed population. Areas with new in-migration—backcountry localities for example—are poorly represented. Such considerations have led historical demographers such as Smith and Michael Haines to push downward estimates of female age at marriage in the United States in 1800 to between 19.4 and 21 years.[10]

An even greater discrepancy between the New World and western Europe is can be observed if one considers the entire female population of the United States. By the later eighteenth century, twenty percent of the female population consisted of enslaved African American women. The marriage system excluded them. For slave women the statistic comparable to mean age at marriage and indicative of family formation is mean age at first conception. One Chesapeake estimate placed the mean age at first conception at between 17.3 and 18.5 years during the eighteenth century.[11]

Young age at marriage is not necessarily inconsistent with patriarchal control of the event. Prerevolutionary China, the Asian subcontinent, and other societies famous for their arranged marriage systems usually register very low female nuptial ages. In these cases, however, newlyweds lived with parents. The European model of marriage identified over thirty-five years ago by John Hajnal, however, had as its most salient characteristic couples forming a new household.[12] Consequently, the young had to delay marriage until parents and the community gave them the means to live on their own. Land availability in America, it is commonly supposed, weakened that system and pushed down marriage age. But as we have learned in the case of workers, land availability did not necessarily translate into a free labor system. In land-rich British America, parents had even more reason to want to hold on to the labor of their daughters and sons. So why didn't they?

Another demographic statistic—the proportion of first births conceived prenuptially—may provide a clue. Prebridal pregnancy, rather than out-of-wedlock births, is chosen as an indicator of sexual norms because of the higher likelihood of it being recorded.[13] The two, it appears, are correlated, so it can be assumed that when premarital pregnancies rose so did what contemporaries would have called bastardy. Needless to say, patriarchal household heads did not find pregnant daughters amusing, unless perhaps they happened to be someone else's heiress gotten with child by their son. Generally, swollen bellies of unmarried daughters reflected negatively on the authority of the paterfamilias. Historical demographers uncovered a pregnant-bride epidemic in late-eighteenth-century America among the white population, an outbreak that correlated closely with a reduction in the penalties for fornication and bastardy. In the seventeenth century, county courts in Massachusetts and Connecticut prosecuted married couples for prenuptial conceptions with punishments of both fines and whippings. Almost all communities showed fewer than one in ten births being conceived less than eight months after marriage. In the later seventeenth century, whippings declined, and after 1740, courts only prosecuted bastardy, a prosecution that fell almost exclusively on the single mother. In the eighteenth century, the proportion of babies prenuptially conceived rose, so that after 1750, between a quarter and a third of births fell into this category. After 1785, single mothers in Massachusetts simply could pay a fine without suffering an indictment, and within the next ten years, the whole procedure changed to a system of paternity suits.

A similar pattern of reduced policing can be found in another colony initially dominated by a dissenter sect, Pennsylvania. Quakers did not take fornication lightly. Whippings, fines, and mandatory marriage faced couples in the early years. As the colony became more diverse, however, some jurisdictions, such as Philadelphia, all but stopped prosecuting the crime. By 1780, fornication prosecutions statewide consisted only of men being sued for support of a child.[14] Quakers had to rely on their meetings to censure errant members. Because of a dearth of non-church-based vital statistics, no estimates exist for the Middle Atlantic aside from those specific to religious sects.

In the Chesapeake, the only other area that has generated much in the way of statistics, the figures on prenuptial pregnancy show much less of a trend. Rather it was always double-digit, with proportions of a third or more not that unusual.[15] Nor did authorities appear to prosecute prenuptial pregnancies. Instead they focused their attention on the pregnancies of their servant girls, which they punished with whippings and extended service. English ratios appear rather similar to the Chesapeake numbers except that the rise at the end of the eighteenth century is more defined.[16] The anomaly then among English and Anglo-American populations is less the eighteenth-century rise than it is the very low level of prenuptial pregnancy in mid- to late-seventeenth-century dissenter communities. In those years, the statistics for these communities resemble those found for French communities throughout the early modern period more than they do those of their own countrymen. The American statistics suggest that when church and state severely punished premarital sex, it deterred daughters and sons from using intercourse as a means to effect a marriage opposed by the patriarch. When punishments grew less harsh, though, it appears that parents had little else in their arsenal.

If demographic patterns imply that the parent exercised little control over household formation, why should we assume fathers managed marriage in British America? A major reason seems to be that western European—especially English—family history often serves as a reference point for colonial family history.[17] The legal systems that became hegemonic in the Americas came from western Europe, and the idea of parental control as well as the notion of its decline originate in models taking Europe as the norm.[18] So it might be worthwhile to review, briefly, recent early modern period research on parental control of marriage, some of which has come out since the local studies of colonial family relations appeared. Three things immediately catch the eye: first, the elaborate legal and familial apparatus surrounding marriages in some continental European countries; second, the difference between those traditions and the early modern English system; and third, the importance that governments in major European countries, including England, attached to strengthening parental control of marriage in the early modern period.

Notarial records from the early modern era spell out in mind-numbing detail the parental involvement in French marriages. Custom and law required a French father to pass on the bulk of his estate to lineal descendants. Because both the prospective families of the bride and groom expected that the other side would contribute to the conjugal fund, the marriage of children became the occasion for setting out intergenerational transfers in a marriage contract. Fathers lost power over property, but because their participation was indispensable, they also played a role in the choice of spouse and the timing of household formation. If the child was a minor, the father had a positive veto. Kin joined in role as well. Previous to the wedding, relatives gathered to learn the amount of the dowry, its composition, the proportion of the dowry that became part of the conjugal fund, the size of the widow's dower, the names of guarantors, and so forth. Those minors with deceased fathers had to negotiate their marriages with kin, usually brothers or brothers-in-law. The greater family retained interest in the couple even after the finalization of the contract and the exchange of vows, because often so much of the dowry had been set aside as lineage property that followed the woman and her heirs. Kin could name guardians of children and intervene in cases where a marriage had broken down. All was justified on the basis of lineage interests, yet it was far from simply a practice of the aristocracy. Even children of domestic servants might have marriage contracts.[19]

The French continued this system of marriage contracts in Canada, and it remained in place until at least the mid-nineteenth century, long after Britain assumed control over the area.[20] The Spanish had a system of agreements comparable to French marriage contracts that protected lineage property. When a couple married, the notary drew up a *carta dotal,* which specified the dowry property, and the groom offered an additional gift, the *arras,* which combined with the dowry constituted the claim of the bride and her lineage on his estate when he died, a system that was also transferred to the New World.[21] German states had marriage contracts participated in by parents and marriage inventories that set out the property of both sexes.[22]

The English system of protecting lineage property developed differently from the Continent's, due to the way family property law evolved after the Protestant Reformation. Because of the 1540 Statute of Wills and subsequent legislation in the seventeenth century, patriarchs could disinherit children at pleasure.[23] Mandatory endowment no longer existed, and consequently fathers had less reason to participate in marriage contracts. It may be, though, that even prior to the laws eliminating testamentary restraints, English fathers and couples of ordinary means did not formally arrange the financial terms of the marriage.[24]

Among the wealthy, what came to be a problem was an irresponsible or foolish patriarch unmindful of his lineage responsibilities squandering the family fortune or dividing it in a way that diluted the clout of the dynasty. Relief was found in equity law adjudicated in chancery courts. Historians have documented the rise in the late seventeenth century of equity's strict family settlement among the English elite.[25] The settlement—normally bearing the signatures of the male heir who was about to marry and his prospective bride's father as well as her eldest brother, the heir to her family's holdings—gave the groom life interest only in the estate, which at the groom's death would pass to the eldest male born to the marriage. The agreement also set the sum of the dowry; provided the succession of the manors and lands to younger children in case the eldest son died without an heir; and, most important, substituted a jointure for the much larger dower rights his soon-to-be wife could have claimed under the common law if she became a widow. For a time in the eighteenth century, marriage announcements in publications such as the *Gentleman's*

Magazine actually listed an amount purporting to be the dowry.[26] The settlements were designed, on the one hand, to keep property concentrated in the patriline and to set limits to the claims of other children and the widow. On the other hand—and this motive explains the timing of the family settlement and relates it to the continental marriage contract—the document laid out what the bride's family would receive for the dowry contribution: specifically, the bride's son as heir and the fate of the estate in case that heir died, as well as the amount she would get when and if she reached dowager status. Wills, which could be changed right up to the day of death, would not serve the latter function. Much less widespread than the continental marriage contracts, these settlements were a crucial element in perpetuating an aristocratic class in England through the nineteenth century.[27]

Both Catholic and Protestant European governments adopted measures that complemented these contracts and settlements by augmenting the power of the household head to control marriage. In most instances, these state actions involved restricting the role of the established church, that quasi-governmental body in charge of marriage. The church's canon law was seen by some as favoring the wishes of the participants over dynastic strategies of the family, because of the priority the church gave to the mutual consent of the couple in deciding what was and was not a marriage. Even a clandestine marriage could be legal if both parties agreed to it. Not that the church operated under a laissez-faire philosophy in the area of marital relations. Policing of sexual behavior before and after the wedding could be quite extensive, and as part of its own reformation at the Council of Trent in 1531, the Catholic Church decreed that legal marriages required public announcement on three occasions and celebration by a priest. The refusal to give patriarchs a veto, however, was what led secular authorities to intervene.[28]

Probably no western European government took more trouble to thwart participant-run marriages than that of France. In the mid-sixteenth century, by royal edict, the age at majority for males rose from twenty to thirty and the age for females from seventeen to twenty-five, and parents gained the right to disinherit minors who married without their consent. The French government ruled marriages accomplished through abduction or *seduction* null and blocked suitors in black robes, such as the Jesuits, from luring minors away from the family fold into religious orders.[29] While the French Revolution temporarily dismantled much of this system of patriarchal control, the Napoleonic Code in 1804 reinstituted and reinvigorated the authority of the household head under the guise of correcting Revolutionary "excesses." Though in the nine-teenth century the age of majority fell to twenty-one for women and twenty-five for men, parents retained the authority to disinherit minors, and a father, without having to demonstrate good cause, could have his underage child detained for up to one year if the father disapproved of her or his actions.[30] Marriage contracts still prevailed, though daughters had lost the right they had during the ancien régime to sue their fathers for failure to provide a dowry.

Developments in France over the early modern period and into the early nineteenth century have their parallels elsewhere in western Europe. In Spain, the principal American colonial power, deference to the church delayed the state's entry into marital policing until the Bourbon reforms of the 1770s. In 1776, the Spanish Crown issued the Royal Pragmatic—operative in both Spain and its American possessions—to counteract the practice of youth making inappropriate marriages in defiance of patriar-chal authority. It allowed parents to disinherit children under the age of twenty-five who married without their consent and required those over twenty-five to notify parents prior to marriage.[31]

In Reformation Germany, Martin Luther's writings indicate exas-peration with the inability of fathers to stop elopements of the young. "Should my child be so available," he marveled," "that any boy, perhaps a stranger or an enemy to me, would have power and free access to steal her?" No boy, he believed, would "be able to win a child from a pious man or presume to become an heir of property that he had not acquired," if clandestine vows had no legal standing.[32] Protestant states revised the marriage law, requiring parental consent for a valid marriage when either the bride or groom "was still under the authority of his or her parents." One study of the marriage courts set up in a German state to adjudicate disputes finds that the cases most frequently heard by these courts did not concern fornication or divorce, but rather were cases brought by parents concerning secret engagements made by their children.[33]

Early modern English legislation also cast a jaundiced eye on clandes-tine unions, especially ones involving propertied women. Parliament in 1558 refashioned old canon law provisions concerning abductions—which according to the Catholic Church constituted grounds for annulment—into an act that applied to any husband who married an heiress below the age of sixteen without the consent of her father or guardian. The law sub-jected him not only to imprisonment or a fine but also to loss of control over her fortune. Almost a hundred years later the Puritans, during the Interregnum, tackled the issue in typically rigorous manner. They passed a law covering all sons and daughters under age twenty-one whose spouse had used "violence or fraud" to effect a marriage. The legislation punished said spouse by loss of estate, life imprisonment, and, for the first time, voiding of the marriage. This last act lapsed in 1657, even before the Stuarts regained the throne. From the Restoration period on, the English landed classes and their representatives in Parliament continually introduced bills to strengthen parental authority over marriage by voiding marriages contracted without a father's consent, but no such acts passed.[34]

The uproar in England over abducted heiresses reached a fever pitch in the mid-eighteenth century. The popular literature of the time reflects this preoccupation with the seduction of heiresses and the inability of patriarchs to control marriage. If—as C. S. Lewis long ago argued—the quintessential love tale in medieval literature concerned adultery, in the early modern period more and more the romantic dilemma involved a female virgin at risk. What began as one of several themes in the theater of Restoration London developed into the central issue in eighteenth-century prose fiction. The most popular novelist of the time, Samuel Richardson, explored both of the possible outcomes: in *Clarissa, or, The History of a Young Lady* (1747–48), the virgin heiress is seduced and ultimately destroyed, while seven years earlier, in *Pamela, or Virtue Rewarded,* he created a girl of more humble origins who manages to withstand the attack on her maidenhood and win a rich husband. Not everyone, of course, saw things the same way. London playwright, magistrate, and sometime-rake Henry Fielding authored a parody of Richardson's classic called *Shamela,* and then published—a year after *Clarissa* appeared—the novel *Tom Jones.* In Fielding's novel, it is the male—as innocent in mind as Pamela is in body—who has to cope with the aggressive sexual behavior of the opposite sex before being united with his true love. To Fielding most of those prattling about safeguarding female virtue were hypocrites who, if men, hoped to seduce the women themselves, and if women, hoped to cover up their indiscretions or benefit monetarily from their real or pretended chastity.

With pressure building, Parliament sided with Richardson rather than Fielding and passed the Marriage Act of 1753, otherwise known as Lord Hardwicke's Act. Under this legislation, fathers could have the clandestine marriages of minor children—those under age twenty-one—declared null and void. Older offspring could marry publicly with banns read or could obtain a special license granted by the clergy. Whatever the case, clergy had to officiate and register the happy couple. Only Jews, Quakers, and the royal family were exempt, three groups that already had more than enough marriage regulation of their own. Clergy knowingly breaking the rules faced a charge of felony and fourteen years transportation. The falsification of marriage records carried the death penalty. According to the Parliamentary debates, members hoped by the passage of this legislation to put out of business the seducer of an heiress, the lying gold-diggers who appeared out of a married man's past claiming a marriage, and the man with a wife in every port.[35] Also, of course, it left with limited options the single mother who had trusted the promise of her children's father that he planned to marry her at a more propitious time. Some have attributed the observed rise in illegitimacy rates to these more stringent marriage standards.[36] The act inaugurated a more uniform and comprehensive national registration system that prevented clergy from allowing the offspring born to couples who never went through the formal procedures to be counted as legitimate. Though those who formerly would have sought out the London Fleet Street marriage mills found a replacement over the Scottish border in Gretna Green, thwarting the patriarchal will had become more difficult. The nullification of the clandestine marriages contracted by minors remained in place until 1822. If the strict family settlement separated the elite from the professional and middle classes, the Marriage Act divided society along the line of respectability. Noncompliance, frequent as it might have been, carried a penalty.

What evidence is there that any of this complex system of parental control over marriage ever got transferred to the thirteen colonies? The most difficult part of the American data to evaluate is the references to parents setting marriage terms. The majority of instances cited as evidence that marriage occasioned intense negotiations between families involve verbal, not written, commitments. Mostly they are examples of seventeenth-century oral agreements going awry, and the only reason they have come down to us is because the injured party tried taking the case to the local county court. Promises of property transfers did not fare well in common law courts when the other side could produce the deed or a will as justification for possession.[37]

Expectations by fathers that a deed of gift should be conveyed prior to marriage crop up occasionally in the first generation of settlement. One of the few examples of a deed actually stating that it was drawn up on the occasion of a marriage is a 1646 document from Plymouth entitled "the condicions of the marriage between Jacob Cooke and Damarise hopkins" that lists the five gifts the groom's father promised to his son. According to probate records, however, the bride already had gotten her portion—about £9 of household goods—two years earlier at the death of her father, so the deed does not seem to have been part of a contract with the bride's family as much as an agreement reached between the groom's father and his son.[38] A Maryland joiner in 1706 deeded his entire estate to his daughter—who was to marry one John Vincent—in exchange for care in his retirement. He was to have "Meat Drinck washing and apparrell in the same manner and noe worse than the said John Vincent himself." While this certainly was a transfer at time of a child's marriage, this artisan was not exactly managing the marriage or negotiating from a superior position.[39] Mostly, though, it seems that fathers grew evasive when prodded to come up with a deed to the farm at the time of their offspring's marriage. A seventeenth-century bargaining session between Simon Bradstreet of Andover and Jonathan Wade—discussed by both Edmund Morgan and Philip Greven—is a good example. Bradstreet—whose daughter had been proposed to by Wade's son—wanted Wade's promise of land in England to take the form of a deed of gift. Wade would only go as far as promising to devise it in his will, indicating just what Bradstreet feared—that ultimately Wade might make some other disposition of the property. Bradstreet balked but eventually had to accept the offer.[40]

Nothing like the strict family settlements appears in the literature on colonial families. The chancery courts adjudicating family settlements in England did not exist in dissenter colonies until the end of the eighteenth century, and in the colonies where they did appear earlier—such as South Carolina—nonprofessionals such as the province's governor and council members sat on the bench. The colonial cases considered by this court consisted mainly of disputes over wills and intestacy divisions.[41] The court also handled suits concerning marriage settlements, a legal device imported from England for very different purposes than the strict family settlement.

Marriage settlements covered approximately 1 to 2 percent of South Carolina marriages, probably the highest incidence in the thirteen colonies. Women drew up these agreements with their prospective husbands—sometimes including third-party trustees and sometimes not—to set aside property in a separate estate exempt from coverture and their husband's control. Rather than a device to safeguard and expand patrilineal holdings, these marriage settlements withheld the bride's property from the patrilineage. Widows—the women most likely to draw them up in colonial South Carolina—could escape coverture and continue to control wealth that had come to them from their first husbands. First-time brides, perhaps with prompting from their parents or guardians, used the instrument primarily to ensure that their wealth descended directly to their future children.[42] Rather than showing parental control of marriage, these settlements suggest parental dismay—with the father seeming to regard the groom in person or fortune inferior to his daughter but lacking the power to stop the marriage—and, at least in the case of widows, female power. For the dynastic ambitions of the groom's patrilineage, the marriage settlement was a disaster—the whole purpose of a man marrying an heiress was to create a conjugal fund that he could manage.

British American fathers overwhelmingly left their estates to their children, but they commonly did so in their wills or according to the intestacy provisions of their colony. Seventeenth-century New England community studies indicate very little inter vivos transfer of land to sons occurred. In this situation, neither they, their spouses, nor their spouses' families could be sure of what might be forthcoming, as a patriarch could always come up with a new will. Family historians have associated this behavior with patriarchal power. True, it did give the household head more control over his *property* for a longer time. Whether it promoted parental control of marriages and kinship alliances, however, is another matter. In the eighteenth century, the inter vivos pattern is more contradictory and less well documented.[43] Whatever the case, no study documents large-scale transfer of property by deed as part of marriage negotiations. The reluctance of fathers to sit down at the table and sign away property before the marriage may have ultimately lessened fathers' ability to control who and when their offspring married. Sons could accumulate wages and had legal rights after age twenty-one to be compensated for work done for their parents. Payments by parents to daughters occurred less often, although daughters had hope chests.[44]

In fact, about the only property that could routinely be associated with the setting up of a new household was the bedding and cooking implements that the bride—through her own labor or through the gifts and work of her parents—provided.[45] While this hope chest might have constituted more of an inheritance than does its twentieth-century counterpart—Westbend pots and pans—and while its absence might have been more sorely missed, only for the very poorest segment of the free population could such items comprise a child's entire inheritance. Nor could one imagine that the transfer of these goods could make or break a wedding for very long.[46]

A father's death greatly exceeded in importance the marriage of children when it came to the intergenerational partitioning of wealth. While it has been suggested that the availability of land in America made the timing of property transfers unimportant, community studies show that much uncultivated land could not easily be taken over for agricultural production. The claims of Indian nations, the engrossing of land by Crown grantees, poor transportation to markets, and the costs of clearing lots and other agricultural expenses all inhibited the flow of settlers westward in many communities during the colonial period. For couples in places such as the seventeenth-century Chesapeake, where fathers frequently died before most children came of age, the retentiveness of fathers made less difference. If the figures shown in table 2 are accurate, most colonial American couples could have had the portion, however humble, of at least one of the partners as they set up their household, courtesy of the grim reaper. In other early American locales, however, the mortality levels appear similar to or even lower than those in western Europe. Consequently the coyness of the paterfamilias right up to his death about signing on the dotted line must have had an impact on the fortunes of the young couple. What it did not do was stop them from setting up a household.

Given the power of household heads in British American society and their need for labor, why didn't patriarchs just pass laws forbidding their children to marry without their consent? Initially most of the founding generation, influenced by English legislation, did write statutes designed to discourage marriages they had not blessed. In the earliest New England settlements—Plymouth, Massachusetts Bay, and New Haven—not only did the laws direct children to obtain the consent of their parents to their marriage without mentioning an age when such consent no longer would be needed, but the laws also forbade men to "inveigle" or "insinuate" themselves into the "affections of young maidens" without consent of parent or guardian to the courtship. Corporal punishment or prison could befall the repeat offender. Providence Plantation in Rhode Island even adopted the Tudor statute equating the "taking away, deflowering or contracting in marriage a maid" under sixteen with man stealing and providing a five-year prison term.[47] County court records through the 1670s contain instances where judges tried suitors for nonobservance of these rules. On occasion the accused tried to turn the tables on the father and allege violation of another law that prohibited parents from "unreasonable" opposition to a marriage.[48] Maryland's 1640 act required an oath that a woman was not "under the government of parents or tutors" before issuing a marriage certificate. The Duke of York's laws of 1665–75—the first marriage regulations for New York, Pennsylvania, and Delaware—also required consent for daughters without giving an age limit. Only

Virginia's 1632 law explicitly limited parental control to age twenty-one. Colonists hoped through the adoption of procedures requiring the publication or announcement of the intention to marry and the payment of fees for registration to stop clandestine marriages and all marital irregularities, including the elopement of sons and daughters. During the ecclesiastically confused period from the Protectorate to the early years of the Restoration, Rhode Island, Maryland, Virginia, and the middle colonies under the Duke of York's laws went beyond Anglican practice and took the severe step of voiding irregular marriages, although only in Rhode Island does the absence of parental consent trigger this penalty. Elsewhere such strictness seemed aimed at strengthening the Church of England's hold over the dissenter community.[49]

Strict laws providing stiff penalties for irregular unions seem a far cry from the marriage law of the early United States as described first by George Elliott Howard and more recently by Michael Grossberg and Nancy Cott.[50] All draw attention to the triumph of the misnamed common law marriage in the early republic, a development that certainly interfered with the objective of patriarchal control over marriage. From independence right up to the 1840s, state legislatures and courts—with the notable exception of Massachusetts—refused to void irregular marriages, including those in which minors had not obtained parental consent. Couples who had lived together openly as husband and wife would be considered married with all the same legal relationships to each other and their children, including the latter's right to their share of intestate property. Indeed, even apart from the issue of voiding underage marriages, the courts seemingly had little interest in even fining the errant ministers. In one of the few appellate cases devoted to the subject, Maryland parents seeking to collect damages provided by statute from an Episcopal clergyman who had officiated at the 1802 marriage of their daughter—who was then under the age of sixteen—had to go through a prolonged extensive appeal process, and in the end their case was dismissed in 1810 on a technicality.[51]

Grossberg, who has written most extensively on common law marriage in the early republic, tiptoes around the question of just how new this development was. He notes that "post-Revolutionary legal authorities were confronted with an ambiguous English and colonial legacy."[52] The ambiguity results from the contrast between the rather stern injunctions of the seventeenth-century marital legislation just recited and what apparently happened in regard to those statutes in practice. In contrast to the number of citations of cases concerning fornication—a type of case among the most commonly prosecuted in the seventeenth-century courts—citations relating to violation of the marriage laws are not thick on the ground. The absence of prosecution might perhaps indicate that all couples wed in glorious conformity with the statutes. The fact, however, that every colony taking a hard line against irregular unions reversed itself before the eighteenth century got underway suggests something different. A 1699 Rhode Island law accused "some persons," of taking "advantage" of those "not duly observeing ye Act of Registering their Marriages" by branding their children as "illegitimate" and thus presumably incapable of inheriting an estate.[53] That these concerns had overthrown the law voiding irregular marriages indicates that more than a few weddings of the propertied lacked some or all of the legal niceties. The preface to Pennsylvania's 1730 act that stated that the previous legislation to prevent clandestine marriages "hath been very much eluded" provides more evidence.[54]

In fact, the so-called "republican" marriage system seems more a continuation of than a departure from the eighteenth-century colonial institution, especially as it concerns parental consent. The third column in table 3 shows the statutes in effect prior to the Revolution. Little pretense of policing remained. Five of the thirteen colonies had *no* explicit reference to parental consent in their marriage laws. Another four only required certain groups of young people to provide proof of parental approval: "children under . . . care and government," "daughters," "heiresses under 16," and those with parents "conveniently" situated. Only Virginia, North Carolina, New Jersey, and Pennsylvania had a law specifying an age (twenty-one) that pertained to both sexes. In *no* colony did a failure to observe the rules void the marriage or interfere with the inheritance or administration of an estate.[55] Instead, as deterrence the colonies relied more and more upon statutes fining the clergy and magistrates officiating at weddings. Of course some statutes—originally inspired by Tudor-period legislation or Puritan principles and never updated—still levied substantial punishments on the groom. South Carolina's adoption of the 1558 English law on abduction meant that a five-year sentence for running off with an heiress under sixteen could be imposed, along with the loss of legal power over her estate.[56] The justice of the peace manuals in many colonies included the text of that English statute. There is little evidence of parties successfully intervening in the courts anywhere, though, except when the girl was under twelve, and those cases pertain to the seventeenth century, not to the eighteenth.[57]

TABLE 3

Colonial and Early Republican Laws on Parental Consent

State	Year	Parental Consent	Year	Parental Consent
Massachusetts	1695	Yes; for children under their care and govt.	1786	Yes; males < 21 Females < 18
Connecticut	1672	Yes; for daughters	1786	Yes; for children under their care and control
Rhode Island	1730	No	1794	No; same as colonial
New Hampshire	1714	No	1791	No; same as colonial
New York	1684	No	1684	No; same as colonial
New Jersey	1719	Yes; under 21	1795	Yes; males < 21 Females < 18
Pennsylvania	1730	Yes; under 21 or tuition	1730	Yes; same as colonial
Delaware	1701	Yes; if they can conveniently	1790	Yes; males < 21 Females < 18
Maryland	1717	No	1777	Yes; males < 21 Females < 16
Virginia	1705	Yes; under 21	1792	Yes; same as colonial
North Carolina	1741	Yes; under 21	1778	No
South Carolina	1712	Yes; heiresses under 16	1712	Yes; same as colonial
Georgia	none	No	1789	No; same as colonial

Sources: Massachusetts, John D. Cushing, ed., *Massachusetts Province Laws 1692–1699* (Wilmington, Del., 1978), and Massachusetts, *The Perpetual Laws of the Commonwealth of Massachusetts from the Establishment of its Constitution in the Year 1780 to the End of the Year 1800* (1801); Connecticut, Cushing, ed., *The Earliest Laws of the New Haven and Connecticut Colonies, 1639–1673* (1978), and Connecticut, *Acts and Laws of the State of Connecticut in America* (1786); Rhode Island, *Acts and Laws* (1730), and *Public Laws of the State* (1798); New Hampshire, Cushing, ed., *Acts and Laws of New Hampshire, 1680–1726* (1978), and New Hampshire, *Constitution and Laws of the State of New Hampshire* (1805); New York, Cushing, ed., *The Earliest Printed Laws of New York, 1665–1693* (1978); New Jersey, Cushing, ed., *The Earliest Printed Laws of New Jersey, 1703–1722* (1978), New Jersey, *Law of the State of New Jersey,* rev.(1800); Pennsylvania, *Laws of the Commonwealth of Pennsylvania, 1700–1781,* vol. 2 (1810); Delaware, Cushing, ed., *Earliest Printed Laws of Pennsylvania, 1681–1713* (1978); Maryland, Cushing, ed., *Laws of the Province of Maryland* (1978), and Virgil Maxcy, ed., *The Laws of Maryland,* vol. 1 (1811); Virginia, *Hening's Statutes at Large,* vol. 3 (1809–1815), and vol. 13 (1823); North Carolina, *The Earliest Printed Laws of North Carolina, 1669–1751,* and Henry Potter, J. L. Taylor, and Bartholomew Yancy, eds., *Laws of the State of North Carolina,* vol. 1 (1821); South Carolina, Cushing, ed., *Earliest Laws, 1682–1716,* vol. 1; Georgia, Cushing, ed., *The Earliest Printed Laws of the Province of Georgia, 1755–1770* (1978), and Georgia, *Digest of the Laws* (1800).

The data in table 3 indicate that after the Revolution the majority of the first thirteen states made no change to their parental consent laws. New York, Pennsylvania, and South Carolina did not even bother to re-draft the statutes. Georgia finally wrote a marriage act but included no penalties for being wed without parental consent. Of the six that made changes, only North Carolina could be classified as liberalizing its law by dropping the provision. Balancing that liberalization is the action of the Maryland legislature, which inserted a clause requiring parental consent for males under twenty-one and females under sixteen, and the expansion of the concept of consent by Connecticut's lawmakers from daughters to all children under the "care and control" of parents. The rest of the states engaged in tinkering: Massachusetts and Delaware substituted specific ages for more vague criteria, and New Jersey simply lowered the female age after which parental consent was no longer needed from twenty-one to eighteen. All in all, these changes represented something less than a revolution in marriage law. No one followed up on Thomas Jefferson's suggestion of adopting Lord Hardwicke–like legislation voiding the marriages of minors who had not obtained parental consent. The colonial marriage laws were loose even in areas that one might think would have been of central concern—miscegenation and incest. The only colony to void interracial marriages was Georgia. By 1800, only Massachusetts and Rhode Island had followed suit.[58] Some colonies did not have statutes listing those degrees of kinship within which marriage was forbidden, and among those that did, not all voided the marriages of offenders.

The casual attitude adopted by the colonies and early states toward transgressions of the marriage law seems quite understandable given the impossibility of enforcement. In order for states to crack down on couples violating the law, they would have had to create a vital statistics bureaucracy to monitor births, marriages, deaths, and divorces. Western European countries relied on established churches. While Protestant toleration and dissatisfaction with the ecclesiastical establishment led to more and more secular regulation, a national network was at least preexisting. The states of the United States had no such base upon which to build. Even the idea of an established church rankled substantial portions of the population in each of the thirteen colonies. Much of the rewriting of marriage laws was an effort to resolve the tension between incorporating everyone in the record—thus accommodating religious differences—and being able to hold certain specific officials responsible for the maintenance of the record.

Look, for example, at the history of marriage legislation in the dissenter colony Rhode Island. In 1647, the Rhode Island representatives passed legislation requiring a couple to obtain parental consent, to then publish their intentions (the banns) twice at town meetings, to confirm it with the "head officer" of the town, and then to have it entered into the town clerk's book. In 1663, a new law directed the general officer marrying them to draw up a certificate and ordered the couple to carry this certificate to the town clerk. Without such procedures, the marriage was void. In 1699, citizens' failure to observe the law forced the assembly to declare legal marriages that had not been registered properly, while still maintaining that all persons marrying should file with the town clerk within ten days of their marriage. In 1701, the legislature passed another act on the publication procedure that involved obtaining written proof from "some person in Authority within ye Township." In 1730, the marriage law enabled "the settled and ordained ministers and elders of every society's denominations of Christians in the colony" to join persons together in marriage. In 1733, the act specifically recognized Presbyterian and Baptist ministers as being eligible for this duty, as long as they observed the publication regulations. In 1794, the Methodists got added. In 1798, the law read:

That all persons within this State, who are desirous of being Joined together in the estate of matrimony, shall make their Application to an Assistant, Justice of the Peace, or Warden, or to some ordained Minister of the Episcopal church, or to any settled and ordained Minister or Elder of any Presbyterian Congregational, Independent, Baptist or Methodist church, society or congregation; or to the ordained Minister of any religious denomination in the town or towns wherein such persons respectively dwell.[59]

These persons all had the authority to publish banns, officiate at the marriage, and provide certificates. The act left it up to the couple to register in the town clerk's office. All three procedures—publication, marriage certificate, and registration—involved the paying of fees, a disincentive to compliance. The act ended by affirming the validity of Quaker and Jewish rites without indicating whether these groups had to conform to the procedures outlined in the law.

The point of this perhaps tedious recounting of Rhode Island marriage law is to underscore the difficulty that American colonies and states experienced in authorizing and recording marriage. Rhode Island, like most of the New England dissenter colonies, originally tried to make marriage a civil procedure. That effort failed, as denominations wanted control over the marriage process. The bewildering variety of Protestant sects, however, made policing difficult, and fees—along with provisions that placed the final marriage registration in the hands of the couple—only exacerbated the problem. The high rates of eighteenth-century pre-bridal pregnancies in New England explain the lack of attention paid to the age of the father and female birth order by couples planning marriages. While failure to stop such behavior might be laid at the feet of the patriarch, it seems to be more associated with a general diminution of religious intensity among the Puritan leadership. Colonies with Anglican antecedents also foundered in their support of the household head. The paucity of ordained Church of England ministers and the proliferation of sectarian congregations made it difficult to police marriages.

And how could the father or guardian know where to look for the publication of banns? A shortage of ordained established church ministers to officiate and register marriages in the locality frequently meant journeying outside one's own community. The multiplicity of Christian sects undercut efforts to develop one set of procedures and records. Sectarians rejected policies limiting marriages to one denomination's ministers, as those colonies in the seventeenth century that tried such restrictions found out. The religious enthusiasm and sense of religious propriety of the population also blocked magistrates from being given the exclusive privilege of solemnizing rites: New England Puritans had originally preferred that clergy from the established church of the province have the sole power to officiate, which had also been the preference of the elite in much of the South. And then, if the couple were to ultimately register their marriage with the civil authorities, what happened to that record? Did the province preserve it? In almost all cases it remained in the locality, waiting to be obliterated by fire, water, air, or neglect.[60]

Anyone trying to check up on a marriage, therefore, faced a daunting task, considering the numbers of persons who might have officiated and the number of places where the event might have been recorded. Some of the more bureaucratic colonies/states, like Massachusetts, required that the person officiating later register all marriages performed with the town clerk. From Laurel Ulrich's careful reconstruction of marriage practices in Hallowell, Maine—then part of Massachusetts—we know that town clerks had a difficult time with compliance. We also know of the large number of persons who married after or only shortly before the birth of their first child. The births of 38 percent of the diarist's midwifery clientele fell into the categories of either premarital pregnancy or bastard birth.

Out of twenty-one intentions to marry filed in the town during 1792, one prompted a written objection by a father. But in the end, he withdrew his opposition—because his daughter was ready to give birth.[61]

The problem of irregular marriages was not confined to the earliest years of settlement or to frontier communities, although probably the enforcement of marriage law was the weakest in sparsely populated areas. Little seemed to improve over the course of the eighteenth century. Christian sects proliferated, and the rate of migration westward reached unprecedented levels from the late 1760s on. Statistics on growth of churches between 1650 and 1775 show population continually outpacing congregations, with 446 persons per church in 1650; 720 in 1750; and 837 in 1775.[62] The rate of expansion did not begin to drop until after 1840, and the courts and legislatures only slowly offered incentives to observe marriage laws. With the free population in such disarray in regard to marriage, it is not surprising that in America—unlike in some other systems of bound servitude, such as Russian serfdom—slaves lacked any means of formalizing their unions.[63] The absence of a marriage system is apparent from the accounts of eighteenth-century slave residential patterns. Except on very large estates, two-thirds or more of adult men and women routinely resided without partners.[64]

Only tightly regulated sects controlled marriage in early America. The best example is the Society of Friends. Couples underwent close scrutiny from relations and members, and their prospective union required the approval of the meeting as a whole. The restrictiveness of the system in the end discouraged matrimony: the group had both one of the highest proportions of women never marrying and one of the highest average ages at marriage. Just as most sects dating from the English Civil War period were mellowing or splintering into "New Light" and "Old Light" groups, diluting the power to patrol marriage, the Quakers in mid-eighteenth century launched a reform movement that made disownment the consequence of failure to conform to the rules of marriage.[65] Sectarianism had its price in terms of influence, however. Quakers lost their hegemonic position in the Delaware River valley, and between 1750 and 1850, they dropped from having the third-largest number of congregations to the eighth. While it might be argued that the ultimate legacy of Quaker reform included a crucial contribution to the creation of a women's right's movement in the United States—a movement that had its impact on marriage formation[66]—the withdrawal of Quakers from the mainstream and their decline in numbers meant less policing of marriage in the region.

Considering the lack of marriage contracts and family settlements in early America; the failure to draft marriage statutes requiring parental consent and to enforce those laws in existence; the frequency of premarital pregnancy; the comparatively young age at marriage; and the exclusion of one-fifth of the population from any kind of marital legislation, it is difficult to characterize the marriage system of early America as parent-run. While the Quakers and certain seventeenth-century New England dissenter communities put barriers in the way of participants controlling household formation, what such groups substituted could be better described as community management than as parental management. In Massachusetts, the observed mid-eighteenth-century breakdown in birth-order marriages and in the association between father's death and son's age at marriage may have had more to do with the weakening of Congregational church influence than with a change in parent-child relationships. Patriarchs, consciously or unconsciously, seemed to have made a choice in the seventeenth century. Running the marriage system meant giving up control over property, and they chose not to set up the mechanisms to do it. To enforce parental consent, fathers would have had to agree to mandatory endowment of children, something from which the 1540 Statute on Wills had liberated them, and to the recognition of an established church or other bureaucratic institution to police the marriage system in British America.

Over time, the father's limited role in marriage negotiations and the failure of the community's elders to set up an adequate governmental system to register and police marriage undermined patriarchal authority over all dependents. The freedom of children to marry was on a collision course with the expanded authority that heads of households had obtained over the portions of sons and daughters, the labor of bound servants, and property of married women. If household heads could not control the household formation of their children—in effect, their children's mobility—how could they control the children of others, such as their servants or apprentices? The gulf between servants and free labor grew wider than in places where marriage and mobility of youth was restricted, and it made slavery more anomalous. Furthermore, if no one kept track of marriage, what was to prevent informal divorce? And, if partners could so easily break up their marriages themselves, what sense did it make for the government to refuse to offer legal dissolutions?

A comparison with colonial Spanish America is instructive, because one could argue that high illegitimacy rates there qualified their marriage system to be labeled "out of control." In many ways it clearly was. It appears that church and state had little control over the coupling of many segments of the population, although in some places such as Mexico that control increased over the course of the eighteenth century. Unlike British America, however, a high illegitimacy rate for the general population was combined with a fairly elaborate system of state-sanctioned patriarchal control over marriage for the Spanish-identified portion of society. Entry into many positions in church, military, trades, and the government depended upon a lineage check. These property arrangements safeguarded the patrimony for the elite. Failure to observe the marital conventions carried a penalty and placed one in a disadvantageous position in terms of mobility.[67] The near-absence of a formal system in the British colonies turned many potential illegitimacies into premarital pregnancies, and regardless of their economic class, couples deciding themselves when to form a households do not seem to have been subject to sanctions.

European observers argued among themselves about the effect of the American marriage system on society. August Carlier—a French observer writing at the time of the American Civil War—viewed marriage very differently from de Tocqueville, who a generation earlier had claimed that "there is certainly no country in the world where the tie of marriage is so much respected as in America." Carlier argued in his 1860 book that the freedom allowed young girls, "[who] must depend upon *themselves* to find a husband" (my emphasis); the lack of paternal authority over courtship; and the loose laws around marriage and divorce produced disrespect for the institution of the family itself, promoted divorce, and ultimately corrupted the morals of the American population.[68] Another generation later, Progressive George Elliott Howard maintained that America's soaring divorce rate could be traced to the failure to celebrate and register marriages. He became America's greatest historian of marriage, but in terms of changing policies, Howard toiled in vain. Not until 1957 did the United States establish national registration, and even now not all states have joined the system.[69]

The volatility of marriage in the United States, still remarked upon by social commentators, has colonial roots that go beyond the very limited marital exits permitted by the Puritans. The absence of mechanisms to control the marriage of the young was a distinctive feature of the American household and one that did more than the American Revolution to bring about the early disintegration in the power of the household head.

5

THE HOUSEHOLD'S CIVIL WAR
IN THE ERA OF DOMESTIC BLISS

MID-NINETEENTH-CENTURY ART AND LITERATURE IN THE UNITED States is famous for its celebration of the joys of domestic life. Novels about loving Victorian families like the one in *Little Women* and paintings such as *The Hatch Family* (fig. 10) of comfortable elite households have enjoyed a continuing popularity. Household cheerfulness so pervades conceptualizations of the period that the title chosen for a contemporary exhibit of nineteenth-century paintings of the American family was *Domestic Bliss*.[1] Images of the household from this time period—rather than from quaint colonial times or the TV family sitcoms of the fifties—seem to be the ones most often preferred, even today, by those romanticizing family togetherness.

What is perplexing about this glorification of household life is that it coincided with a variety of expressions of deep dissatisfaction with the then current system of household organization. During these years, Americans advocated more strongly than in any other time period in their history the use of custodial institutions for the placement of indigent men and women, their children, and the infirm. This institutional movement contained an explicit criticism of how household government worked among poor families. More important, in the twenty years before 1860 and the twenty years after, an unprecedented amount of conflict erupted in legislatures and courts as Americans slowly dismantled much of the legal edifice supporting the household head's rule over his dependents. The states, not the federal government, had the principal jurisdiction over the laws governing domestic relations. The time it took to effect change corresponds closely to the forty-year period American political scientists have found it normally takes to push legislation through all the states of the union. In this case, though, a bloody civil war had to be fought before

10 Eastman Johnson, *Alfrederick Hatch Family* (1871).
COURTESY OF THE METROPOLITAN MUSEUM OF ART, NEW YORK, GIFT OF FREDERICK H.
HATCH, 1926

recalcitrant regions pledged to the status quo altered their laws.[2] Also in
this period, a series of utopian schemes for family reorganization surfaced
with panaceas ranging from a return to biblical patriarchs to the forming
of free-love communities. The question is, what set off these battles over
household government and how, in the end, amidst the carnage did such
a positive image of the family triumph?

The story seems to start prior to the 1840–80 period of legislative
change, when a variety of groups with a variety of concerns about the
household tried to alleviate those concerns with measures other than ones
that directly took power away from the household head. Obviously the
primary form of antislavery activity at this time, the American Colonization Society—which sought to send those of African American descent
back to Africa—falls into this category. Another example—less often associated with the household—is the rise of institutionalization. In the
1820s, state and local officials in the most populous northern states began
issuing a series of reports—in Massachusetts, the Josiah Quincy and
State Prison at Charlestown reports; in New York, the Yates and the Society for the Prevention of Pauperism reports; and in Pennsylvania, the

Philadelphia Guardians of the Poor and Bache's Pennsylvania Penitentiaries reports—promoting and justifying the use of institutions such as poorhouses and prisons for housing and ruling dependent groups in the population. David Rothman's influential 1971 book, *The Discovery of the Asylum,* discussed many of these reports, and under his editorship, Arno Press issued reprints of the documents, making them generally available to scholars. Rothman—writing at the height of the late-twentieth-century de-institutionalization movement—regarded these documents as the origin of the attitude that institutions were "an inevitable and sure step in the progress of humanity."[3] He contrasted these impersonal, massive fortresses that cordoned off the poor with a colonial welfare system in which Americans "relieved the poor at home or with relatives or neighbors."

Subsequently historians have criticized the "golden age" aspects of Rothman's interpretation. Colonists had supported the use of the almshouse with more enthusiasm than he had perhaps appreciated. Almshouses and workhouses had existed in the major port cities throughout the colonial period, and even some parishes and townships in the countryside erected houses for that purpose, although often use of the establishments lapsed over time. Closer examination of the accounts of overseers of the poor from colonial localities also puts a different spin on what it meant to be "relieved" "at home or with relatives or neighbors."

Townships or parishes did provide tax exemptions and distributed food, clothing, and fuel to individual households in need. Money payments for the care of a very young, very old, or completely disabled family member might occur, but rarely was the compensation designed to support fully an entire family. Rather, as described earlier, local officials frequently auctioned off the aged or infirm to the lowest-bidding householder; paid premiums to households to take infants and toddlers; and bound out children of the poor as early as age four to a master who could make legal use of their labor up to age twenty-one (or even older, if they were African-American, Indian, or biracial), pushing the mother into servitude as well. Sometimes payments for infants and aged parents enabled a poor family to stay together, but more often the payments went to better-off households that had the means and the room to house the welfare recipient. Payments of support to these households were much more generous than the sums granted directly to the poor living in their own homes. Even so, the overseers frequently had problems convincing household heads to take on the task, and many indigent people changed caretakers every year, moving from place to place.[4] The only way over-seers could justify giving out-relief directly to an indigent family was if it was cheaper than dismembering the household through apprenticing and boarding out.

The whole idea was not to preserve families, but to preserve orderly family government, which often meant encouraging small, weak house-holds to disband and join up with larger, stronger ones. This system of boarding out the incapacitated and indenturing the able resembled En-gland's poor relief, except that it appears that in the colonies the author-ities indentured children at an earlier age and never did provide as much out-relief directly to needy families as did the English parishes adopting the Speenhamland system.[5] It also appears that in America the English-model network of almshouses and workhouses for the poor had difficulty spreading much beyond the major port cities. Rural communities exper-imented with them, but most early American counties and townships re-verted back to auctions and binding out. After the Revolution, state gov-ernments put pressure on localities to erect poorhouses. Southern states transferred jurisdiction over the poor from the parish to county govern-ment, making it economically more feasible for local governments to take the institutional route. The abandonment of warning out—the colonial practice of notifying newcomers to town that they were not eligible for poor relief and encouraging them to leave—in places like Massachusetts gave added incentive for townships to find a place to make poor relief as unattractive to potential claimants as possible. As a result, jurisdictions in the countryside gradually built institutions for the poor or contracted out with one family to care for the community's poor.

Rothman is probably justified, though, in seeing the 1820s reports as something of a watershed, if not exactly for the reasons he suggests. The advocacy of institutions by the authors was—by direct statement and im-plication—a condemnation of household government for the poor. The officials were not simply attacking the old targets—sturdy beggars and vagabonds. In the call to end out-relief, they wanted to stop the array of payments, exemptions, and in-kind assistance given directly to poor households that kept them together, but they also wanted to end all pay-ments to families taking in the indigent, claiming that the institutions provided more cost-effective and superior care. In regard to out-relief, they had only to invoke the experience of the former mother country as evidence "that of all modes of providing for the Poor, the most waste-ful, the most expensive, and the most injurious to their morals, and destructive of their industrious habits, is that of supply in their own families."[6] Absent are recitations about the worthy poor such as widows. Rather, the discussion involving female-headed households focused on unwed mothers, a group never deemed appropriate to head households in the first place. In earlier times, corporal punishment, public humiliation, and extended labor terms for servants fed the community's hunger to penalize these errant females and relieved the community of some of the requests for support. Now towns faced greater demands, or so they felt. The tone of the report from the Philadelphia's Guardians, for example, turned nasty as it treated the subject of single mothers, whom the Guardians claimed had been cut off from any support other than that provided in a workhouse by all other major cities.

Let anyone whose convictions on this point are not sufficiently clear, attend at this room on the day when the committee on bastardy pay the weekly allowances to their pensioners, and mark the unblushing effrontery, that some of them exhibit. The thanklessness with which they receive their allotted stipend; the insolence with which they demand a further supply, arrogantly exacting as a right which ought never to have been granted, even as a charity.[7]

An even more striking departure was the attitude toward male household heads. Support for poor and unemployed male-headed households became support for intemperance. The New York State report of 1824 cites 6,896 permanent paupers and finds that 1,585 of them "became so from the too frequent use of ardent spirits" and that this group, clearly comprised of adult males, "brought into poverty with them 989 wives and 2,167 children," meaning that "intemperance produces more than two-thirds of all the permanent pauperism in the State."[8] All of the northern states with large urban populations identified intemperance as the major cause of poverty, and, by doing so they targeted the behavior of the white adult working-class male, including those who headed families. The fact that some fell into the category of "worthless foreigners" no doubt made it easier to lash out at the group, but no one suggested that immigrants alone generated all the intemperance in society.[9]

The most strident condemnation of household government, however, is found in the prison reports, which present case studies of the inmates. As Rothman notes:

The 1829 and 1830 reports of the Auburn penitentiary contained 173 biographies, and in fully two-thirds of them, the supervisors selected and presented the data to prove that childhood made the man. Almost always a failure of upbringing—specifically, the collapse of family control—caused deviant behavior.[10]

No matter how old the criminal, the problem had begun with an absent father, a prostitute mother, an abusive stepfather, a master whose failure in discipline had caused his charge to run away, or some other situation resulting from a poorly governed household.

Consequently, the most enlightened suggestions for institutional use emphasized specialization. The poor families should not remain intact in the poorhouse but should be separated based on their age, sex, and situation, with the able going to workhouses separated by sex; drunks going to houses of intemperance; and, most important, children being directed to a child refuge or orphan asylum (even though they were not orphans) to be educated and trained in industriousness before being bound out. The movement to establish separate institutions for children to remove them from corrupting influences meant rescuing them from their parents or parent.

Perhaps most surprising is the rejection of boarding out and the skepticism about indenturing, the backbone of the welfare system for centuries. The Josiah Quincy report on Massachusetts considered boarding out of the poor to be "applicable to only to very small towns." The report completely dismissed the argument of the community of Chilmark that "the poor being sometimes boarded with those, who are in want themselves, it is not lost to the town," and used their response as an illustration of "how liable to abuses it is."[11] The New York report regarded boarding out as being not only "wasteful in regard of economy" but also "cruel in regard of the paupers themselves." Here the household head of the host family—"the keeper"—was portrayed as being guided by pecuniary motives and as often behaving barbarously to the inmate. Almost all of the writers on the subject of pauperism, claimed the author of the report, "have condemned these modes of providing for the support of the poor."[12] Moreover, even indenturing of children to household heads was faulty because

the education and morals of the children of paupers, (except in almshouses) are almost wholly neglected. They grow up in filth, idleness, ignorance and disease, and many become early candidates for the prison or the grave. The evidence on this head is too voluminous even for reference.[13]

Notice the phrase asserting that "except in almshouses," the education and morals of children of paupers were neglected, a statement peculiar to this time period. By mid-century, the almshouse and prison experience engendered more skepticism, although the specialized institution—orphanage, reformatory, mental asylum—continued to garner support.

In the United States—with its proud colonial and then republican tradition of small government—how had institutions suddenly grown so popular? The increased perception of a severe poverty problem, especially in northern towns and cities, seems to be at the core. Early age at household formation and little parental or community control over marital unions increased the proportion of low-income households in the American population. Youthful households and poverty were not new, but, as discussed in the previous chapter, the liberties of free sons and daughters had a withering effect on servitude of all sorts. Decline in the indenturing of immigrants and mercantile apprenticeship, as well as the abolition of slavery in the northern states, all contributed to increased numbers of youth and laborers on their own. Welfare systems that no longer warned out newcomers and operated at the county rather than local level made it more difficult to place poor in neighbors' households and facilitated migration into towns and cities. Of groups likely to be low income—free blacks, free young men of all races, and female household heads—disproportionate numbers can be documented from the 1790s on as living in urban areas such as Philadelphia, New York, Boston, and Baltimore.[14] The increasing number of young European immigrants pouring into the port cities after 1820 only exacerbated the problem. In 1824, nearly a quarter of New York State's long-term paupers and over one-half of those needing occasional support lived in the city of New York, even though the city claimed no more than 13 percent of the population. In Pennsylvania circa 1820, Philadelphia's poverty rate was three times that of surrounding counties. Forty percent of Rhode Island's poor in 1850 resided in Providence.[15]

By 1850, the first year in which solid national statistics on individuals are available, 10 percent of the American population lived in cities of twenty-five thousand or more, but 30 percent of inmates resided there.[16] Getting paupers into poorhouses had been fairly successful, according to the census, with two-thirds of those so identified living as inmates rather than being boarded in private families or receiving poor relief at home.[17] By 1850, over 96 percent of those running afoul of the law resided in correctional facilities, and 44 percent of those labeled insane had been put in asylums. Very small percentages, however, of persons suffering from other mental and physical disabilities lived in institutions at mid-century. Of course, the impact of the institutions on the population was greater than the 1 percent or less who at any one time showed up as inmates. Turnover was brisk. Many older and sick inmates died; and young people waited out the winter and high unemployment periods and then reentered the workforce. Almost all children going to institutions in this period were eventually bound out for service unless their family managed to reclaim them.[18]

Immigrants were overrepresented in institutions, but nonetheless, two-thirds of inmates had been born in the United States.[19] Patricia Cline Cohen's wonderful study of the antebellum New York world of Helen Jewett, an Augusta, Maine, servant girl–turned-prostitute and her clientele of middle-class male clerks on the make reveals some of the travails of native-born white youth who came to the big city. Neither sex as portrayed in Cohen's book could enjoy the good life without resort to criminal activity.[20] For most women, only the oldest profession offered pay sufficient to live independently in a room of their own. Males could more easily escape their masters' abodes and reside in boardinghouses. But unless they had substantial family resources to augment their meager clerks' pay, about the only amusement affordable after work was reading evangelical Christian tracts borrowed from the Apprentices' Library, an institution that thoughtful employers set up to encourage their boys to stay on the straight and narrow. Pay was two dollars a week, a shared room perhaps one dollar a week, a night with the former Maine maid Helen Jewett, five dollars! Girls of the town, the theaters where they could be propositioned, and the champagne and gifts necessary to close the deal were out of reach for all but the embezzler. Indeed, even less fashionable and satisfying forms of entertainment would seem to require clerks engaging in some sort of petty larceny. Helen for her part had expenses: the costs of stylish clothing and a weekly rent of twelve dollars for a fancy brothel room. The madams rented from the first families of New York, who apparently had no qualms about profiting from such a business. Working-class men unable to gain admission into this world of entertainment at all sometimes stormed their way in, accumulating records of disorderly conduct or assault in the process. None of the social groups mentioned above, save the landlords, was a stranger to the criminal justice system and the inside of New York's jails. As they grew older, some of these men and women along with small children would no doubt encounter the poorhouse as well.

How can this seeming promotion of big government be reconciled with the aversion to it exhibited in nineteenth-century republican and liberal ideology? The nature of the institutions explains a lot. In 1850, 65 percent of inmates lived in institutions managed by benevolent associations or religious denominations. Though privately run, they often received government payments on a per-inmate basis. The institutional heads used volunteers for many management tasks and recruited the more able-bodied inmates for manual labor. As immigration from Catholic Ireland soared, so did the participation of the Catholic Church in institutional development. With its religious orders dedicated to promoting charitable institutions, a whole social group arrived on the scene that had hitherto barely existed in the United States.[21] If taxes had been required to construct all these institutions and pay full-time employees, the development might have been slowed considerably.

The attack on out-relief and the growth of institutions to care for dependents demonstrated to contemporaries the poor job that household heads had done. The intemperate husband and father, the sluttish unwed mother, the neglectful master, boardinghouse keeper, or brothel proprietor—all had failed to govern their realm. Whether or not such failures were deliberate, they made it easier for would-be reformers to argue not only for poorhouses and jails but also for the removal of abused wives and youth—whether sons, daughters, or servants—from a system of household governance. If the state had little interest in promoting household government—either by keeping poor families together on out-relief or sending family members into new larger households rather than institutions—then why should dependents be denied right of exit? The cataclysmic impact of the Civil War on the lives of both masters and slaves has obscured the other losses sustained by the household head. No military battles or constitutional amendment preceded the other alterations in his status. Instead, they occurred piecemeal on a state-by-state basis. While western European nations outlawed slavery earlier than did Americans, the states experienced a mid-nineteenth-century surge in legislation weakening the head's power over all his other household dependents that proceeded at a much faster clip than in the "Old Country."

Table 4 displays the chronology of the legal blows to the American household head. In 1865, after four years of war, the states ratified the Thirteenth Amendment to the Constitution, which banned slavery and involuntary servitude in the United States. Two years after the abolition of slavery, the United States Congress passed the Debt Peonage Act, outlawing so-called "voluntary servitude." This legislation brought an official end to the two-century-long expansion of the powers given masters under the English common law. The indenturing of western European servants had, for all intents and purposes, come to end by 1830, not because of lack of demand, but because the supply had dried up. With a better economic situation in the Old World and the lower cost of steamship travel, the business apparently no longer attracted recruiters or recruits.[22] Soon after, the practice of offering indentured service in lieu of prison to debtors lost its legal standing. Delaware, at mid-century, was the last state to outlaw this type of adult servitude.[23] At the same time, debtors' prisons also disappeared, so masters might well have wondered what legal recourse they would have if an adult indentured servant just quit. The indentured servitude that accompanied gradual emancipation of slaves and their children in the northern states after the American Revolution had about run its course. Just as the auctioning off of poor people grew more problematic, the traditional placing out of white native-born youth to work in the household of others seemed on the wane.

According to the one census available for Maryland at the time of the Revolution, not just slave children, but also 15 percent of free white boys from five to fourteen and 11 percent of free white girls lived in the households of nonrelatives, presumably working as servants. Among the free population of the same age in 1850, under 4 percent, including institutional inmates, fell into that category. Comparing the situation of free youth aged seventeen to twenty-six—the prime years in which males and females either married or worked for others to save up for marriage—about half of the unmarried males and nearly 40 percent of the unmarried women lived with nonrelatives at the time of the Revolution. In 1850, this situation still obtained among free black and foreign-born youth, but if one looks at just white native-born young people—the group predominating in the 1776 census of Maryland—less than 20 percent (19 percent of males and 15 percent of females) lived with nonrelatives in private households. The remainder of 1850 youth was working elsewhere and living at home, with relatives, or in group quarters. The traditional labor system that had involved binding out poor children in the households of the more affluent and the placement of youth in domestic, agricultural, or artisanal service to a master was in decay among the white native-born population.[24]

The Thirteenth Amendment banning slavery in the United States did not eliminate the "voluntary" indentures contracted by a servant and master. Congressional records indicate that some members saw nothing wrong with contracts where consenting adults worked without wages to pay off a debt or for room and board. When Indians in the New Mexico territory fell victim to this kind of service, and masters called upon the

TABLE 4
Collapse of Legal Support for Household Government

Role Affected	Legal Change	Date	Persons or Area Affected (%)*
Master	Free from enslavement	1840	13 (% black pop.)
		1850	12 "
		1860	11 "
		1870	100 "
		1880	100 "
	Debt Peonage Act bans vol. servitude	1867	all U.S.
Husband	Cruelty as ground for absolute divorce	by 1840	41 (% states & terr.)
		by 1850	40 "
		by 1860	48 "
		by 1870	53 "
		by 1880	66 "
	Drunkenness as ground for absolute divorce	by 1840	17 (% states & terr.)
		by 1850	26 "
		by 1860	45 "
		by 1870	53 "
		by 1880	66 "
	Wives' right to separate estates	by 1840	0 (% states & terr.)
		by 1850	31 "
		by 1860	38 "
		by 1870	55 "
		by 1880	87 "
Father	Child custody determined by court	by 1840	4 (% states & terr.)
		by 1850	32 "
		by 1860	51 "
		by 1870	50 "
		by 1880	60 "
	Free public education	by 1840	6 (% states & terr.)
		by 1850	6 "
		by 1860	31 "
		by 1870	74 "
		by 1880	96 "

Sources: Servitude—Robert Steinfeld, *The Invention of Free Labor: The Employment Relation in English and American Law and Culture, 1350–1870* (Chapel Hill, 1991), chap. 7; Divorce—George Elliott Howard, *A History of Matrimonial Institutions*, vol. 3 (Chicago, 1904); Carroll D. Wright, *A Report on Marriage and Divorce in the United States, 1867–1886* (Washington, D.C., 1891); Separate estates—Joan Hoff, *Law, Gender, and Injustice: A Legal History of U.S. Women* (New York, 1991), 379–82; Richard Chused, "Married Women's Property Law, 1800–1850," *Georgetown University Law Journal* 71 (1983); B. Zorina Kahn,

TABLE 4
(continued)

"Married Women's Property Laws and Female Commercial Activity: Evidence from United States Patent Records, 1790–1895," *Journal of Economic History* 56 (1996): 362–64; Sara Lynn Ziegler, "Family Service: Labor, the Family, and Legal Reform in the U.S." (Ph.D. diss., UCLA, 1996); Child custody—Howard, *History of Matrimonial Institutions*, vol. 3; Joel Prentice Bishop, *Commentaries on the Law of Marriage and Divorce*, vol. 2 (Boston, 1873), chap. 35; Michael Grossberg, *Governing the Hearth: Law and the Family in Nineteenth-Century America* (Chapel Hill, 1985), chap. 7; Peter W. Bardaglio, *Reconstructing the Household: Families, Sex, and the Law in the Nineteenth-Century South* (Chapel Hill, 1995); Mary Ann Mason, *From Father's Property to Children's Rights: The History of Child Custody in the United States* (New York, 1994); Public education—Clifford Lord and Elizabeth Lord, comps., *Historical Atlas of the United States* (New York, 1953), 84–85, 174–75.
*In 1840, there were 29 states and territories covered; in 1850, 35; in 1860, 42; and in 1870 and 1880, 47. Child custody, however—which required that states and territories had already given the courts jurisdiction—had fewer areas that qualified: 26 in 1840; 28 in 1850; 35 in 1860; 42 in 1870; and 43 in 1880.

United States Army to return runaways, the Republicans decided that all ambiguity needed to be removed in regard to this type of "voluntary" service and passed the 1867 law. Masters traditionally had had the right to restrain or physically punish servants, and the state had intervened to bring back indentured servants who had unilaterally decided to terminate a labor contract. The new law not only shut the door on centuries of expanded master-servant law but also reversed many of the traditional common law provisions regarding a master's authority and his ability to call upon the state to enforce it.[25] The new, mostly immigrant, contract labor, however, was different on two counts. First, as Robert Steinfeld points out, these wage-earning workers who earned wages (minus transportation costs) now faced liens on property or wage forfeiture rather than penal sanctions if they broke their contract.[26] Second—and what has attracted less notice—is that these laborers typically worked in mills, mines, railroads, and ships for employers, not for a head of household. Exploitative labor relations did not necessarily cease, but the venue and the relationship changed. Economic necessity might discourage exit, but legal household dependency no longer did.

In contrast to the situation with bound servitude and slavery, the federal government declined to take jurisdiction over husband/wife or father/children relationships unless forced by other constitutional mandates to do so. In those instances, Congress assumed a quite conservative posture. Its rejection of polygamy in Utah can be counted an antipatriar-chal stance, but it also represented the status quo of a millennium.[27]

Essentially, the battle for change occurred in the states, one by one. As a consequence of laws eventually passed on the state level, husbands could be deprived of control over their wives' wealth and could be di-vorced for abusive behavior. Other state-by-state actions broke the fa-ther's monopoly over the custody of his children and his supervision of their labor.

During the middle decades of the nineteenth century, legislators and judges argued long and hard about the husband's control over the person and property of his wife. The rules governing divorce and coverture played a central role in this debate. The much-vaunted departure from the "till death do us part" tradition of Christian marriage in the post-Revolutionary period actually turned out to produce few absolute di-vorces for wives, because success as a petitioner normally depended upon a husband disappearing or living adulterously for many years with an-other woman.[28] For husbands, disappointing behavior on the part of his wife could be countered with moderate physical correction or economic sanctions, as he had legal control of the purse. Creative legal tactics occa-sionally provided a way out for wives in similar situations, but the statis-tics indicate that the odds were not good.[29] Expanding the grounds of divorce to cruelty and drunkenness along with giving wives the right to hold separate property notably increased women's ability to exit le-gally without having to wait to be deserted. These became largely female grounds for divorce. In the period 1867–86, courts granted women 88 percent of the decrees issued for the former cause and 90 percent of those for the latter. Adultery remained more of a male complaint, with 56 per-cent of decrees going to husbands, even though Victorian mores and prostitution statistics would suggest the incidence to be higher among married men than married women.[30]

Table 4 indicates that a substantial number of states and territories, around 40 percent, had already added cruelty as a legitimate cause for divorce by 1840. In a few states, like Vermont, it became an important ground for divorce, but elsewhere that was not the case.[31] States where the judiciary granted a high percentage of divorces to complainants were also states that restricted absolute divorce to the standard adultery or de-sertion pleas.[32] Most states allowing cruelty as a ground for divorce prior to 1840 usually set the threshold for prosecution at the level of "extreme cruelty"—the spouse had to be at risk for maiming or death—or the procedure involved such a complicated set of requirements that few obtained a divorce. For example, Alabama accepted cruelty petitions from 1820 on, but for any divorce to be final in that state, two-thirds of the legislature had to concur. Kentucky allowed petitions for cruelty as early as 1809, but every divorce case had to have an attorney representing the public interest by arguing against the termination of the marriage, even when both parties wanted it. Louisiana before 1857 required a two-year waiting period before a divorce on the grounds of cruelty would be final. Both Ohio and Pennsylvania were also early in recognizing cruelty as a plea, but their judges granted divorces to fewer than half of those petitioning.[33]

For all these reasons, no clear upward trend in the divorce rate occurred much before 1850,[34] but thereafter the situation changed. States lowered the threshold for the cruelty plea, and new states jumped on the bandwagon. Drunkenness surfaced as a popular ground after 1840, and by 1860 a majority of jurisdictions had amended their divorce statutes to include it. As a plea it proved easier to document than cruelty. When the first national statistics appeared in 1867, 22 percent of the divorces obtained by women were for husband's cruelty and/or drunkenness. By 1886, that share had grown to nearly one-third. The increase in divorces given wives for cruelty and/or drunkenness in this 20-year period far exceeded the overall percentage rise in divorce.[35]

Table 4 also shows that in the four decades under scrutiny nearly all states passed married women's property acts that allowed wives inheriting wealth from fathers or first husbands—and, later, those who had earned wages—the legal means to wrest control of their separate property from their husbands and to exit a marriage.[36]

Finally, table 4 reveals the extent to which the patriarch's control over his minor children had been reduced by actions of the states during the middle decades of the nineteenth century. Under the English common law, which had no provision for divorce, a couple's children, being of the patrilineage, belonged to the father. As separations and divorce came into the legal tradition in Britain and the United States, the issue of what to do with the offspring of the couple arose. When states passed divorce legislation and, in the first half of the nineteenth century, moved toward having divorces handled by the judiciary rather than the legislature, they also gave to the courts the right to settle custody. Initially that authority meant little, though, because judges inclined toward maintaining the common law tradition of keeping children in the custody of their fathers, even when said father had been the "guilty" party in the breakup of the marriage, as long as he had not abused the child or children.[37] The father was the one who had to support the child. What male judges knew—and what divorced women with children later found out—was that little support would be forthcoming from a man who lacked custody rights. Clearly fears about the fate of one's children kept many miserable wives in marriages. As late as 1840, only one state court, New York's—out of twenty-six jurisdictions where courts had the right to act on custody as part of the divorce or separation procedure—had clearly challenged the father's automatic assumption of custody. And even in that state judges questioned whether a patriarch should be subjected to what they called "household democracy."[38] State actions repudiating *patria potestas* cropped up in more and more states, however, during the 1840s. By 1850, about one-third had passed statutes or issued judicial opinions in cases that weakened the paternal claim to custody. In some states, the judges genuflected before the principle that he father's right was paramount but then went on to list so many exceptions to that right—tender years of the child, sex of the child, wishes of the child, being the person at fault in the dissolution of the marriage, and so on—that the right came to mean little. More and more, though, judges simply claimed that the welfare of the child—not the father's rights—was the first criterion when awarding custody to the mother or to a third party. By the last quarter of the nineteenth century, mothers much more often than fathers received the custody of children in divorce proceedings. Nevertheless, the courts had not simply substituted the authority of the mother for the authority of the father as mid-century women's rights advocates had argued they should do. Nor—despite judicial opinions citing the importance of consulting the wish of children—did sons and daughters make the final decision. Instead the power went to what Michael Grossberg termed the "judicial patriarchy."[39]

States also removed fathers from complete control over the training and labor of their young. In 1840, only Massachusetts and Maine had passed laws mandating free public schools in every locality. By the 1870s, as table 4 indicates, only a few of the territories lacked such legislation. Every state had approved them. Truancy rules on the local level and compulsory education acts on the state level followed on the heels of this legislation.

The clamor for free public schooling did not come from eager young scholars. Rather, it sprang largely from white Protestant middle-class, middle-aged professionals in northern states, who warned that the household head would or could not furnish education for his young and that the state had to step in if a law-abiding democracy were to survive in the United States. School officials did worry about being accused of interfering with parental authority. The first compulsory education acts targeted manufacturers who employed children all year around, not their parents, even though most reformers considered the parents to be the root of the problem. Soon, though, educators directed their attacks at the parent. "The parent is not the absolute owner of the child," declared the Boston School Committee in 1853 as it took measures to ensure universal schooling. The secretary of the Connecticut State Board of Education in 1872 dismissed the argument that compulsory attendance interfered with the "liberty of parents."

The child has rights, which not even a parent may violate. He may not rob his child of the sacred right of a good education. . . . In ancient Greece, the law gave almost unlimited authority to the father over his offspring. The same is true in some semi-barbarous nations now. In all Christian lands . . . the duty to educate is as positive as to feed and clothe.[40]

The first report of the national commissioner of education in 1870 canvassed superintendents of instruction in the various states. School officials regretted their lack of authority to compel attendance. The report from Maine, arguing the necessity of compulsory education laws, drew an analogy between criminals and truants.

The state builds prisons and penitentiaries for the protection of society and taxes society for the same. But does she stop here, leaving him who has violated law to be pursued by the community in a mass, to be apprehended by a crowd, and borne by a throng to the place of incarceration? No, she pursues the criminal through legitimate instrumentalities.[41]

Becoming the provider of education to children meant taking responsibility for seeing that they got that education. Some school superintendents shrank from that responsibility, but most, like the official from Maine, urged passage of such legislation. This debate foreshadowed the post–1880 struggles in other social service agencies over how fully the state should fill the power vacuum left by the reduction in the authority of the household head.

Who objected? Individual fathers refusing to send children to school do not show up much in the court records. Instead, most of the cases involved parents accusing police or truant officers of assaulting their child or of having the child sent to an institution as a vagrant because he/she was not in school.[42] The biggest fights were over who should replace the authority of the father in educational decisions. White southerners in control of state governments wanted no such intrusion into their households of free and slave children and mostly kept common schools out until the Civil War.[43] In the Northeast, the Protestant-dominated school administration fought continually with the Catholic Church and the Democratic Party over control of the schools and compulsory education, just as the Republicans and Democrats in the postbellum South struggled over funding for the schools of freedmen's children. The Catholics charged that the supposed nonsectarian schools actually inculcated Protestant practice by conducting Bible readings and hymn singing. The Whig/Republicans feared that the Catholic Church would obtain public monies for its own school system—just as tax dollars already went to Catholic institutions for the indigent—and that the values of republican ideology would be threatened by priestly education. *Harper's Weekly* during the 1870s regularly produced cartoons in which simianlike Catholic politicians and priests tried to undermine the educational system by their objections to the use of the Protestant bible in the schools. In figure 11, a Thomas Nast cartoon shows rude Catholic children, egged on by a priest, reveling in their ignorance and kicking the Bible out of school.[44]

If one glances over the entire record revealed in table 4, it appears that on most issues about half of the states and territories that made changes stripped power from the head of household prior to 1860 and about half did so in the twenty years after. Southern jurisdictions clearly closed the door on any changes that might be viewed as antipatriarchal during the 1850s as the battles over slavery grew more intense. Consequently, during Reconstruction—when radical Republicans took charge—most southern legislatures passed provisions that had already been enacted in the North. By 1880, not only had involuntary and voluntary servitude been abolished, but two-thirds of the states allowed divorce for abusive behavior on the part of the husband and 87 percent presented roadblocks in the way of husbands trying to claim their wives' capital over the wives' objections. Sixty percent had ruled that courts had the ultimate determination over child custody. Ninety-six percent of the states and territories took over the education decision from the household head by passing legislation providing for free public schools. All in all, these were not banner decades for the paterfamilias.

The various conflicts over legal dependency reinforced one another.

Some did so directly. Clearly, the antislavery movement influenced other organized movements against patriarchal power. For example, most of those gathering at Seneca Falls, New York, in 1848 to argue for women's rights were abolitionists, and antislavery agitation had provided them with the tools and the experience to develop a group consciousness and publicly to demand change. Antislavery advocates applied contract theory to the labor relationship and the marital tie, while some women's rights advocates drew the connections to divorce.[45]

Those on the other side drew similar connections for the opposite reasons. Globally, slavery was far from an unknown status. What made it "peculiar" in mid-nineteenth-century United States is that it was *not* combined with concubinage, debt servitude, lifelong minority status for unmarried children, and other practices that kept wives and youth in a subservient position. Arguments to increase further the freedom of other dependents made slavery all the more anomalous. If white antebellum household heads had not been in a downward spiral regarding control over the labor and the household forma\tion of their sons and daughters and the bodies and property of their wives, they would not have had

11 Thomas Nast, *Don't Believe in That* (*Harper's Weekly*, 23 December 1871).
COURTESY OF UNIVERSITY OF VIRGINIA LIBRARY COLLECTIONS, CHARLOTTESVILLE

such a difficult time justifying the chattel slavery of their African American servants. Contemporaries understood the connection. Apologists for slavery stressed the importance of supporting the authority of not only the master but also the father and husband against incursions by the state. Northern reformers, complained one southern journalist in 1855, "divide the household into separate interests." The southern states, another warned, had already gone too far in emulating "Northern ideas on the subjects of divorce and the independency of married women, through separate estates and exclusive revenues" and that historically, similar acts had been what brought down the Roman republic.[46] Sarah Hale, the editor of the widely read *Godey's Lady's Book,* attacked both women's rights and abolition.[47]

By no means did the turmoil that resulted in free white men confronting one another in Congress, state legislatures, judicial chambers, and ultimately battlefields go unexpressed in the literature and art of the time. The best-selling American novel of the era, *Uncle Tom's Cabin,* focused upon the incompatibility of Victorian domestic values and chattel slavery. Temperance images in novels and art also dealt with the theme of the derelict household head. Those who thought that the problem rested more with the dependents than the head also got their say, projecting their fear for the future of a society replete with divorce petitioners, man tamers, insolent free blacks, and little street urchins. In Currier and Ives's *Age of Iron: Man As He Expects to Be . . . after His Wife's Emancipation* (1869) (fig. 12), men are left to do the washing, mending, and childcare, while the wife hails a coach driven by a whip-wielding woman to go out on the town. Other prints show women dominating the polling places while men stand idly by holding babies or women luring men into marriage only to sue for divorce and alimony a short time later. Anti-abolitionist cartoons feature the free African-American male turning the tables on the white man by claiming the white woman and lording it over a household of mixed-race children. In the paintings of David Gilmour Blythe—a specialist in portraying the new common school juvenile delinquent—the horror of the emancipated child is revealed. Slate and notebooks under arm, the scamp brazenly uses the cigar he is smoking to light a firecracker.[48]

Actual alternatives to antebellum household organization burst forth in the 1840s. While utopian groups—the Shakers, George Rapp's Rappites, and Robert Owen's communal socialists—traveled to America from the late eighteenth century on to take advantage of the lower cost of

12   Currier and Ives, *Age of Iron: Man As He Expects to Be . . . after Wife's Emancipation* (1869).
COURTESY OF LIBRARY OF CONGRESS COLLECTIONS, WASHINGTON, D.C.

land and the freer religious environment, not until the 1840s did native-born American men throw themselves wholeheartedly into founding sects with innovative familial arrangements. These endeavors—varied in their prescriptions for domestic happiness—had one common characteristic: they were led by charismatic, northern WASP males who saw their opportunity to restructure households in an even more grandiose way than before and in way that removed monogamy as a centerpiece of the system. Some of this generation's frustrations surfaced in the "Young America" movement's incoherent attack on the "old fogy," but the utopian movement men had much greater ambitions.

One obvious way to restructure the household was to restore the primitive Judeo-Christian church and with it patriarchal powers. The most famous and the most substantial in terms of numbers were the Mormons, a group organized in 1830 by Joseph Smith in Palmyra, New York, around his abilities as a prophet and his claim to be the finder of lost biblical scripture. Smith's Book of Mormon, published in that same year, had family disorganization as a constant theme but denounced polygamy. Subsequently Smith warmed to the idea of a more collectivist, though still hierarchical, society that included a redefinition of marriage. An "Angel of God" prompted this redefinition. Smith told of the visit by one who "stood by him with a drawn sword" and warned that unless Smith moved forward and established polygamy, his "priesthood would be taken away from him and he should be destroyed." Practical problems in part led to Smith's need to control marriage. Converts would come into the Mormon enclave having left behind unconverted spouses and children. These people needed to be married off, even though they had not ever been properly divorced.[49] When Joseph Smith announced his revelation in 1843 and began soliciting brides from among the relatives and even wives of his church leadership, the shock of not only his original wife but others in the hierarchy suggests that the demand for this system had not come from within the flock but from their leader and his communications with his deity. He died the next year at the hands of an angry mob outraged by his unorthodox views, and the successful implementation of his vision of "celestial marriage" was left to others. Brigham Young took control of the community and moved with his followers from the hostile environment around Nauvoo, Illinois, into the wilderness of Utah. In 1850, the census showed the population of the territory to be eleven thousand. Two years later, the Mormon leadership formally admitted to plural marriage, and it remained the policy among the Mormons until the federal government forced its end in 1890, at which time two hundred thousand people had been added to the Mormon population.

Joseph Smith claimed the gift of prophecy, and he dominated the family, friends, and converts whom he brought into the faith. His family, originally from Essex County, Massachusetts, moved to western New York as they tried to cope with the effects of the post-Revolutionary depression. In a biographical statement Smith wrote in 1832—twenty-seven years old and already a successful prophet—he described a childhood of "indigent circumstances," in which he was "obliged to labour hard for the support of a large Family" and "deprived of the bennifit [sic] of an education."[50] Most of his personal writings are not in his hand and those that are show very limited skills in spelling, grammar, and syntax. It is believed that Smith made up for the absence of formal education with liberal doses of Bible reading and with the study of perfectionist doctrines and the hermetic lore indulged in by fringe evangelical Protestant sects in the Burned-Over District of upstate New York.[51] An intensely ambitious man without the proper credentials to be accepted in a mainstream church, Smith recalls the seventeenth-century Quaker leader

George Fox, who also claimed to have a hotline to the Almighty. Fox wrote of his own epiphany in an English field, where "I saw that being bred at Oxford or Cambridge did not qualify or fit a man to be a minister of Christ; what then should I follow such for."[52] Smith's ministry even more than Fox's rested on revelations and his ability to convince others of their legitimacy.

Even before Smith decreed the Mormon adoption of polygamy, he organized the Mormons hierarchically and by gender. He set up orders of elders, the Aaronic and then the Melchizedek Priesthood, which were open exclusively to men. The celestial marriage doctrines that Smith began discussing openly in the 1840s privileged the church's male elite, and only this elite knew about the change in policy at the beginning. According to the new rules, none but celestial marriages sealed by the Mormon Church's leaders would continue in heaven. Men married under this system would be the great patriarchs, similar to those in the Old Testament. In the hereafter—surrounded by their large families of wives and children—they would rule, and those men of the lower orders who had not contracted such a union were condemned to being servants in perpetuity. On earth, wives of such men could better themselves by agreeing to a celestial marriage to a husband higher up without having to go through a formal divorce. The establishment of celestial marriage was necessary in order to bring on the Second Coming of Jesus Christ.

Thus the Mormons, or Latter-day Saints, from the 1840s to at least 1890 offered a definite alternative to the household system in the United States, an alternative that modeled itself after the Old Testament patriarchal households with multiple wives and children. In *The Peacemaker*—an 1842 justification of a new household system for Mormons—the anonymous author argued that patriarchal authority in home and society must be restored to prevent social disintegration. Women had usurped authority in the household, which had produced disobedient children and male desertion. Biblical standards of divorce and marriage should be adopted to allow men to reassert their leadership.[53]

While the general population of the United States may have been outraged by Mormon marriage laws, the Utah territory, inhabited almost exclusively by Latter-day Saints, grew from 11,000 in 1850 to 144,000 in 1880. In that year, the census reveals the population of the territory to be a settlement of families, with those bearing the designations head of household, spouse, or child constituting 90 percent; in the rest of the West only 73 percent fell into those categories. Utah—compared to the

region as a whole—also had a more balanced sex ratio and an almost exclusively non-Hispanic white population.[54] If the ability to marry was
perceived as a great advantage, then Utah had something to offer. For
those over thirty, a lower proportion remained single in Utah than in the
rest of the Far West. The benefits, however, were much more dramatic
for men than women. Only 14 percent of Utah men in that age group had
never married, while in the rest of the West, the figure was 35 percent. For
Utah women over thirty, a mere 3 percent had never married, but the
West generally married off its females, with just 6 percent of those over
thirty left unwed. Utah women had a higher household headship rate,
15 percent compared to 5 percent elsewhere in the West. Most of these
women presumably formed part of a plural marriage in which their husband resided with another wife. Altogether about 13 percent of households where the head was married appear to be involved in polygynous
practices.

Surprisingly, the foreign-born constituted a third of the Utah population in 1880. Most had come from Britain and Scandinavia, where the
Mormons had missions. These converts had entered the United States
in the 1840s and 1850s, before the word of plural marriages had crossed
the Atlantic.[55] Thereafter, membership abroad plunged and immigration dwindled. Meanwhile, in the United States, opposition to polygamy
and other Mormon policies kept domestic in-migration very low. As a result, by 1880, 54 percent of this newly formed territory's population was
Utah-born.[56] Only 13 percent had entered from other states in the nation,
probably most of these as part of the founding group. The great period of
growth through conversions occurred prior to widespread knowledge of
the celestial marriage system. Thereafter growth in membership depended on retention of those already in the group and high fertility.

Mormons were not the only ones pushing for alternative forms
of household organization based on a return to the primitive Christian
Church. John Humphrey Noyes's Oneida communities, begun in 1843,
offered that option through "complex marriage." From the same area and
the same generation as Joseph Smith, Noyes was richer and better connected than the Mormon founder. He attended Dartmouth College,
and—after a born-again conversion experience at a revival meeting—he
spent the decade of the 1830s moving in and out of theological seminar-
ies at Andover and Yale and preaching a brand of perfectionism. Rejection by a woman he intended to marry, it has been argued, inspired his for-
mulation of a new theory of Christian sexual relations. He wrote in 1837

that "in a holy community, there is no more reason why sexual intercourse should be restricted by law, than why eating and drinking should be."[57] Noyes's writings collected in *The Berean: A Manual for the Help of Those Who Seek the Faith of the Primitive Church* (1847) show him to be no free-love bohemian. He attacks the leading liberal clergy of the time as well as the evangelical reformers such as Theodore Weld for their support of abolition, women's rights, and temperance. "A people," he wrote, "whose political and social institutions constantly teach them that independence is their chief glory, and that subordination is disgrace" will not be properly subservient to God or to the Bible.[58]

In order to pursue his vision of a true Christian community, Noyes married Harriet Holton, who provided him with the funds to begin his project. Supplementary monies came with the death of his father in 1841. By 1846, his system of complex marriage was in place. He brought in associates as well as his sisters and a brother, arranging marriages and pressuring even his mother to recognize him as her spiritual leader. The community, which moved from Vermont to Oneida, New York, grew to approximately three hundred people and lasted for a generation. Its group marriage practices, reproduction, and communal childrearing were all closely monitored by Noyes and leaders chosen by him.[59] Over time, he began publishing tracts on socialism and writing less on complex marriage, but the movement had originated in his desire for a Christian communal family to replace the individual households in American society, and in his opposition to reform movements seeking to free household dependents from subordination to the household head.

A third movement involving innovative household relationships gained initial inspiration from Charles Fourier but developed under the tutelage of a small group of men, the most prominent and voluble being Albert Brisbane. Yet another upstate New Yorker, born around the same time as Noyes and Smith, Brisbane became a crusader against the evils of the "isolated household." A freethinker rather than a born-again Christian, Brisbane presented Fourier's communitarian beliefs in an 1840 volume, modestly entitled *The Social Destiny of Man*. Fourier had hoped to take society beyond the stage of civilization celebrated in eighteenth-century Enlightenment narratives—one which valued the isolated household and marriage—into a new world of association based on a network of communities, phalanxes of 1,620 people each, the number derived from the number of personality types in his theory multiplied by two. "The root then of social incoherence," wrote Brisbane, following

Fourier's ideas, "is to be found in our system of separate households."[60] The first division of "non-producers" in society was comprised of women, children, and servants. Brisbane advertised the book as being about a new way to organize labor and played down the sexual liberation aspect of the theory, specifically, Fourier's thoughts on the "New Amorous World" in communal life. Not until the 1960s did these writings find a publisher in the United States. Nonetheless the connection of marriage with a defective, passé system and the advocacy of communal nurseries for infants clearly sent a message different from that favored in respectable Victorian opinion. Brisbane converted Brook Farm in Massachusetts to a Fourier phalanx and over twenty more sprang up in New York, Pennsylvania, and the Midwest during the 1840s. By the 1850s, enthusiasm waned, although four new groups had cropped up. About four thousand in all joined communes, and thousands more became members of Fourier clubs. Men outnumbered women almost two to one in the phalanxes, and nearly all of the women were married, suggesting the experiments appealed primarily to males. Contemporary comments from women indicated suspicion about the motives of the movement. Sophia Peabody, fiancée of Brook Farm member Nathaniel Hawthorne, feared that the Frenchman's ideas would undermine the stability of the family and marveled "that among learned men, who are interested about public morals and civic institutions, no one should take the trouble to read what Charles Fourier wrote."[61] Brisbane, of course, knew quite well what Fourier had written and seemed unfazed by popular notions of public morals. He never put down roots in any community; instead, while serving as a cheerleader for the investments of time and money by others, he traipsed back and forth across the Atlantic with a long succession of wives and mistresses. Dying in 1890 at the age of eighty-one, he had fathered ten children, three of them out of wedlock.[62]

Traditionally, historians have portrayed these movements as reactions to the dog-eat-dog world of antebellum economic stress, capitalism, and industrialization. Utopians' criticism of the family as too selfish and their adoption of innovative sexual arrangements were interpreted as an offshoot of the class analysis of society, a secondary objective that had come out of close daily contact in communal settings.[63] Another way to look at these projects, however, is to see them as responses by northeastern white males to changes they perceived happening to the household and the authority of its head, each appealing to different socioeconomic groups— from the poorly educated men of rural America to the leading intellectuals in its towns and cities. However different, all espoused a vision of the

household more grandiose than that expressed in the typical northern domestic circle, and all sought to reverse what they considered a move to a
smaller, more individualistic family.

In the midst of the controversy swirling around the household, an image of domestic bliss emerged that steadily gained in acceptance and
eventually erased much of the historical memory of a "household civil
war." This image came to epitomize the "modern family," remained relevant to the majority of the population until at least the mid-twentieth
century, and continues to be perceived as reassuring to a certain segment
of American society.

A particular group of antebellum female writers and artists—white,
educated, middle-class easterners—can be credited with foisting images
of "domestic bliss" on an uncertain American public. Ann Douglas first
drew attention to these women who edited women's magazines and wrote
"woman's fiction." They have become one of the most heavily studied
groups in literature departments, just as the cult of domesticity and
separate spheres prescriptive literature has became a staple of women's
history courses. Douglas accused them—along with downwardly mobile
Protestant ministers—of feminizing American culture by pushing a sentimental, vapid view of domestic life on the reading public, encouraging the writing of treacle-laced mush, lowering the level of intellectual
discourse, and paving the way for a culture dominated by soap-opera
consumers.[64] Douglas's slightly over-the-top analysis had the virtue of
recognizing the influence and determination of a group that hitherto had
been dismissed as "female scribblers." Subsequent study of these authors
by others absolves them from some of Douglas's charges and also suggests
that their influence, while considerable, had its limits in a public sphere
still safely dominated by men. What they did do was refashion the concept of the household and its power relationships.

Nina Baym presents us with a comprehensive analysis.[65] She focuses on most of the best-selling novelists of the time—Sarah Hale, Susan Warner, Maria Cummins, Augusta Evans. *Woman's fiction,* as Baym
uses the term, does not mean all stories written by or for women, although
it probably includes the most popular works and the lion's share of the
best-sellers. The "woman's fiction" novels differed from other work avidly
read by women. Unlike the gothic or historical novel, "woman's fiction"
was set in more mundane, present-day settings. The "woman's fiction"
writers drew a sharp distinction between their aims in these works and
those expressed in the seduction novel, of which they heartily disapproved
and which has a much clearer link to the soap opera of the twentieth

century. In the seduction novel, the heroine was weak or wily, but in either case she had little object in life but snagging a rogue, who in some cases was redeemed but in most cases brought her to degradation and death. In contrast, the heroine in "woman's fiction" was, or became in the course of the novel, a strong independent woman who did not waste herself in the pursuit of unworthy men. She might or might not work outside the home or have a career, but her most important goal was triumphing over adversity and emerging as a person who could give not only love but moral guidance to others in need, usually by creating a supportive household environment for children, husband, and other friends and relatives. One can argue about whether to call this domestic individualism or not: the novel is about a woman becoming a strong individual, but she accomplishes this by giving to others, and her aim is the re-creation of a domestic community that has been lost or damaged.[66] It is, however, clearly a separate sphere domain.

A rather striking example of how the product of one woman's pen changed over the period—going from a portrayal of a weak-willed heroine in a 1791 seduction novel to a depiction in 1828 of the good, useful woman—can be found in the work of best-selling novelist Susanna Rowson. In *Charlotte Temple,* the reader is given the typical beautiful but pathetic victim of male irresponsibility who has no power over her life and pays for her sexual indiscretions with death from a broken heart. A sequel—appearing a generation later, at the end of Rowson's life—*Charlotte's Daughter; or The Three Orphans* reflects the transformation in sentiment. Lucy is the model lady bountiful who survives, chastely, a tragic love affair and substitutes good works for male companionship.[67]

These female authors did not advocate a dismantling of the legal authority of the household head. They opposed not only abolition but women's rights as well. *Uncle Tom's Cabin* caused problems for both northern domestic fiction writers who ignored the issue and for southern writers who obscured it by passing off slaves as domestic help.[68] Mainstream authors from both regions attacked the 1852 book and the abolitionist position. Northerners like Hale favored getting rid of the problem of African American household members through Liberian colonization. Popular antebellum southern writers, who—unlike southern novelists after the war—tended to pit their female heroines against patriarchal planters, had an even bigger problem in writing contemporary fiction. To exclude the subject seemed more and more absurd, while to include it changed the focus of the book. The main point, though, is that this type of literature transcended sectional conflict to an amazing degree.[69] Its seemingly northeastern white middle-class milieu apparently attracted any female with access to a book regardless of demographic difference. Despite the political conservatism of the fiction, male writers, when they took notice, had little good to say about women's literature. "What is the *mystery* of these innumerable editions of the *Lamplighter?*" whined Nathaniel Hawthorne about Maria Cummins's most famous novel. Cummins—whose book sold four times more copies in the first month than Hawthorne's *Scarlet Letter* sold in his lifetime—wrote about a young orphan, Gerty, who accedes to the dictatorial presence of an elderly surrogate father, a Mr. Graham, because she wants to help his kindly, blind daughter, Emily. Upon attaining adulthood, however, Gerty is determined to show her independence and leaves the household to teach and live on her own in a boardinghouse. Not that she is a career woman. As is usually the case, once independence is proven, it can be sacrificed in order to make a home for a properly moral young man, in this instance one Andrew Sullivan, who loves her for her character, not her sexual charms. The novel is full of improbable subplots and reunions, including the resurfacing of Gerty's supposedly dead father.[70]

Men did not write novels of this sort, even though they authored women's conduct books and seduction novels. Baym comments:

I theorize that they avoided woman's fiction because it made them uncomfortable. Representations of gender behavior in woman's fiction, no matter how retrograde they seem today, were challenging the male-defined status quo. Then, as now, most male writers would rather write about vapid angels and malign temptresses than about what Louisa May Alcott called "good, useful women"; and they prefer to represent women as men's auxiliaries rather than center them in worlds of their own.[71]

To get the full sense of the sexual politics at work in this literature, though, one has to consider the presentation of the male characters. For the first time, women have taken control of a genre, and they marginalize men just as women were marginalized in the masculine tales of ambition. Indeed, for men these novels contained few good roles, in either the literal or the Hollywood sense of the term. Males fell into three categories: tyrants who expected total obedience from their women; incompetent household heads who lost the family fortune and left their women folk to reconstruct the domestic circle; or mealy-mouthed ciphers, usually the moral, good young man whom the heroine chooses at the end of the book for purposes of nest building. Whoever the male might be, he is treated to a continual barrage of good Christian advice and behavior intended to guide him in shaping up his life. The moral incompetence of the men appearing in "women's culture" books hardly helped the cause of patriarchal authority, even though their authors showed no love of either Seneca Falls types or abolitionists.

Douglas especially notes the opposition to this kind of writing from male authors such as Melville and women intellectuals such as Margaret Fuller. Unlike Hawthorne, many of the best-known American male writers of the time, sensing that no good could come of literary fiction based in the household, made a concerted effort to escape the household entirely. They put male characters in historical settings or in the outdoors—preferably on a horse in the West or out on the water—far from the domestic scene. The fate of the paterfamilias or the exploration of household relationships was not what many men wanted for recreational reading, as Herman Melville discovered when he switched from whales to unflattering depictions of mothers and the problems of incest. Nor did Walt Whitman's first novel on temperance lead to fame and fortune. Each sex had its separate sphere of popular literature. Newspapers, sporting magazines, and adventure tales faced only weak competition from the more "serious" male literature treating issues between men and women.

The pictorial images of domestic bliss correspond closely to the portrayal of domestic conventions in women's literature, even though the artists were, with a few important exceptions, male. The conversation piece that displayed real people talking or at play in their own gardens, estates, or houses—as opposed to generic types stiffly posed in front of the conventional pillars with drapes opening out into a pastoral setting, as was typical of the straight family portrait—came into its own in the United States during the Victorian period.[72] It may be that as photographers took over the job of documenting for posterity the likenesses of sitters, the well-heeled consumers of paintings began to seek something different from artists working in oils. However, that they chose the conversation piece and changed it in the way they did suggests a political connection, because, once again, it was a form that rose circa 1840 and dwindled in popularity in the United States by the 1880s.

As noted in chapter 2, early America—unlike Britain—had very few family paintings in which the head of the household was prominently positioned amidst swarms of family and servants.[73] The head appeared either in the foreground or the center of the picture, standing apart or taller than the rest, recognizable by the richness of his dress, by the nature of his gestures, and/or by having one or more dependents looking to him.

Still, these paintings were intended to represent informal moments, and the household head is often at play. Yet the viewer is not left wondering who heads the family or to whom these persons, objects, and structures belong. In the eighteenth-century conversation pieces in which the background is a specific family estate or domestic interior, the head of household always appears.[74] Wives and children by themselves in and around the house were represented, even though women then as in the nineteenth century primarily cared for children, not men. Women and children could be lumped together in a regular portrait, while the father appeared alone in his own picture. But when a painting depicted the household domain, the head—who had almost always commissioned the painting—had to be in the picture as the presenter of the scene. The picture demonstrated how a refined environment led to cultured and civilized family behavior. The switch from formulaic backdrops of pastoral scenes to actual landscapes and domestic interiors made that point more emphatically.

The great advantage of the conversation piece for the social historian is that it provided the artist and the client much more latitude than did the large formal portrait in presenting the subject and in suggesting relationships among household members and their setting. Conversation pieces conveyed the household more in the way that the head wanted it to be portrayed. Genre pieces had a fictional base and could be more easily manipulated by the artist to send a message that would find a ready audience or otherwise suit the painter's purposes. Such paintings express norms but in the process also sometimes mask the ambivalence that can be found in the conversation piece.

In 1840 America, stilted conversation pieces still had the head of household directing the action from center stage with the background full of stock iconographic symbols.[75] But over time, especially after 1860, conversation pieces emerged that definitely possess that reassuring look of the comfortably well-off Victorian family. Some do such a good job that they earn subtitles such as "Christmastime" that indicate that the artist marketed them as genre pieces. Nearly all of the characteristics are found in the most famous of this kind of painting, Eastman Johnson's 1871 conversation piece *The Hatch Family* (fig. 10), mentioned earlier in the chapter.

The most important change in this new type of conversation piece is that the household interior with upholstery, lighting, carpeting, and, preferably, a piano has taken over the center stage that had been the household head's. A holiday also helps make the picture more festive. The prime age (30 – 60) household head wears a dark suit and either stands on the side or, more often, is seated with a newspaper; he is not foregrounded, centered, or standing tallest. His demeanor is serious, not playful; he is observant, but not directly engaged in any family interaction. Children are playful. Finally, servants—if they appear at all—tend to be young white female domestics. There are no African Americans and no prime age white male servants to serve as ugly reminders of race or class differences, despite the fact that the wealth of the room implied a household needing a staff.

Alfredrick Hatch—who commissioned the painting and who later became the president of the New York Stock Exchange—was the nineteenth-century equivalent of the London commercial magnates featured in the early modern British conversation pieces discussed in chapter 2. The painting finds the household head back in a corner turning away from what appears to be a desk. He depends upon the sumptuousness of his parlor at Christmastime and the size of his well-dressed family to tell us about his importance. He lacks a newspaper, but his father—who along with Hatch's mother-in-law has been recruited for the picture—holds up one. A number of pictures with similar characteristics appeared in the 1860s and 1870s: Johnson's *The Blodgett Family* (1864); John B. Whittaker's *Mr. and Mrs. John Tousey and their Children* (1869); Seymour Guy's *William H. Vanderbilt Family* (1873); and Lucius Rossi, *William Astor Family* (1878).[76] In these paintings, the domestic background, not the paterfamilias, overwhelms the canvas. He is most often seated with a newspaper. Even in pictures where a complete family with husband, wife, and children is not shown, if a prime age male is placed in a parlor, it is thought best to give him a newspaper, as Eastman Johnson has done in figure 13, *The [James] Brown Family* (1869).[77] The newspaper shows Brown's membership in the outside world, where his "real" job is.

These depictions of Victorian families are different in another way from the conversation pieces and family portraits produced in later eighteenth-century England and the thirteen colonies. In the "Mr. Sensitive" portraits discussed in chapter 3, the head of household adopted a playful demeanor or indicated by the stylized gestures he made a gentlemanly stance of informality. The fashion that emerged showed the head of household in a positively affectionate interchange with wife and children. Two of the best examples of colonial American family portraits—Charles Willson Peale's *John Cadwalader Family* (1772) and John Singleton Copley's *Sir William Pepperrell and Family* (1778) (figs. 6 and 7)—feature this

13 Eastman Johnson, *[James] Brown Family* (1869).
COURTESY OF NATIONAL GALLERY OF ART, WASHINGTON, D.C., GIFT OF DAVID EDWARD
FINLEY AND MARGARET EUSTIS FINLEY; PHOTOGRAPH ©2002 BOARD OF TRUSTEES

sort of portrayal of household relations. By most historical accounts, the Victorian family exceeded the Georgian in display of affection, yet, over the course of the nineteenth century, the household head in family portraits becomes more serious and less demonstrative, not more affectionate.

A rich domestic environment also takes on a new meaning as the head of household recedes and assumes a serious air. That seriousness connotes security for the family, but it does not work as well if the home looks barren or less well appointed. An example of a work in which a more modest or gloomy interior makes the father's staring off into space seem as if he is a loser or emotionally disturbed is figure 14, *The Joseph Mabbett Warren Family* (1874). Also painted by Eastman Johnson, this work shows a newspaper that has fallen to the ground, revealing a morose, disoriented fellow who would rather be someplace else.[78] In some of the more opulent and festive environments one sees the same sort of faraway eyes, but in those works the surroundings compensate for the alienation.

14   Eastman Johnson, *Joseph Mabbett Warren Family* (1874).
COURTESY OF SHELBURNE MUSEUM, SHELBURNE, VERMONT

A take-off on the man with the newspaper was produced in this period by one of the few prominent female genre painters, Lily Martin
Spencer. The painting is *The War Spirit at Home* (fig. 15), in which the
mother in the kitchen is reading about the Battle of Vicksburg, while her
children are celebrating and her maid is working.

By the 1880s, most conversation pieces are of women and children,
and by the early twentieth century the form disappears altogether. The
only example from the mid-twentieth century in Mario Praz's collection
of over three hundred conversation paintings is a self-conscious reinven-
tion: a collector of eighteenth- and nineteenth-century family portraits
commissioned one of his own family being served coffee by a black servant in his luxurious Palm Beach drawing room.[79]

Over time, heads of household—whether intellectuals or bourgeois
capitalists—disappear from the interiors of homes in genre pictures as
well, resolving all anxieties about how to portray them. The interiors are

15 Lily Martin Spencer, *War Spirit at Home* (1866). Newark Museum, New Jersey.
COURTESY OF COLLECTION OF THE NEWARK MUSEUM, PURCHASED 1944, WALLACE M.
SCUDDER BEQUEST FUND

for women and children. Middle-aged white men seem reluctant to go beyond the threshold. In the genre paintings shown in the *Domestic Bliss* collection of family life from 1840 to 1910, almost none shows households with prime age (thirty to sixty) male household heads in the picture. Most are fictional domestic scenes of common household events or rituals with mothers and children, only children, or mother, children and grandparents. When fathers are present, they tend to be so elderly that they look like grandparents. Blacks in domestic genre pieces move from inside, to the doorway, to their own cabins, where the reticence about showing a prime age male in a noncommanding situation disappears.[80] In the few instances in which white household heads appear in a domestic interior, they are like the father in the 1867 *The Four Seasons of Life* print (fig. 16), coming home to or off on the edge of the family circle. Well into the twentieth century, the most popular Currier and Ives family prints

16   Currier and Ives, *The Four Seasons of Life: Middle Age* (1868).
COURTESY OF LIBRARY OF CONGRESS COLLECTIONS, WASHINGTON, D.C.

that included the head of household were those in which he is entering the house, not settled in it.[81] Viewers today may think of Currier and Ives as a big purveyor of domestic scenes, but it turns out that they produced many more lithographs of the sporting life—prints of horse racing, for example—than of domestic scenes, and when domestic scenes did appear, they usually lacked the father figure. Instead, mothers and children predominated.[82] The contrast with the dominant forms of representation a century earlier is striking. Artists avoided the depiction of a head of household in domestic settings, and when an adult male figure appeared, the artists left obscure his place in the family and its structure of authority. The patrirch had become a problem. The solutions are indicative not only of the nature of the issue but of why the household's civil war ultimately resolved itself in the way it did.

Removing the paterfamilias from the picture while retaining the environment that says he is still around is a strategy that parallels the literary one of having father away during most of the action. According to Baym, about the only novel that survived for posterity from the genre she calls "woman's fiction" is *Little Women*. Baym attributes its survival to the fact it was directed to a juvenile audience, where the "woman's fiction" mode continued longer. There are other characteristics, however, that separate Alcott's novel from both the standard "woman's fiction" product and other more heavily Christian novels for girls such as *Elsie Dinsmore* that account for its continued popularity.[83] *Little Women* encourages girls to become those strong, useful Christian women whose presence Baym has identified as the most salient characteristic of the genre. Also, as in "woman's fiction" books, the characters in *Little Women* did not discuss either slavery or women's status. Alcott came from a strong abolitionist and women's rights background, and though the novel dealt with the situation of white northern women during the Civil War, creating characters who shared Alcott's family's unpopular social views would have only killed the market for the book. Alcott did not depart from "woman's fiction" by being more assertive, but less. Strength came not from constantly showing the male head of household the error of his ways, but from being loving, generous spirited, and helpful to others, like Marmee, one of the most reassuring figures in American fiction. Still Alcott would have been faced with the problem of how to present strong, useful women in a traditional male-headed household, if she had not taken advantage of the Civil War and sent the father away through most of the story. Those familiar with the details of her life may also be aware that her own father, Bronson, was a constant headache for the family due to his penchant for utopian schemes that invariably failed. About the only way to depict a cheerful middle-class household was to keep him in the background. Using her father's incompetence as a provider to attack women's legal disabilities would have been personally destructive to them both. Although few had as radical a background as Alcott, her solution for presenting domestic bliss—placing the family in a traditional home with the patriarch away—was in fact followed much more often in the representation of the household than is perhaps recognized. It was also a solution that ensured greater longevity for her novel than other strategies for dealing with a problem or tyrannical paterfamilias.

What I am suggesting here is that most of those engaged in mid-nineteenth-century social reform can instead be thought of as political reformers of household government. They are reacting to what they see as a problem of the head's authority over dependents, although their assessment of whom and what was to blame differs greatly. The attacks on the management style of the head by the advocates of the asylum, abolition, women's rights, and the common school are countered by a different kind of reformer promoting more grandiose schemes, patriarchal and otherwise: slavery apologists, sectarian prophets, and communitarians.

These battles eventually erupted into the formal political arena as court decisions, legislation, and ultimately, war.

The cultural manifestations of this household civil war appeared in print and image. When the dust had settled, about the only conception of household government that enjoyed support in every community regardless of geography, race, gender, age, religion, and economic status was that bound up with separate spheres domesticity, a view broadcast in the most popular forms of "woman's fiction" and in genre painting. Traditional sources of power and conflict are removed from the household environment by keeping the paterfamilias out of the action or in the back of the picture reading a newspaper. Considering this situation, it is not surprising that late-nineteenth-century male artists and intellectuals identified domesticity as the antithesis of modernism.[84] Not resolved in this period, however, was where the authority was to go and how support might be maintained for a sphere that had seemingly marginalized the head of household.

6

AFTER THE WAR

*Shrinking Census Households and
the Institutional U-Turn*

THE NOTION THAT THE CIVIL WAR PERIOD AND RECONSTRUCTION REP-
resented a radical departure from the past is now a commonplace in
American historiography,[1] but so is the notion of brakes being put on reform and even a reversal of trends thereafter. Dependents were not mir-
aculously transformed into equals of the household head. Indeed, the
story of the struggle for full citizenship continued well into the twentieth
century, as has been amply documented by historians of civil rights in
modern America. From the postbellum period into the depression era, a
continual redefinition of legal status sheltered former dependents from
the pain and the privilege of full equality. This shifting legal status expressed itself for married women in protective labor legislation, marriage
bars, and spousal rights to social security; for freedmen in paternalistic
economic procedures, strict vagrancy laws, and segregation; and for those
previously governed by master-servant law, in protection against collective bargaining.[2]

Nor has the work of most family historians strengthened the argument that significant change in the family structure occurred after the
Civil War. During this field's heyday in the 1970s, the degree to which
households in the United States or elsewhere could be described as extended and the point at which households converted into a more nuclear form only briefly dominated the discourse on family history. Going
back to the sixteenth century, scholars soon found that the majority
of families consisted of just pop, mom, and the kids, the so-called nuclear form. Slaves were not included in the framework. In fact, almost
none of the legal changes discussed in the last chapter was considered of
particular relevance to household structure save divorce. The tiny households of contemporary life, it has been argued, reflect longstanding

desires blossoming under propitious economic and technological circumstances. Deviations from the norm of pop-mom-kids—as occurred in the African American family or in the working-class family during industrialization—could be attributed to economic stress, but not to legal constraints.[3]

Without question, to consider the mid-century legislation and court rulings as having an important impact on household members requires that the problem of exit be taken seriously. When that is done, the U.S. population censuses show that important changes occurred in the size and composition of households in the later nineteenth century. Perhaps more unexpected is that the place where one can identify definite retrenchment in terms of household exit is with the one group whose dependent status had never been contested—children. The mid-nineteenth-century efforts to remove white children from households and place them into appropriate institutional residences—perhaps the single most radical change in American household government with the exception of slave emancipation—came under fire and then full attack during the Progressive era. This turnabout had major repercussions for the household and the welfare state in the United States.

That it is possible to make detailed analyses of United States households is due almost solely to the efforts of a group of University of Minnesota historians, most notably Steven Ruggles. It is he who has kept the issue of American household structure alive over the past two decades, arguing most vehemently that much of the work on household size and composition has, perhaps inadvertently, encouraged an ahistorical view of family life and kinship. Ruggles has assembled what is perhaps the most extensive series of quantitative data existing for the study of United States history: thirteen (to-date) public-use samples of the decennial federal census stretching from 1850 to 1990, samples that can be studied for a number of purposes, including household structure over time. He maintains that kinship underwent a greater transformation in the later twentieth century than commonly believed. The stem family—a type of extended family where a parent or parents cohabit with the family of one of their children—is a form that Ruggles believes prevailed until recent times whenever the demographic conditions dictated its need. In the past, mortality and fertility patterns, including marriage characteristics, greatly limited the number of generations that could live together. If significant numbers of parents died prior to their children marrying—either through short life expectancy or late age at marriage or both—then obviously three-generational extended households would be few. Similarly, if the average married woman bore seven children, and all of the children married and set up separate households, only one could have the parents in residence. To judge intent, the analysis must be restricted to elderly parents who survived and had adult children (the population at risk). When looked at in that way, not until after 1940 did a majority of the elderly live apart from a grown child or children. Whether due to material or emotional considerations or both, a majority of those over sixty-five lived in stem families until the era when Social Security benefits and pensions became common. Coresidency, to Ruggles, is the most reliable indicator of the kinship bond, and when the analysis is limited to the population at risk to be in the household, a definite change can be seen to have occurred during the course of the twentieth century in multigenerational living.[4]

Ruggles's argument that important variations have occurred in U.S. household composition over time and the magnificent data sets that his project at the University of Minnesota has made available encourage a rethinking of the history of household structure in the United States. What has become apparent from the evidence accumulated in this book is that such a history depends on the legal rights of household heads, the power of members to enter and exit, and the vigor of residential institutions outside of the household. The early expansion of the household in the colonial environment—an expansion spurred by not only a high fertility rate but also the popularity of unfree labor and the lack of institutional quarters—was remarkable.[5] Average household size—between four to five in British communities—registered above seven in eighteenth-century America.[6] Thereafter, it was on a slow downward trajectory (see appendix 2), but there is more to the story than that.

The previous chapter focused on the decline in the legal authority of the household head in the forty-year period between 1840 and 1880. The public use data sets put on-line by Ruggles provide an opportunity to see how these changes correlate with alterations in household composition. Sometimes lost in the process of tallying extended kin are the changes in the nuclear family prior to the 1880s and in the long-term behavior of those unrelated to the household head: unfree persons and also those outside of private households, people voluntarily or involuntarily residing in what the Census Bureau has come to call "institutions and other group quarters." Much research on household composition removes all these persons before proceeding with analysis, yet in some years the most significant changes involve them.[7]

So what new do the censuses tell us? Supporting the view of the importance of the 1840–80 period for household change is the transformation during those years in how the census enumerated the population. In 1840—as in all earlier decades going back to 1790—only the household head merited a listing by name, because what linked members was that they all were ones "who by nature or law are placed under the authority of a single person."[8] Others in the household simply were tallied in the columns showing number of persons in each household by age group, sex, color, and whether free or slave. In 1850, the census broke with tradition and instituted the most sweeping changes ever implemented in the structure of the population census. For the first time the Census Board instructed its enumerators to list the names and specified characteristics of every *free* person in each household. This individual enumeration did not meet with universal approval. The Census Board had originally proposed, in addition, a second schedule listing the name and characteristics of each enslaved person, but southern congressmen beat back that initiative.[9] Slaves were removed from the household count and placed in a separate schedule, but they were not named or described. These alterations reflect the changes in the legal relationship between the head and his dependents, and the furor over the separate schedule for slaves foreshadows the coming of the Civil War. With the abolition of slavery, the 1870 census included full information about all inhabitants except Indians living in their own national groups. Finally, in 1880 the remaining piece of data key to understanding familial organization appeared—relationship to the head of household.

Table 5 shows the distribution of persons over the various household categories. It follows the practice of colonial historians rather than that of nineteenth-century historians in its depiction of household composition. In 1850 and 1860, I include the slave population in the column "nonrelated," where by law they belonged. What this inclusion does is give a very different cast to the series. First, it focuses attention on the truly most remarkable thing about the history of United States households: the large number of unrelated dependents they contained prior to the Civil War. Household size in early America was comparatively large (see appendix 2). The households of the seventeenth-century Atlantic migration actually grew larger as they organized on the eastern seaboard of North America and as the jurisdiction of the household head increased. Unrelated persons, not just more offspring, account for this rise. I have explored this subject in the earlier chapters of this book. While changes in household size and composition are mostly gradual and lack drama, that cannot be said of the period from 1850 to 1880. In terms of household size, the single decade between 1850 and 1860 witnessed a reduction in size about comparable to what it had previously taken sixty years to accomplish. The drop between 1860 and 1870 — which reflects emancipation — brought the single greatest reduction in size, a whole person's worth, 6.05 to 5.01.

Household composition was of course affected. Slaves became freedmen and then heads, spouses, or children in their own households rather than remaining as servants to their former masters. African Americans went from comprising 2 percent of household heads in 1850 to 11 percent

TABLE 5

Distribution of United States Population by Status in Household, 1850–2000

Year	Number in Sample	Head (%)	Spouse of Head	Child of Head	Parent or Other Relative of Head	Nonrelated, Including Slave Inmate, Group Qtrs
1850	[197,736*]	15.4	12.8	44.0	6.7	21.4 (7.7)[†]
1860	[135,862*]	16.6	13.6	44.0	5.8	20.0 (7.3)[†]
1870	191,627	19.8	15.8	49.2	6.7	8.4
1880	502,840	20.3	16.2	49.6	5.7	8.4
1890	n.a	n.a.	n.a.	n.a.	n.a.	n.a.
1900	100,425	21.3	16.6	47.4	6.3	8.5
1910	366,239	22.0	17.4	45.1	6.3	9.1
1920	521,131	23.1	18.4	44.1	7.1	7.3
1930	n.a.	n.a.	n.a.	n.a.	n.a.	n.a.
1940	1,351,732	25.9	19.8	40.9	6.8	6.5
1950	n.a.	n.a.	n.a.	n.a.	n.a.	n.a.
1960	1,799,890	29.4	22.0	38.7	5.6	4.2
1970	2,029,633	31.3	21.5	38.6	4.3	4.3
1980	2,267,320	35.4	21.6	33.7	4.1	5.2
1990	2,500,052	36.8	21.3	31.6	4.5	5.8
2000	281,000,000	38.0	19.0	30.0	6.0	8.0

Sources: IPUMS <http://www.ipums.umn.edu> webpage codes; frequencies for variable RELATE; U.S. Bureau of the Census, *Historical Statistics of the United States* (Washington, D.C., 1975), 15–18; *Los Angeles Times*, 15 May 2001.
*Free population only. Census figures for slave population added to get percentages.
[†] Percentages in parentheses are the nonslave unrelated

in 1880. This change is one obvious reason why in the thirty years between 1850 and 1880 the proportion of the population falling into the "household head" category jumped at a faster rate than in any other comparable period until the span from 1960 to 1990, going from 15.4 to 20.3 percent of the population.

A second reason for the rise in the "household head" category shows up in the slight but growing gap, during these years, between the percentage claiming headship status and the proportion claiming to be a spouse. That happened because the proportion of women as household heads went up. Women started the period as 9 percent of household heads and ended in 1880 at 12 percent, a 33 percent increase. Admittedly, this large proportional rise benefited from a low base. It was an increase, however, that did not continue to grow. It fluctuated around 12 percent for sixty years before resuming its secular trend upward in 1940. The proportion classified as children grew because young African Americans now appeared as children of their parents, not in the "nonrelated" category. After 1880, however, the fertility decline began eating away at the proportion.

It is more difficult to measure the exit from household government of apprentices, servants, and other employees who traditionally fell under master-servant law, because no means exist—before the identification of relationship to household head in the 1880 census—to separate them from lodgers. Being a lodger did not involve the same kind of legal dependency. Both appear in the last column as "nonrelated persons," a category that also includes institutional inmates and those in more voluntary group quarters such as rooming houses, barracks, dormitories, and convents. From 1850 to 1880, the percentage of free persons unrelated to the household head rose slightly from 7.7 to 8.4 percent. In 1880, the first year where relationships to the household head are clearly designated, 39 percent were boarders or lodgers, and 34 percent were in the employ of the household head. By 1910, those percentages had changed to 63 and 22 percent, respectively, as boarders came to outnumber greatly those giving service in the household. One suspects that trend did not begin after 1880 but had started earlier, and that servants, apprentices, and other employees had been a majority of those unrelated to the household head in 1850.

The least drama over time occurs in the column entitled "parent or other relative" in table 5. Extended kin comprised from 4 to 7 percent of the population from 1850 to the present. Never more than 2 percent of the population and usually less were in a household as parts of a stem arrangement—parent(s) taking in a married child and spouse or the adult child taking in a parent or parents.[10] In the nineteenth century, some of this coresidency appears to be related to farming and agricultural production, but mostly it reflects problems experienced by one or another of the generations. Is the glass half full or half empty? While it may be that the majority of people over sixty-five with adult children resided with at least one child and his or her family, the number of people in that demographic category is quite small in the nineteenth and the first third of the twentieth century.

The numbers in the "nonrelated" column are more interesting, not only because of the tremendous change that occurred with emancipation, but also because—from the vantage point of 1850—one might have predicted a very different trajectory for them than the one evident in table 5. Commonly changes in household size and composition have been associated with a decline in the functions performed by the household and with the rise of outside institutions. This link is a staple of modernization theory—the shrinking household not only ceased to be a center of economic production, but it passed off many of its education, nursing, social welfare, and disciplinary duties to schools, healthcare professionals, social workers, and law enforcement officials. More than just diehard adherents of that theoretical disposition ascribe to this notion. In fact, it is hard to argue with the conclusion that few people are any longer home-schooled, nursed through life-threatening illnesses by housewives, or physically chastised by masters. What can be questioned, however, is the assumption that the decline in household services necessarily should produce a steady long-term decline in the size of residential units. One could actually make the reverse projection—based on what was initiated in the mid-nineteenth century—arguing that as households offered fewer services, more people would seek out communal living arrangements or become institutional residents.

So what happened to these household alternatives, to these forms that appeared to be growing in the nineteenth century during the household's civil war? Can that change be documented? And if so, what happened subsequently? The burst of enthusiasm for communal groups aroused an almost immediate backlash, due largely to the threat such groups posed to monogamy, and the federal government forced the most notorious and successful experimenters—the followers of the Church of Jesus Christ of Latter-day Saints—to conform to more traditional notions of household organization.[11] Institutional solutions to social problems, however, had a much more respectable and powerful group of advocates, and one might presume that increasing proportions of the population would end up in these establishments. The belief that institutions rather than households could better manage not only the criminal and the insane but also poor men, women, and children, as well as the elderly, sick and disabled who previously had been boarded or indentured in households, marked a radical departure from the past. The movement to replace household government with institutions began before the onslaught of legal changes in the status of dependents. It was one of the signals that trouble was afoot. The creation of new households and the reduction in the proportion of household members whom the head had legal responsibility to support would, all other things being equal, place added stress on the welfare system. The growth of this type of problem in northern cities earlier in the nineteenth century had prompted the call for institutionalization. The hue and cry for the poor to go to institutions rather than to receive out-relief in the antebellum period accompanied the declining propensity of white native-born youth to enter households as servants, the emancipation of free blacks in the northern states, and the continuation of little parental control over early marriage.[12] Out-relief, contemporaries claimed, only faciliated drunkenness in male household heads, promiscuity among female single parents, and hooliganism in youth.

With little abatement in the social problems dogging urban areas and with the collapse of the economy throughout the South, institutional solutions should have gained new advocates after the Civil War, and indeed—from the what we know about the legislation abolishing out-relief and the founding of benevolent establishments in the immediate postwar period—the enthusiasm for such solutions continued, as did the movement begun before the war to siphon off from the all-purpose public poorhouse subgroups of those who fell into the worthy or potentially salvageable category and to place them in separate institutions, usually sectarian or private.[13] Publicly funded mental institutions, hospitals, infirmaries, and sanitariums grew in number, but reformers devoted most of their energies to privately run orphanages, arguing that poorhouse children should be moved there whether they had a mother or father or not, so they might not acquire the indolent habits of their parents and others around them.[14] As William Pryor Letchworth, New York State Charities Board member—the man welfare historian Michael Katz has identified as "the most famous advocate of children's causes of the day"—reported in 1874:

In some poorhouses, I find that the children have one or both parents with them, and the kind heart of the keeper, or mayhap, of his amiable wife, who is a mother herself, protests against the separation of the child from the parent. But . . . the antecedents of the parent were such as to make it evident that the only hope of rescuing the child from a life of pauperism was to separate it from its parent or parents.[15]

The justification for removal, then, was not the squalor of the surroundings, but the fact that families living in poorhouses defeated the purpose of those institutions: punishment and rehabilitation of the adults and separation of the children from a corrupt environment. Nationally, in 1850 more children aged five to fourteen went to the poorhouse than to special asylums. In 1880, children's facilities attracted the majority, and by 1910, almost no children are listed as almshouse residents.[16]

The public-use samples of the census enable us for the first time to observe the trend in institutionalization, and the results are somewhat surprising to anyone familiar with the heated debates in the postbellum period. Table 6 shows very small proportions of people—whether children or adults—going into institutions or group quarters throughout the nineteenth and twentieth centuries.[17] The range is from a low of 1.8 percent in 1860 to a high of 3.6 percent in 1900. The figures for "persons in other group quarters" are very inconclusive, because they represent such a diversity of residential communities, and because the census counted them so differently in different years. The figures for "inmates in institutions," while hardly problem free, have more consistency over time.

The proportion counted as inmates—those in prisons, mental asylums, poorhouses, orphanages and industrial training schools, residential hospitals, and other specialized homes—inched up slowly. It increased 50 percent between 1850 and 1880, probably due to the increased specialization of institutions and more people being sent to prison. In 1850, half of the institutionalized lived in poorhouses. By 1880, only 23 percent did; the ill, the disabled, children, and indigent Civil War soldiers had been channeled elsewhere. These specialized institutions also picked up some additional inmates who in earlier times would have been maintained in households. The peak came in 1900 with a full 1 percent of the population institutionalized, as the same trends continued and as the populations of infirmaries and sanitariums soared. Then we find a retrenchment and no growth for most of the twentieth century. By 1940, two-thirds of the institutionalized were either in prison or in mental institutions. Poorhouses and orphanage numbers had declined dramatically. In the 1970s, the de-institutionalization movement hit mental hospitals and homes for those with physical impairments, though total numbers do not reflect it because of growth in residential treatment centers, convalescent homes to care for the increasing numbers of very elderly, and, finally, a rising prison population.[18]

Looked at closely, these figures document a steady increase in people living in nonhousehold units through 1900, then a decline, and, finally,

TABLE 6

Percentage of U.S. Population in Group Quarters,
1850–1990

Year	Inmates in Institutions (%)*	Persons in Other Group Quarters (%)†	Total (%)
1850	0.4	1.8	2.2
1860	0.5	1.3	1.8
1870	0.5	1.4	1.9
1880	0.6	1.6	2.2
1890	n.a.	n.a.	n.a.
1900	1.0	2.6	3.6
1910	0.9	1.8	2.7
1920	0.9	1.6	2.5
1930	n.a.	1.1	2.4
1940	0.9	2.1	3.0
1950	1.0	n.a.	n.a.
1960	1.0	1.7	2.7
1970	1.0	1.8	2.8
1980	1.1	1.4	2.5
1990	1.3	1.4	2.7

Sources: Figures up to 1950 from unweighted public use samples supplied by IPUMS, University of Minnesota Project. Figures for 1950 are from *Historical Statistics of the United States* (Washington, D.C., 1975), 43; figures for 1960–1990 are from U.S. Bureau of the Census, *Statistical Abstract of the United States: 1994.*

*Prisons, labor camps, reformatories, mental institutions, institutions for the mentally and physically disabled, poorhouses and poor farms, orphanages and training schools, Indian schools, old age and nursing homes, other homes for dependent populations, hospitals, sanitaria, infirmaries (differs slightly from those group quarters defined as institutions by the University of Minnesota Project).

†Rooming/boarding houses, military barracks, dormitories, worksites, religious houses.

a stabilization based largely on prison inmates. While at its height, only 3.6 percent resided in institutions or other group quarters at one point in time, the number of persons who had that experience during the twelve-month period might be double that due to constant turnover. The percentage would go even higher if one looked at the experience of the population over a group of years or looked at urban populations, a subject to which I will return. Anyway, regardless of how innocuous the census percentages seem, some Belle Epoque observers began to find them alarming. Why?

Welfare historians trace the first criticisms of the institutional solution to a group of children's charity volunteers in the Northeast, where the orphan asylums were proliferating.[19] Always mentioned in accounts of this group are liberal Protestant Charles Loring Brace of the New York Children's Aid Society and his 1872 book, *The Dangerous Classes of New York and Twenty Years' Work among Them.* While others worked to set up orphanages, child refuges, and training school alternatives to almshouse and prisons, Brace's organization undertook the mass exportation of Manhattan's street children into midwestern and southern rural areas to work in the households of farmers. Sending them away from their families and one another on the so-called "orphan trains" gave them a new start and rid the city of criminals. Brace criticized the cost of institutions, but even more he stressed their suppression of individuality and their spreading of bad habits. "In large buildings, where a multitude of children are gathered together, the bad corrupt the good, and the good are not educated in the virtues of real life. . . . the best of all Asylums for the outcaste child, is the *farmer's home.*"[20]

Also prominently featured as advocates for children's welfare in welfare histories is a group of elite Protestant women who dedicated themselves to being unpaid yet professional and scientific "visitors" and board members of watchdog organizations in New York and Massachusetts—people such as Josephine Shaw Lowell, Louisa Lee Schuyler, Grace Hoadley Dodge, Clara T. Leonard, and Elizabeth Cabot Putnam. They took it as their mission to point out abuses in the administration of public and publicly funded private institutions for children. It was not that these women wanted the government to return children to their mothers and fathers, for they disapproved most heartily of what was called "outdoor public relief." Rather, the problem of indigent families, in their view, should be solved by dispensing charity to the worthy poor, who recognized that the support came from the benevolence of those in better circumstances and was not their right as citizens; and, in the case of drunken or irresponsible parents, by taking their children from them and placing the children in respectable homes as servants. Family tutelage, not that of institutions, was what was needed.[21] As Leonard put it, "children cannot be raised in masses. The gradual acquirement of practical knowledge and manual dexterity so essential to future usefulness is hardly possible where the number of children in a house is largely disproportional to that of adults. . . . "the machine life [of the institution] . . . creates a spirit of dependence, and stultifies the affections and moral qualities." Working in households provided "a more natural form of life."[22]

This new enthusiasm for the placing out of children not only increased support for orphan trains and undercut funding for orphanages, but it led to the development of general adoption laws, a procedure that had no standing in the English common law. To counteract birth parents tracking down their children who, in the view of charity workers, had been placed in homes better equipped to raise youth, legislators passed adoption laws in over twenty states in the last half of the nineteenth century, the first being Massachusetts in 1851.[23]

Most historians draw a contrast between these civic leader types and the new coalition of child welfare agency professionals and settlement house workers who began appearing on the scene in the 1890s. The general impression one receives is that the institutionalization movement and its early critics were a kind of prehistory, a stage that had to be worked through before reformers saw the light and pushed for a "genuine" welfare state: mothers' pensions, unemployment insurance, child labor laws, and old age insurance. In the words of Michael Katz:

The 1890s mark the start of a new era in the history of social welfare . . . scientific charity and family break-up had failed miserably. . . . The first major alternative was child-saving. . . . the welfare of children unified social reformers around campaigns to which contemporaries were more likely to refer as "child-saving" than "progressivism." Almost overnight, it seemed, children became the symbol of a resurgent reform spirit, the magnet that pulled together a diverse collection of causes and their champions into a new loose, informal—but very effective—coalition.[24]

The best-known professional spokesmen shared their predecessors' dislike of institutional care of children, but they expressed themselves in more academic, neutral language and undertook scholarly studies of the institutional situation. Amos Warner, a Stanford professor of economics and social science and former charity director in Baltimore and Washington, published *American Charities* in 1894. He reminded readers that "the people of the United States have a larger share of administrative awkwardness than any other civilized population." Obviously sharing some of that discomfort, Warner argued that children just did not develop normally in institutions. "They do not feel at home outside of the sheltering walls, and shrink from the rough contact of ordinary life. . . . life is made too easy."[25] Much better, in his view, was to place out children in private homes. Michigan-born, Harvard-educated Homer Folks spent the decade running public charity agencies in Pennsylvania and New York. In his 1902 classic, *The Care of Destitute Neglected and Delinquent Children*, Folks tempered his criticism of orphanages but clearly preferred placing out. He complained about the size of orphanages and the rivalry between religious bodies for children, and he charged that "new institutions were incorporated for the purpose of receiving these public funds," referring to the subsidies that states such as New York provided to private institutions.

Parents by placing their children in institutions . . . were virtually receiving public aid . . . and many of the parents, particularly those of foreign birth, came to regard the institutions somewhat in the light of free boarding schools. . . . The institutions . . . naturally were inclined to retain the children until thoroughly instructed and trained in the faith.[26]

Like the Lowells and the Putnams, Folks and Warner had an aversion as well to using public funds for welfare or "outdoor relief."

From the histories it seems that the impetus for moving the 1890s child-savers off into a new direction did not emanate from these male professionals, but rather from the new breed of college-educated women that congregated in settlement houses and undertook paid social service. These women—Jane Addams, Lillian Wald, Julia Lathrop, and Florence Kelley are among the most famous—formed what has been called a "female dominion" that changed American child welfare policy.[27] Utilizing maternalist arguments, they advocated governmental action to improve the lot of poor children. They were among those called to the 1909 Conference for the Care of Dependent Children, an immensely influential meeting of over two hundred child welfare specialists convened by President Theodore Roosevelt. The report emanating from the conference is said to have set the agenda for child-saving in the following decade. The report stated first that children should not be removed from their own families except for urgent and compelling reasons, and that families should receive financial aid (preferably private charity, but the statement left the door open for public assistance) if the only reason for breaking up the home was poverty.[28]

This initiative struck a responsive chord in the press and with middle-class mainstream organizations such as the National Congress of Mothers and the Federation of Women's Clubs, who lobbied hard for what became known as mothers' pensions, which would provide public aid to widows and deserted wives with children. Suddenly a broad spectrum of female civic leaders questioned why government money should go to either child asylums or foster homes that boarded children when children's own mothers could keep them, if the mothers had the means. Apparently state representatives agreed; over 80 percent passed mothers' pension legislation by 1920. The welfare state was launched with lightning speed at the state level on the theory that it would preserve the household, even a female-headed one. New Deal Social Security policies built on this foundation of support to preserve households, although some scholars see a dilution of female influence and a two-track system privileging the male household head in the later Social Security versions of ADC (Aid to Dependent Children) and then AFDC legislation.[29]

This story, however, of the failure of the institutional alternative to household living and the politics behind the decision to support women's pensions at the conference is complicated and in some parts actually contradicted by an avalanche of books that have appeared in the last decade on the orphan experience.[30] First of all, both the reformers' attacks on orphanages—on their size, on their lack of individual concern, and on their producing in the children who lived there an inability to fit into the outside world—and the reformers' claims for the superiority of placing out run counter to the depiction of the institutional situation for children in the late nineteenth and early part of the twentieth century.

Most child asylums did not have hundreds of inmates, and private establishments far outnumbered public. Catholics and Jews ran the largest of the private institutions, and the size of those institutions resulted from the large numbers of parents of those faiths requesting places for children whom they could not support.[31] Most other institutions, including state homes, had some form of Protestant sectarian indoctrination, and the majority of families taking in children also were Protestant. The issue of faith aside, parents usually preferred orphanages to placing-out agencies, because from orphanages they could more easily reclaim their children. Commonly 75 to 80 percent of children in orphanages had at least one parent living. Children did not stay in the asylums for more than several years before a family member or friend reclaimed them: they were sent to a public school during the day or they were sent to a resident industrial school; or the institution, pressed for space, placed them with a family. Thus the likelihood of the children never knowing any experience other than the orphanage was probably not great.

While a parent's concern for a child's individual development undoubtedly exceeded that provided by a busy matron in an institution, the solicitude extended by householders who took children in for their labor or for the boarding payments they would provide cannot be easily determined. What value did these children derive from their work experience on midwestern and southern farms, given the limited opportunity and high out-migration of young people from rural areas in this period? The mass exportation of the orphan train children has raised uncomfortable questions. This placing-out process differed very little from the British and colonial practice of parish apprenticeship, or indenturing the children of the poor to farm families that needed labor. Even the long distances covered by the orphan trains have their parallel in the transatlantic indentured servant trade. For younger children, the parish sometimes paid the household head to take them in just as they would pay for a household to care for an ill or disabled person.[32] In fact, the descriptions of placing out by Brace, Putnam, and even Warner and Folks as innovative and a new departure in child welfare strike anyone familiar with the operation of colonial welfare as extremely odd.[33]

Most important, what comes out of the orphan histories and the statistics from the late nineteenth and early twentieth centuries is the strength, and the apparent success, of those institutions run for and largely by European immigrants and children of these immigrants, particularly Catholic ones. By 1890, the Catholic Church and its religious orders sheltered over half of all children in institutions. Over the course of the twentieth century this percentage dropped, but even in the 1930s, Catholics housed the most inmates. In the cases of Catholic religious orders and Jewish benevolent society leaders, a positive attitude toward resident institutions prevailed. The establishments existed due to a need in their religious communities, but beyond the concerns about their groups' children being turned against their own religious traditions by Protestant foster families, they also enunciated the social, psychological, and educational advantages that their institutions could offer.

And in the case of the Catholic nuns, brothers, and priests, this commitment to a communal lifestyle extended to themselves as well. Women were particularly important. Though seldom mentioned as part of the "female dominion" of reform because they pursued a different strategy and had a much lower public profile, the sisters probably exceeded their Protestant counterparts in numbers. Between 1850 and 1910—while the population increased fourfold—the number of females in convents grew tenfold. Fifty thousand women in religious orders served in Catholic institutions at the beginning of the twentieth century, the staff equivalent of two thousand Hull Houses. Catholic leaders reminded their critics that its workforce largely provided services for free, a system that would be hard for Protestants to match.[34]

Historians of the Progressive era have long made a point of the fact that reformers such as Brace, Lowell, Folks, and other opponents of government support to private institutions and private families were biased against Catholic immigrants and wanted to impose their own standards of behavior on them. What has been less clear is the degree to which the institutional U-turn correlated with the rise of Catholic domination of child welfare in major cities of the Northeast where the debates raged the most vociferously; whether the view of institutions was less disparaging in other parts of the nation; and the degree to which the emergence of so-called welfare state policies represented efforts of Republican Progressives to reach an accommodation with Catholic leaders and their Democratic Party allies.

Much of the anti-institution rhetoric came out of New York City, where the incidence of child inmates departed dramatically from that in the rest of the nation. The 1850 census showed six times as many New York City children in institutions as was the case in the general population of five to fourteen year olds (see table 7). By the time of the 1880 census, New York City housed 2.8 percent of its children in institutions, seven times more than among children of that age nationally. Of course, the total number of children who might have an institutional experience sometime during their youth was greater. If we assume a complete turnover every two years in the five to fourteen age category, then for New York City children in 1880, perhaps 14 percent of that age group at some point entered an institution. Nationally, though, no more than 2 percent would have. The drop for New York City in 1910 suggests that the investigations and withdrawal of public monies from private orphanages had taken their toll. By 1940, the New York City percentages fell below the national average.

Interestingly enough, it was the liberal Protestant, pillar-of-the-community type who in the first half of the nineteenth century worked as-

TABLE 7
Percentage of Children 5–14 in Institutions,
1850–1940

Year	U.S. (%)	New York City (%)
1850	0.3	1.9
1880	0.4	2.8
1910	0.7	1.7
1940	0.4	0.3

Source: Integrated public use samples, United States
decennial censuses, University of Minnesota IPUMS
Project. The 1850 figure refers only to the free population. For institutions included, see table 6.

siduously to build institutions to place the indigent and in the last half labored just as hard to dismantle them. Charles Loring Brace, the orphan train's best friend, did not, initially, attack orphanages. His 1853 circular announcing the formation of the New York Children's Aid Society indicated that the group would be helping by "opening Sunday Meetings and Industrial Schools, and, gradually as means shall be furnished, by forming Lodging-houses and Reading-rooms for children, and by employing paid agents whose sole business shall be to care for them."[35] But by 1872, after twenty years of battling Catholic institutions for the hearts and minds of the young and as the first Irish Catholic took over the leadership of the city's Democratic Party, Brace saw a conspiracy between the party's bosses and the priests to nurture for their own purposes what would become young "ruffians."

At present, they are like the athletes and gladiators, of the Roman Demagogues. They are the "roughs" who sustain the ward politicians, and frighten honest voters. They can "repeat" to an unlimited extent, and serve their employers. They live on "panem et circenses," or City-Hall places and pot-houses, where they have full credit.[36]

New York's system of poor relief allowed some state aid to private institutions, and Catholic orphanages were becoming a disproportionate beneficiary of this underwriting. To Brace, institutions were a natural for Catholics and epitomized all the stereotypic shortcomings of the faith. "Asylums are a bequest of monastic days," he wrote. "[They] breed a species of character which is monastic—indolent, unused to struggle; subordinate indeed, but with little independence and manly vigor."[37] Here Brace borrows from a tradition going back at least a century to the "enlightened narratives" of eighteenth-century secular Protestants and agnostics who regarded the Catholic Church as a threat to societal progress.[38] Three years after Brace's book came out, New York's legislature passed an act requiring all children to be taken out of almshouses and voted per capita subsidies for those placed in private orphanages, meaning an even greater expansion of the "monastic" influence. The flow of public money to private, largely Catholic, institutions further infuriated the charity establishment, people like Josephine Shaw Lowell, who fought to stop these subsidies as well as all public outdoor relief.[39]

Massachusetts, a state with a similarly large number of Roman Catholic immigrants but a weaker Democratic Party presence, dealt differently with what one of the women on the state board of charities referred to as "R.C. aggression," her term for the vigilance of Catholics concerning the fate of Catholic children placed in Protestant-run state institutions.[40] Catholic leaders demanded Catholic religious instruction instead of Protestant services for these inmates. Protestants and Catholics alike believed that children in state institutions needed religious instruction; at issue was which denomination would provide the instruction. Placing children, most of whom had one or more parents alive, in foster homes was the solution favored by the Protestant-dominated State Charities Board, and in 1882 the state legislature passed an act subsidizing the boarding out of children under the age of ten. Massachusetts became the first state to more or less do away with state-supported orphan asylums and to establish instead a state network for placing out. The private Catholic asylums consequently housed many fewer children due to the expense of support.

What happened with American Indian children, though, casts some doubts about the consistency of the anti-institutionalists' arguments. In the 1880s—just as Massachusetts was doing away with residential institutions for children—the commissioner of Indian affairs, Thomas Morgan, a former Baptist minister, hoped to assimilate the entire Native American population into the mainstream of American life by upgrading the schooling given Indian children. In effect, that meant placing the Indian children in boarding schools. Residency of Indian children in the schools run by the federal government or, less often, by missionaries soared. By 1900, over twenty-one thousand Indian children lived at one of these institutions, probably a third of all Indian children of school age. Instruction included Christianization in a nonsectarian Protestant framework, with a heavy emphasis on Bible reading, prayer, and song. In the case of Indian children, no one suggested that an upbringing in a household was best.[41] The growth of private preparatory schools in the Northeast in the late nineteenth century is another contradictory example.

Just how much this debate about institutions resonated in other parts of the nation is still to be determined.[42] Big cities felt the Catholic presence in the school system, and that presence may have spurred anxieties about welfare institutions too. Figure 17 from *Harper's Weekly*—where Thomas Nast's anti-Catholic cartoons had become a regular feature—shows some of the spillover in New York City.[43] Uncle Sam tells the Catholic priest who is railing against the public schools that he should investigate "these institutions," meaning the House of Refuge, prison, penitentiary, and almshouse shown in the background, which the priest will find "filled from the 'Greek' and Roman Schools."

A recent study estimates that in 1880 the fifteen largest cities had an average of 29 percent of the children of school age enrolled in parochial schools;[44] such a percentage obviously frightened Protestant majorities on the eastern seaboard. Elsewhere among the administrators of state institutions such as child asylums it is unclear how polarizing the issue had become. Over half of the states in a 1904 survey reported spending

17 Thomas Nast, *Foreign Church (Roman) Declaring War upon Our National Public School* (*Harper's Weekly*, 8 November 1873).

five thousand dollars or less of public money annually on support of orphanages. Only ten states had as many as two thousand children in homes of all sorts, these ten having 75 percent of the inmates.[45] Many midwestern states had set up state and county child asylums, and their administrators tended to argue for the need for some institutional presence and also pointed out the poor monitoring and abuses of the placing-out system. Throughout the period from 1880 to 1910, the vast majority of children—from 91 to 92 percent—lived with parents or a parent, and another 5 percent lived with relatives. Of the small numbers remaining, children were at least twice as likely to be living with an employer or boarding with a family as to be inmates in an institution.[46]

While the institutional population including children grew during the last half of the nineteenth century, where it grew fastest was in the minds of East Coast reformers of Protestant background. When President Theodore Roosevelt forwarded recommendations from the 1909 Conference on the Care of Dependent Children to Congress, the statistics he used from a special 1904 Census Bureau report reversed the proportion of private home placements to institutional inmates that appeared in the decennial census, making it seem as if most children went into institutions, whereas most went into private homes.[47] Many areas of the country had been slow to climb aboard the benevolent institution bandwagon. The Jim Crow South offers one such example. Immediately after the Civil War, almshouse residency soared in some communities. White local officials argued that impoverished freedmen were the federal government's problem. The Freedmen's Bureau—the agency in charge of supervising the transition from slave to free in the years immediately following emancipation—pushed marriage, hoping that by creating two-parent households, the orphan problem would be reduced. Planters hoped to solve the problem of supporting indigent African American children by indenturing them and wanted former masters to have first rights. In fact, older children had been taken from their parents—despite parents' ability to take care of them—to meet the shortage of cheap labor. The Reconstruction Congress tried to stop courts from allowing the apprenticeship of black children under circumstances that would not apply to white children. After the Reconstruction period, however, indenture probably was the primary means of "welfare" for African American youth lacking kin to take them in.[48] Given the disenfranchisement of African Americans, it has been argued that black women continued to devote their efforts to building private institutions—schools, old age homes, and hospitals—

after white women had begun focusing their energies on changing governmental policy.[49] In 1890, nonwhites (largely African Americans) comprised 12 percent of the total inmate population, a percentage very near their proportion of United States residents. If one looks more closely, however, it appears that that percentage is as high as it is because nonwhites represented 30 percent of the prison population. When it came to those in benevolent institutions, only 4 percent were nonwhite. Orphanages might take in black children, but in towns where African Americans represented a significant proportion of the population, institutions were segregated, offering African Americans many fewer places than their numbers and poverty might have justified. The attack on institutions seen among some white child-reform advocates does not seem a feature of the African American response to social welfare.

When Northeast corridor white Protestants, Irish Catholics, Jews, a few African Americans, midwestern state asylum administrators, and settlement house women descended on Washington, D.C., in 1909 for the Conference on the Care of Dependent Children, James West, the principal organizer—a child-rescue volunteer and a former orphan inmate himself—intended that the conference would serve as a platform for a national policy recommending foster home placement and charity handouts over institutional life and outdoor poor relief. The conference report did favor the home over the institution, but the surprise was the privileging of the child's own family over all the other options, even if it meant the provision of private or public assistance. This position represented a great compromise for the two major sides, who apparently came to terms for fear of falling into something worse. From the perspective of Catholics, that worse would be Protestant foster homes; from the perspective of the WASP establishment, it would be the Catholic orphanage. While men of Protestant background affiliated with private children's aid societies comprised the majority of the two hundred or so participants, all the caregiver communities were represented with one glaring omission. Fifteen percent of the participants were women and 15 percent were Catholics, but it appears that only one Catholic woman received an invitation, and she was not in a religious order.[50] Catholic nuns cared for more dependent children than did any other group in the United States, but they did not participate. Given their orphanage and educational work, one wonders if they would have been as ready to compromise by identifying institutions as the least attractive option in the conference report as apparently had been their primary spokesmen, Catholic laymen. For a long time, the Catholic Church had defended institutions for Catholic children whose parents could not care for them. Obviously, those who had dedicated their lives to Catholic religious orders found positive value in large numbers of people living communally in a regimented environment for a common purpose. Almost no other group in American society would be inclined to make such an argument, and the Catholics, in doing so, encountered hostility and a campaign to diminish their influence, despite the popularity of the institutions among their own constituency. Institutions, from this period on, never really regained momentum. The one growing segment after 1920, mental institutions and treatment centers, were the longest lived, and even they got hit by the de-institutionalization movement in the 1970s. By that time, even voluntary institutions like boarding schools had come to be seen as somewhat unnatural.

The household civil war of the 1840–80 period permanently altered the composition of American households, increasing the number of heads and reducing size and the number of legal dependents. The substitution of institutions or "other group quarters" for household government, however, did not materialize in any significant way. The "other group quarters" inhabitants—those living in rooming houses, barracks, dormitories, religious houses, and so on—are such a diverse and inconsistently documented group about whose historical fate it is difficult to generalize at this point other than to observe that it was not a highly expansive one over time. More can be said about trends in formal institutional living. The institutional alternative, if not strangled in the cradle, barely escaped obsolescence, as its dangers and disadvantages came to be seen as greater than its benefits. In large northern cities, Protestant Republicans—the same group that earlier had been so enthusiastic about institution building as a way to reform errant household heads—reversed their political position as the Democrat-supported Catholic Church proved so successful in the activity. In the Protestant South, the issue postemancipation was race rather than religion, but the race issue dampened enthusiasm and sapped fiscal support for institutional solutions.

Religious diversity in America once again affected social policy. In countries with an established church, the nineteenth century witnessed a battle to secularize already existing institutions. In the new United States, there had been no established church and little in the way of existing social welfare institutions. Instead, most states had relied on a household system of care. Attacking that system and trying to build institutions in the nineteenth century proved costly and controversial. With a Protestant majority made up of a bewildering number of weak denominations and with growing Catholic and Jewish minorities in the North, Midwest, and West, secular would really have to be secular. No consensus could be reached on the appropriate religious moral guidance, yet nearly everyone considered such guidance an essential part of a successful institutional experience. The secularization of day schools enjoyed the most success, although public school support has had a troubled history up to the present day in any area where there is substantial ethnic, racial, and religious diversity. Residential institutions took the biggest hit as the nation returned to the household for solutions: boarding out would be refashioned as foster care and adoption; and, more significant, money payments to female household heads would begin, a policy initiative launched at the 1909 Conference on the Care of Dependent Children, a pivotal event in United States welfare history.

The opponents of institutional residency had to rehabilitate the household as a welfare site and ultimately had to sanction a modest redistribution of wealth in the form of government payments to keep the poor in their own households. The wholesale placement of Indian children in government- and religiously funded boarding schools, however, undermines the arguments of the anti-institutional WASP reformers that any home was preferable to an institution.

Racial diversity, no longer hidden within the perimeters of the household, also weakened support for public institutions in the South and in nonsouthern communities with growing populations of African Americans. The Freedmen's Bureau briefly offered welfare assistance, but they placed their emphasis on strengthening the black family. Later, segregation meant no unified residential institutional system and a very weak financial base to draw on for the population most in need of assistance.

Support for institutional living took a U-turn in all parts of the United States as the costs and the compromises necessary to fund alternative sites became clear. The much-vaunted strength and resiliency of the American family exists because of welfare policy, not in spite of it.

7

THE TROUBLESOME ALTERNATIVES

ONE OF THE MORE BEWILDERING DISCOVERIES MADE BY THOSE WESTern Europeans who ventured around the world bearing glad tidings from their king, god, and chartered trading company was how many cultures allocated power and authority within the family very differently from the way they themselves did. Those who first set foot in the Americas— mostly soldiers, missionaries, or sea captains—seldom headed conventional households: the mere choice of these professions marked them off as placing other priorities above hearth and home. Yet even their journals indicate a less than playful attitude toward innovative roles for husbands, fathers, wives, mothers, and children.

Chapter 2 contains a discussion of some of their comments, which I attribute largely to the gut reactions of those accustomed to patrilineal households coming into contact with more matrilineal systems. For most of these men, the relations among Indian family members were not of pressing concern. They simply expressed their disapproval and moved on without investigating the issue further. The responses of those in Catholic religious orders proved the exception. In their journals, the reader comes across the kinds of information about kinship that later became the obsession of anthropologists. For example, Gabriel Sagard, missionary to the Huron, noted that "the children do not succeed to their father's property; but the fathers constitute the children of their own sisters their successors and heirs." [1]

The grand culmination of these anthropological efforts came in 1724 with the publication of Jesuit Joseph-François Lafitau's *Moeurs des sauvages amériquains, comparées aux moeurs des premiers temps,* an impressive work of two volumes that compared the customs of the Indians with those of the earliest societies described in classical Greek and Roman sources. [2]

Lafitau, son of an affluent Bordeaux wine merchant and banker, joined the Jesuits at age fifteen and, after a full course of study in rhetoric, philosophy and theology, petitioned to be sent to an Iroquois mission in New France. He stayed nearly six years. During that time, Lafitau had ample opportunity to observe Iroquois groups in the area firsthand as well as to quiz other Jesuits in the missions about their experiences. In his book— which he wrote upon returning to France—Lafitau devoted considerable attention to the household government of the Indians. He labeled Iroquois society a "gynocracy." "Nothing is more real," he alleged, "than the women's superiority. It is they who really maintain the tribe, the nobility of blood, the genealogical tree, the order of generations and conservation of the families." When a couple married, they did not set up a family and residence apart. Each one remained at home, and any children born of the union were counted as being of the wife's lodge and family. At a later point, Lafitau grew even more detailed about the lineage arrangements of the Indians.

Among the Iroquois and Huron, all the children of a household regard as their mother all their mother's sisters, and as their uncles, all their mother's brothers, for the same reason they give the name of father to all their father's brothers, and of aunts to all their father's sisters. All the children on the side of the mother and her sisters, and the father and his brothers, look upon each other likewise as brothers and sisters; but as for the children of their uncles and aunts, that is, of their mother's brothers and their father's sisters, they put them only on the footing of cousins.[3]

The practices outlined in these passages eventually fueled the major debate on the evolution of the household recounted in chapter 1, but Lafitau had concerns other than the invention of kinship theories. To the Jesuit, the importance of what would later be called the matrilineal and matrilocal customs of Indians such as the Iroquois derived from the support their practice gave to the theory that Indians had descended from ancient societies in Europe such as the Lycians, who had also reckoned descent through the mother. If the Indians could be linked with postdiluvian groups mentioned in early classical texts, the Native Americans could be placed historically, and the threat of Indians as a separate creation challenging the omnipotence of the Christian god disappeared.

To Lafitau's way of thinking, the obviously non-Christian institution of a gynocracy reflected the degeneracy that occurred whenever groups wandered to the far reaches of the earth and acquired bad habits. Lafitau speculated that this is what had happened with the ancient Greek peoples who had traveled through Asia and adopted heathen practices prior to settling in the Americas. Through most of the book, Lafitau—whose discussion moved back and forth between Indian behavior and that of ancient peoples in Europe and Asia Minor—tried to play down the divergences between the practices of these groups and Christians in order to make his point that all had come from one god's creation. Thus he minimized the likelihood of incestuous sister-brother relations among these apostate groups, citing the kinship system that caused cousins to be referred to as sisters and brothers. Nowhere, though, did Lafitau offer an analysis of why the Indian groups may have adopted their gynocracy. The point of his lengthy descriptions was only to make the connection with the European groups that had already been fitted into the creation and propagation of humans by the biblical god.

Half a century later, the Scottish Enlightenment writer John Millar made use of Lafitau and a wide variety of other authors to demonstrate the direct relationship between women's status and progress in society.[4] The one point that gave him pause, though, was the independence women in some rude societies exhibited toward the father of their children and the authority they exerted over those offspring, who reckoned their genealogy through the maternal line. Millar, in a short chapter, puzzled over these reports of the "mother as the principal person in the family."[5] It was not, however, until the renewal of these evolutionary theories in the mid-nineteenth century and the disintegration of the household government system that Lewis Morgan "invented" kinship.[6] As the discipline of anthropology developed—with functionalists and structuralists replacing cultural evolutionists—theories about the meaning of kinship systems changed. Yet long after most anthropologists rejected the notion that matriliny was an evolutionary stage located lower on the rung of human progress than patrilineal forms, and after a female anthropologist, Margaret Mead, impishly introduced the case of Samoa where none of the rules seemed to apply, the message that matriliny was trouble continued to run through the mainstream literature.

In the late 1950s, the Social Science Research Council sponsored a summer seminar on matrilineal kinship, and in 1961, the participating structural anthropologists produced a heavy tome on the subject. Using a sample of the world's cultures, the editors found that matrilineal forms appeared about a third as often as patrilineal ones.[7] The lead editor, David M. Schneider, underscored how attitudes had changed over the one hundred or so years that separated the work of Morgan and his contemporaries from current research. Schneider rejected the notions of stages and of any association between matriliny and greater female authority. Rather, what interested these anthropologists was the extent to which uncles and brothers of the female competed with her husband for power in the woman's descent group and the degree to which this competition produced instability. Schneider created a group of theoretical statements that could be derived from what had been discovered about matrilineal groups. As one reader penciled in on the last page of the copy I checked out from the library: "Bottom line is—less conflict in patri than matri." In other words, Schneider, like his predecessors, leaves the distinct impression that matrilineal forms are trouble.

Another body of research—studies of the African American family— delivered that message in an even more pointed manner. While academic attention to the subject dates back to W. E. B. Du Bois's 1909 *The Negro American Family*—one of a series of studies that Atlanta University produced on different aspects of black life—E. Franklin Frazier's 1939 book on the same subject focused attention on the matriarchal tendencies of the black household. The dates of the follow-up research, however, make it appear that social scientists did not really pick up on Frazier's analysis of the black family until after 1960, when the civil rights movement, poverty programs, and the women's movement made the topic an important academic and policy issue.[8] Why the black family's reliance on extended household forms? Did it originate in Africa? In slavery? In the migration to northern urban centers, where black men, particularly, faced a discriminatory job market? Whatever the answer, the question—as formulated by most scholars and policymakers in the following decades—implied a problem: a scarcity of male household heads made it difficult for African American children to be properly supported financially and emotionally.[9]

By the 1980s, the concern about female heads broadened from highlighting the behavior of African American women to including young unmarried mothers of all races. Rising welfare costs obviously motivated this concern, since single mothers much more often required public assistance than did two-parent households. Critics could point to the fact that in 1960 only 8 percent of American families with children were headed by a single parent, but twenty years later this number had grown to 22 percent, with all racial groups contributing to the rise, not just African Americans. Under President Ronald Reagan, conservative think tanks had replaced liberal ones. The conservatives blamed AFDC (Aid

to Families with Dependent Children) for encouraging irresponsible behavior on the part of both fathers and mothers, a charge reminiscent of
the nineteenth-century analysis of the deleterious effects of "out-relief."
This time, however, the only kind of institutions proposed were jails for
those who failed to pay child support. "Out-relief"—or more accurately,
benefits paid by AFDC—should be only temporary. In 1996, responding
to new statistics that showed that one in three families with children had
a single-parent head, Congress passed the Welfare Reform Act, drasti-
cally altering the welfare system. Under this legislation, aid to a parent or
parents of dependent children could last no longer than two years, after
which time the parent had to find the means to support her or his family.

With 32 percent of households having children under eighteen being
headed by single parents, many have concluded that some profound
change in social relations has taken place in the United States. Furthermore, statistics on female-headed households in many other countries
suggest that what is happening in America is happening elsewhere with
results made even more disastrous by the precarious economies in many
parts of the globe.[10]

So in the new millennium is the United States—accompanied by
much of the rest of the world—moving toward female-headed households as the modal type, with men detached and unattached to their families? Is this the ultimate legacy of the household's civil war in mid-nineteenth-century America?

Let's take the global situation first. The data are so dreadful that rather
than allowing one to generalize from them, they require one to make a
statement about diversity. The majority of nations in the world either do
not take anything that might be remotely described as a reliable census,
or, if they do, they fail to arrange their data in a way that allows the sex of
those in single-head households to be determined. In other instances, the
number of single-head households has questionable validity because so
many in the population have dual residences.[11] Consequently, statistics
indicating that one-third of households worldwide are headed by women
cannot be taken seriously. Even efforts to give regional percentages based
on countries in the area that have reported figures seem problematic, as
so many populous nations fail to report numbers, and those that do often
report them irregularly.[12] It turns out that if one looks at only those nations in the last decade citing 30 to 45 percent (the highest proportion reported) of households with a female head, different underlying demographics have produced similar statistics.

If the nations with 30 percent or higher female headship were shown on a world map, the areas of the world that would be highlighted—North America above Mexico, the Caribbean, Scandinavia, a few eastern European states, and southern Africa—would include some of the wealthiest nations in the world and some of the poorest (see appendix 3 for a list, by nation, of percentages of female-headed households, ca. 1990). Those suspicious of easy generalizations point first to the fact that the designation *female head* includes not only single mothers with children but also older women who have outlived their husbands and have the means to live on their own rather than as dependents in their adult children's households. Certainly an important part of the numbers in North America and Scandinavia is comprised of such people. Second, of the other nations reporting, many have much lower rates: almost all of Asia, the most populous continent; North Africa; and most of South America. Governments strongly influenced by Islamic law tend to have a low proportion of female-headed households, as do East Asian societies with a tradition of strong patrilineages. It is unclear how new the high rates in southern Africa are and in what direction they are going, given the recent political upheaval in the region and the devastation from the AIDS epidemic. None of this discussion is meant to suggest that calculation of headship or other measures meant to provide information about living standards are a waste of time; nor does it suggest that the current system of child support is equitable and beneficial.[13] It is simply intended to point out that it is currently impossible to document a rising tide of female headship around the globe. Whatever is happening in the United States has to be explained without direct reference to a worldwide phenomenon, although obvious comparisons can be made with particular countries.

Fortunately the data for the United States provide more directional guidance. Table 8 shows headship rates for black and white women in the United States for about 150 years. Changes reflect not only the declining popularity of marriage but also other phenomena, especially the increased tendency of older women to outlive their husbands and reside by themselves. A few generalizations are obvious—headship has increased over time and for both African Americans and whites. African American women have always had much higher headship rates than white women with or without the AFDC. Steven Ruggles's in-depth analysis of decennial census samples shows that going back as far as 1850 free black families had a much higher proportion of children living with one parent—usually the mother—or in a relative or employer's household, than did

TABLE 8
Female Headship in the United States, 1850–1999

Year	All Female Householders (%)	White Female Householders (%)	Black Female Householders (%)
1850	9	9	25*
1860	9	9	26*
1870	12	11	18
1880	12	11	18
1890	14	n.a.	n.a.
1900	13	12	19
1910	12	11	18
1920	12	11	18
1930	13	12	19
1940	15	14	22
1950	15	14	24
1960	17	17	29
1970	21	20	35
1980	26	24	44
1990	28	26	47
1999	30	27	49

Sources: 1850–1880, 1900–1920, 1940, 1950, University of Minnesota IPUMS Project, 1960–1999; U.S. Bureau of the Census, *Statistical Abstract of the United States: 1982–83* (Washington, D.C., 1982), table 65; ibid., *1999*, table 74; ibid., *2000*, table 62.

*Free blacks only

white children.[14] Donna L. Franklin has correlated these patterns with specific economic and social policies and programs from those of the Freedmen's Bureau to the late-twentieth-century welfare reforms to account for the trends.[15] Table 8 also shows that the last half of the twentieth century brought the greatest increase, and that the rate of increase began declining in the last two decades. It was during the 1960s and the 1970s that things really changed.

Limiting the households to those with children under the age of eighteen to eliminate any increases due to widows on Social Security and more unmarried women—allows one to make the point even more strongly (see table 9). Between 1960 and 1999, mothers of both races increased their headship of families with children about threefold—from 6

TABLE 9
Percentage of U.S. Families with Children
under Eighteen
Headed by One Parent, 1960–1999

Year	Total (%)	White (%)	Black (%)
1960	8	7	23
Father	1	1	2
Mother	7	6	21
1970	13	9	33
Father	1	1	2
Mother	12	8	31
1980	22	17	52
Father	2	2	3
Mother	19	15	49
1990	28	23	61
Father	4	4	4
Mother	24	19	56
1995	31	25	64
Father	5	4	6
Mother	26	21	58
1999	32	27	63
Father	5	5	6
Mother	26	21	57

Sources: U.S. Bureau of the Census, *Statistical Abstract of the United States: 1982–83,* tables 73, 60, 65; ibid., *2000,* table 64.

to 21 percent for whites and from 21 to 57 percent for blacks, but the transformation appears to have occurred in the later sixties through the early eighties. The trend toward single-mother headship tapered off in the 1990s, before the new welfare act could have shown any impact. Another trend to note is the slow but steady increase in the percentage of single-father heads. Same-sex couples with children do not yet appear on the census radar screen.

Based on numbers like those in table 9, it is difficult to determine whether the United States is charted for single mothering or single parenting, or whether a new plateau has been reached for this type of family. Without tipping my hand on what I suspect the answer might be, I will simply point out that there are probably more proponents of Satan worship in the United States than there are advocates of matrifocal family structures. The fear of a society of single-mother households goes beyond the anger over welfare costs and extends into anxieties about young men being left to their own devices and causing mayhem.

An argument could certainly be made that American national politics from Lyndon Johnson forward has been dominated by a struggle over policies to improve the government of children—*the last legal dependents*—in households that are headed by single parents or ones perceived to be dysfunctional. All the so-called "social issues"—abortion and contraception, welfare reform, gun control, the war on drugs, capital punishment, compulsory imprisonment—that are landmines for any aspiring presidential candidate relate primarily to fears about the misbehavior of youth and unhappiness with parents who have failed to control them. Americans know that female minors are the most likely age group to be single mothers and that male minors are more likely than any other males to be arrested for a serious crime.[16]

Whether these statistics are the cause or the result, the individual rights of minors in the late twentieth century have steadily eroded since the youth revolution of the 1960s and 1970s. Indeed, the trend in recent decades has been to increase the authority of the parents, and when parents seem to act inappropriately, of the schools and other governmental agencies. In a trend that began with states reinstituting twenty-one as the legal age for drinking, other minors' rights—such as the rights to drive, to use contraceptives, and to have abortions—have all been restricted in new ways. Municipalities have toughened curfew and freedom-to-congregate laws. Schools have curtailed students' rights of free speech and freedom from against search and seizure, and judges have increasingly taken advantage of adult sentencing options for youth. Movie theaters, under heavy political pressure, have been forced to adopt a rating scale that prohibits the entry of minors unaccompanied by their parents to a wide spectrum of major studio films. Devices now enable parents to police the television shows their children watch and the Internet sites they access. Some of these restrictions have increased the authority of household heads over their young dependents, while others take away authority that has been judged poorly exercised and give it to others. As households have shrunk in size, more and more attention has focused on adults' management of children.

The legacy of the household's civil war is in the eye of the beholder. There has been one persistent trend, however. In no decade, even at the height of the baby boom in the 1950s, has household size risen.[17] The big question is, When might that trend reverse itself, either by returning to bigger family households or adopting more group quarter living or by making another institutional U-turn? Humans may be social animals, but Americans, increasingly, have preferred living by themselves. Or is preferred the wrong word?

Historians and social scientists have offered up a curious mixture of assumed human emotional needs and inexorable economic and social processes to explain change in the American household. The cliché of the family ceasing to be a productive unit and narrowing its function to the provision of psychological support and affection is often given as the reason for the size and composition of residential units. Land availability and republican or democratic revolutions frequently provide the basis for explaining national peculiarities such as high fertility, the emphasis on companionship in marriage, and rising rates of divorce.[18] Here I have argued that examining the changing laws and policies governing households and other residential institutions is a much-needed antidote to the overgeneralized mega-explanations for household change. I have particularly stressed the importance of looking at the power of the household head to control the exit of dependents over the past four centuries.

What, then, is new about the story of the American household that I have told here? First, the concept found in most general histories of the family that a rigid Old World hierarchical household landed on American soil and over the course of the colonial period grew looser and freer seems to overlook the fact that household size increased over this time period and not simply because of higher fertility rates. Bound servants, both indentured and enslaved, have to be counted as part of the household because of their relationship with the head, their master and the person who controlled their entry and exit. The laws concerning these dependents, moreover, were more restrictive and confining than their English and western European counterparts. Household size also increased because the British colonies were particularly devoid of nonhousehold sites for residence. In many respects, the American household head's power increased in comparison to his opposite number across the Atlantic.

In contrast to most recent accounts of American family history, my version downgrades the importance of the American Revolution in effecting change in household relationships by upgrading other departures from the norm found in the pre- and post-Revolutionary periods. Drawing on an earlier research project involving American inheritance, I find that the testamentary freedom available through English law to propertied colonial heads of household influenced behavior more than in Britain, because few or no accompanying devices such as the strict family settlement existed to blunt its impact.[19] Stated simply, American fathers did not have to endow their children at marriage. The removal of this obligation enhanced the power of the household head in the New World, but it also left him with fewer weapons to stave off premature household formation by his sons and daughters. This situation—when combined with the absence of one established church to license, record, and police births, marriages, and deaths and with the exemption from any marriage rules of the 10 to 15 percent of the population who were slaves—goes a long ways toward explaining the existence of what some describe as the freer, more egalitarian, and more companionate family and marriage system, as well as its high marital instability. That low density and republican ideological traditions reinforced these tendencies is no doubt true. The point is that when looking for influences on family behavior, it is good to begin with the laws, policies, and practices most closely impinging on the family and to work outward from there.

The legislation and court activity of the period from 1840 to 1880 I consider to mark an important watershed in household relations. Because of the current sentimentality about the image of the family during these years—an image that was cultivated in much popular writing and art of the time—to find such a comprehensive repudiation of the authority of the household head seems surprising. A closer look at family portraiture and the literary products of that group of mid-nineteenth-century women writers most identified with Victorian sentimentality, however, confirms what others have argued, namely, that their defense of the family quietly undercut patriarchal authority. This context of turmoil over the powers of the household also illuminates the preoccupations of the American leaders of the utopian communities of the 1840s—men such as Joseph Smith, John Humphrey Noyes, and Albert Brisbane—and their varied male constituencies, all of whom seemed interested in alternatives to the monogamous marriage system in the United States and the agenda of the good, useful women.

In the histories of the American family, it seems to have proven very hard to get the needle to jump the conceptual groove. Quite understandably, considering its statistical preponderance historically, the heterosexual two-parent household is at the center of all narratives. The problem with this focus lies in ignoring the reasons that it has persisted for so long.

Organized opposition to institutions and group quarters and what is perceived as the regimented lifestyle they encourage has surfaced at various points in American history. In only one period did substantial numbers of public policymakers promote institutions other than prisons. The so-called "rise of the asylum" in the antebellum period resulted in the construction of a number of public and private institutions to care for the poor, the young, the old, the ill, and the disabled. The phenomenal success of Catholic religious orders in their institutional work with children, however, created a backlash. This institutional U-turn at the end of the century stopped the growth of children's homes and led to the resumption of the practice of boarding children in need at private homes. Successive waves of de-institutionalization gradually diminished the clientele for all the other institutions aside from correctional facilities. The exceedingly negative view of institutions had its origins in the exposés about late-nineteenth-century orphan asylums. Recent research has presented a much more mixed picture of the orphan trains and foster homes that supposedly represented a superior solution. Suspicion about the motives involved in the de-institutionalization movement seems warranted by the growth of boarding schools for American Indians at the very time that institutional care was being condemned as by nature inferior to the warmth of a private home, even, apparently, the home of a stranger. Why were the Indian boarding schools that removed children from their parents deemed beneficial, while the Catholic children's homes for Irish American youth were labeled a bad mistake?

Putting aside obvious inconsistencies, the institutional U-turn circa 1900 had a significant impact on the twentieth-century welfare state. Specifically, this legal shift protected the right of parent(s) to exert authority over a child within a household. Having the government pay, however poorly, to have children in households rather than in institutions also ensured that the commentary associated with female-headed households would become the longest-running public policy soap opera in American history, a soap opera that is now being expanded in interesting ways with same-sex parents and the single male parent. No analysis of the rights of parents versus the state or of the school versus children is offered here, only this question: Will the household's last legal dependent ever rise up?

APPENDIX

TABLE A
Female Age at First Marriage: Early Modern Europe and British America, 1550–1820

Place	Cohort*	Mean Age

Mid-Sixteenth Century to circa 1750

ENGLAND AND W. EUROPE[†]

England (43)	pre-1750	25.0
Belgium (10)	pre-1750	25.0
France (24)	pre-1750	24.6
Germany (5)	pre-1750	26.4
Scandinavia (6)	pre-1750	26.7

BRITISH AMERICA

New England

Ipswich, Mass.	1652–1700	21.1
	1701–1725	23.6
	1726–1750	23.3
Rowley	ca. 1660–1700	24.1
	ca. 1700–1750	23.2
Topsfield	1701–1725	23.3
	1726–1750	25.3
Wenham	1701–1725	22.2
	1726–1750	23.6
Boxford	1701–1725	22.8
	1726–1750	23.7
Andover	ca. 1660–1700	22.3
	ca. 1700–1750	24.5
Brookline	1710–1730	23.0
	1731–1750	23.0
Hingham	1681–1700	22.0
	1701–1720	24.3
	1721–1740	23.3
Dedham	1640–1690	22.5
Nantucket	1680–1739	20.0
Plymouth	b. 1600–1625	20.6
	b. 1625–1650	20.2
	b. 1650–1675	21.3
	b. 1675–1700	22.3
Deerfield	1721–1740	19.9

Place	Cohort*	Mean Age
Northampton	pre-1700	20.6
	1700–1749	23.9
Sturbridge	1730–1759	19.5
Hampton, N.H.	1655–99	21.5
	1700–1719	23.3
Bristol, R.I.	before 1750	20.5
Windsor, Conn.	ca. 1660–95	19.8–21.8
	ca. 1690–1705	23.0
Mid-Atlantic		
Quakers	pre-1730	22.0
	1731–1755	22.8
N.J. and N.Y. Dutch	1685–1759	21.2
South		
Maryland	1650–1700	16.8
	1700–1750	18.6
Charles Co., Md., natives	b. 1640–1693	17.8
Somerset Co., Md., natives	b. 1648–1669	16.5
	b. 1670–1711	17.0
Tidewater, Md., natives	b. 1680–1699	18.2
	b. 1700–1719	18.5
Middlesex Co., Va.	b. through 1679	18.8
	b. 1680–1699	20.0
	b. 1700–1719	20.6
	b. 1720–1729	20.9
Perquimans, N.C.	b. through 1680	18.7
	b 1680–1699	20.7
	b. 1700–1719	22.3
	b. 1720–1740	20.3

1750 to Early Nineteenth Century

ENGLAND AND W. EUROPE†

England (17)	1740–1790	25.3
Belgium (11)	1740–1790	24.8
France (51)	1740–1790	26.0
Germany (4)	1740–1790	26.9
Scandinavia (3)	1740–1790	25.5

Place	Cohort*	Mean Age
England (17)	1780–1820	24.2
North Belgium (3)	1780–1820	27.9
France (33)	1780–1820	26.7
Germany (17)	1780–1820	27.5
Scandinavia (3)	1780–1820	29.8

BRITISH AMERICA/UNITED STATES

New England

Topsfield, Mass.	1751–1775	24.3
Wenham	1751–1775	23.7
Boxford	1751–1775	22.8
Concord	1750–1770	21.1
	1771–1790	23.9
Hingham	1741–1760	22.5
	1761–1780	23.2
	1781–1800	24.5
Nantucket	1740–1779	20.9
	1780–1839	22.6
Sturbridge	1760–1779	21.6
	1780–1799	23.6
Northampton	1750–1799	25.5
Deerfield	1741–1760	21.1
	1761–1780	23.1
	1781–1800	23.9
Greenfield	1741–1779	18.5
Shelburne	1741–1779	23.7
Bristol, R.I.	1750–	21.1

Mid-Atlantic

Quakers	1756–1785	23.4
Germantown, Penn.	1750–1759	25.0

South

Tidewater, Md.	b. 1740–1790	21–22.5
Northern Neck, Va.	b. 1740–1765	20–21.8

Place	Cohort*	Mean Age
Middlesex, Va.	b. 1730–1739	21.3
3 backcountry districts, S.C.	ca. 1760–1800	19.1–19.8
All United States (estimate)	ca. 1800	19.4–21.0

Sources: Michael W. Flinn, *The European Demographic System, 1500–1820,* 124–27; Robert V. Wells, "The Population of England's Colonies in America: Old English or New American?" *Population Studies* 46 (1992): 88–89; Darrett B. Rutman and Anita H. Rutman, *A Place in Time: Explicatus* (New York, 1984), 65; Allan Kulikoff, *Tobacco and Slaves: The Development of Southern Cultures in the Chesapeake, 1680–1800 (Chapel Hill, 1986), 56;* David Hackett Fischer, *Albion's Seed: Four British Folkways in America* (New York, 1989), 76, 285, 487, 675; James M. Gallman, "Determinants of Age at Marriage in Colonial Perquimans County, North Carolina," *William and Mary Quarterly,* 3d ser., 39 (1982): 179–81; Michael R. Haines, "Long-Term Marriage Patterns in the United States from Colonial Times to the Present," *History of the Family* 1 (1996): 34.

*Indicates marriage cohort unless *b.* is used to indicate birth cohort

†Weighted mean for group of parishes

TABLE B
Private Household Size in the United States, 1790–1990

Year	Households	Mean Household Size	Mean Household Size, Free Population	1 Person (%)	2 Persons (%)
1990	93,347,000	—	2.63	24.6	32.3
1980	80,776,000	—	2.75	22.7	31.4
1970	62,874,000	—	3.14	17.0	28.8
1960	52,610,000	—	3.33	13.1	27.8
1950	43,468,000*	—	3.37	10.9	28.8
1940	34,949,000	—	3.67	7.1	24.8
1930	29,905,000	—	4.11	7.9	23.4
1920	241,654	—	4.34	4.8	17.9
1910	80,333	—	4.43	5.1	17.1
1900	15,963,965	—	4.60	5.1	15.0
1890	12,690,000†	—	4.93	3.6	13.2
1880	101,225	—	4.86	4.2	13.0
1870	37,822	—	5.01	3.1	11.5
1860	25,838	6.05	5.22	2.7	10.5
1850	35,360	6.46	5.47	2.1	10.0
1790	557,889	7.04	5.74	3.7	7.8

Sources: 1790 and 1900, U.S. Bureau of the Census, *Century of Population Growth, 1790– 1900* (Washington, D.C., 1909), 996–98; 1890 and 1930–1970, U.S. Bureau of the Census, *Historical Statistics of the United States to 1970* (Washington, D.C., 1974), 42; 1980 and 1990, from U.S. Bureau of the Census website http://www.census.gov/population/socdemo/ hh-fam/htablHH-4.txt/. Other years from University of Minnesota IPUMS datasets.

*Covers related persons only; not strictly comparable with other years
†Includes group quarter households

3 Persons (%)	4 Persons (%)	5 Persons (%)	6 Persons (%)	7 or More Persons (%)	Female Heads (%)
17.3	15.4	6.7	2.3	1.4	28.4
17.5	15.7	7.5	3.1	2.2	26
17.3	15.8	10.4	5.6	5.1	21.1
18.9	17.6	11.5	5.7	5.4	17.3
22.6	17.8	10.0	5.1	4.9	15.1
22.4	18.1	11.5	6.8	9.3	15.1
20.8	17.5	12.0	7.6	10.9	12.7
19.5	17.9	13.9	9.9	16.1	11.8
19.0	17.2	13.8	10.1	17.7	11.9
17.6	16.9	14.2	10.9	20.4	12.5
16.7	16.8	15.1	11.6	23.0	14.4
16.2	16.5	14.8	12.0	23.4	12.0
15.8	16.7	15.3	12.7	24.9	11.9
14.4	16.3	15.5	12.8	28.0	9.4
14.0	14.9	14.4	13.0	31.6	9.3
11.7	13.8	13.9	13.2	35.8	6.9

TABLE C
Percentage of Households Headed by Females, by Nation, circa 1990

	Household size	Female-headed (%)
Africa		
Benin	5.8	19
Botswana	4.8	47
Burkina Faso	6.2	9
Cameroon	5.2	18
Central African Republic	4.7	21
Comoros	6.2	25
Cote d'Ivoire	6.0	14
Djibouti	6.6	22
Egypt	4.9	13
Eritrea	n.a.	31
Ethiopia	n.a.	23
Gambia	8.8	11
Ghana	4.8	26
Guinea	7.2	16
Guinea-Bissau	6.5	38
Kenya	5.2	24
Madagascar	4.5	20
Malawi	4.3	26
Mali	9.0	7
Mauritania	5.0	24
Morocco	6.0	15
Mozambique	n.a.	27
Namibia	5.2	39
Niger	7.1	8
Rwanda	4.7	25
São Tomé and Principe	4.3	33
Senegal	10.0	20
South Africa	5.8	28
Swaziland	6.3	40
Uganda	4.6	25
Tanzania	6.1	11
Zambia	5.6	24
Zimbabwe	5.2	33
Central and South America and Caribbean		
Argentina	3.7	22
Belize	4.2	22

	Household size	Female-headed (%)
Bolivia	4.6	24
Brazil	4.2	18
Chile	4.0	25
Columbia	4.5	24
Costa Rica	4.3	20
Dominican Republic	4.5	25
Guatemala	n.a.	20
Haiti	5.0	39
Jamaica	n.a.	38
Netherlands Antilles	3.3	34
Paraguay	4.7	21
Peru	5.2	23
Asia		
Bangladesh	5.5	9
Hong Kong	3.4	27
Macao	3.6	21
India	5.5	9
Indonesia	4.5	13
Iran	5.1	6
Kyrgyzstan	4.7	26
Malaysia	4.8	18
Nepal	5.6	13
Republic of Korea	3.7	17
Turkey	5.0	10
Uzbekistan	5.2	22
Vietnam	4.8	32
Yemen	5.8	12
Oceania		
Papua New Guinea	n.a.	8
New Zealand	2.8	37
Europe		
Czech Republic	2.5	26
Denmark	2.3	42
Finland	2.5	42
France	2.6	24
Greece	3.0	20
Hungary	2.7	35
Ireland	3.3	26

	Household size	Female-headed (%)
Luxembourg	2.7	26
Norway	2.4	34
Poland	3.1	31
Portugal	3.1	20
Romania	3.1	22
Slovakia	2.9	23
Slovenia	3.1	44
Sweden	2.2	37
Yugoslavia	3.6	22
North America		
Bermuda	2.8	34
Canada	2.8	30
United States	2.6	36

Sources: United Nations, *The World's Women 2000: Trends and Statistics;* International Bank for Research and Development, 2000 (available from Lexis-Nexis); U.S. Bureau of the Census, International Database Table 88.

Note: Only countries that had data on female-headed households from the 1990s are listed. Some of the household size averages date from the late 1980s.

NOTES

Preface

1. Readers before the twentieth century would not understand the distinction I am making here, because by the term *family*—which was used much more commonly than *household*—they meant what I refer to with the term *household:* those dependent upon or subject to the authority of the same head.

1. The Household Gets a War and a History

1. Quoted in George Feaver, *From Status to Contract: A Biography of Sir Henry Sumner Maine* (London, 1969), 44.
2. John Fiske, *Darwinism and Other Essays* (Boston, 1885), 215–16; and even later, in *Essays Historical and Literary* ([Boston, 1902], 30), Fiske refers to the "beautiful writings of Sir Henry Maine."
3. Sir Henry Sumner Maine, *Ancient Law: Its Connection with the Early History of Society and Its Relation to Modern Ideas* (London, 1930; orig. pub. 1861). Maine had begun working on the project in 1854 (Feaver, *From Status to Contract,* 41). R. C. J. Cocks, *Sir Henry Maine: A Study in Victorian Jurisprudence* ([Cambridge, 1988], 1) has this quotation from A. W. B. Simpson, "Contract: The Twitching Corpse," *Oxford Journal of Legal Studies* 1 (1981): 268.
4. Maine, *Ancient Law,* ix, 180.
5. Ibid., 140.
6. Ibid., 180.
7. Adam Kuper makes a similar point in "The Rise and Fall of Maine's Patriarchal Society," in *The Victorian Achievement of Sir Henry Maine: A Centennial Reappraisal,* ed. Alan Diamond (Cambridge, 1991), 101.
8. For a discussion of this usage, see William James Booth, *Households: On the Moral Architecture of the Economy* (Ithaca, N.Y., 1993), pt. 1.
9. Mathew Hale, *The Analysis of the Law* (London, 1716), 41–50; William Blackstone, *Commentaries on the Laws of England,* 3d rev. ed., ed. Thomas M. Cooley (Chicago, 1884), bk. 1, 422. Hale died in 1676, and his work was published posthumously. Blackstone's *Commentaries* appeared in 1765.

10. Zephaniah Swift, *A System of the Laws of the State of Connecticut* (1795; reprint, New York, 1972), 1: 183–224; Tapping Reeve, *The law of baron and femme; of parent and child; of guardian and ward; of master and servant; and of the powers of courts of chancery* (New Haven, 1816); James Kent, *Commentaries on American Law*, 13th ed. (Boston, 1884), 2: 129–266. On *domus*, see David Herlihy, *Medieval Households* (Cambridge, Mass., 1985), 3.

11. This usage of the term *family* goes back at least to Greco-Roman antiquity; see Herlihy, *Medieval Households*, 2–4. See also discussions by David Hackett Fischer, *Albion's Seed: Four British Folkways in America* (New York, 1989), 274–80; Robert J. Steinfeld, *The Invention of Free Labor: The Employment Relation in English and American Law and Culture, 1350–1870* (Chapel Hill, 1991); Daniel Scott Smith, "The Meanings of Family and Household: Change and Continuity in the Mirror of the American Census," *Population and Development Review* 18 (1992): 431; Christopher L. Tomlins, "Law and Authority as Subjects in Labor History," working paper no. 9,312, American Bar Foundation (1993); and Mary Beth Norton, *Founding Mothers and Fathers: Gendered Power and the Forming of American Society* (New York, 1996), sec. 1.

12. For discussions of these debates, see George Elliott Howard, *A History of Matrimonial Institutions*, vol. 1 (Chicago, 1904), chaps. 1–4; Rosalind Coward, *Patriarchal Precedents: Sexuality and Social Relations* (London, 1983), chaps. 1, 2, 4; and Thomas R. Trautmann, *Lewis Henry Morgan and the Invention of Kinship* (Berkeley, 1987), chap. 8.

13. Fustel de Coulanges published *The Ancient City* in France in 1864.

14. Johann Jakob Bachofen, *Myth, Religion, and Mother Right: Selected Writings*, trans. Ralph Manheim (Princeton, 1967), 69–119.

15. Trautmann, *Morgan and the Invention of Kinship*.

16. Lewis H. Morgan, *League of the Ho-dé-no-sau-nee or Iroquois* (New York, 1901; orig. pub. 1851), ix.

17. Morgan worked and reworked his theories from the late 1850s and throughout the 1860s until they finally appeared as *Systems of Consanguinity and Affinity* in 1871. See Trautmann's *Morgan and the Invention of Kinship*, which its author describes as a "biography" of Morgan's great study (1–3).

18. Lewis H. Morgan, *Ancient Society* (New York, 1878), vii.

19. John Ferguson McLennan, *Primitive Marriage: An Inquiry into the Origin of the Form of Capture in Marriage Ceremonies*, ed. Peter Riviere (Chicago, 1970; orig. pub. 1865).

20. The most comprehensive account of this literature is in Howard's *A History of Matrimonial Institutions*, vol. 1, pt. 1.

21. See the references in note 12 and also Ann Taylor Allen, "Feminism, Social Science, and the Meanings of Modernity: The Debate on the Origin of the Family in Europe and the United States, 1860–1914," *American Historical Review* 104 (1999): 1085–113.

22. See Edward Shils, "Henry Sumner Maine in the Tradition of the Analysis of Society," in *The Victorian Achievement of Sir Henry Maine*, ed. Diamond, 151.

23. Richard Hofstadter, *Social Darwinism in American Thought*, rev. ed. (Boston, 1955; orig. pub. 1944), 13–15.

24. Trautmann, *Morgan and Invention of Kinship;* Ross, *The Origins of Social Science,* 53–58.

25. Coward, *Patriarchal Precedents,* 26.

26. Father Joseph-François Lafitau, *Customs of the American Indians Compared with the Customs of Primitive Times,* 2 vols., ed. and trans. William N. Fenton and Elizabeth L. Moore (Toronto, 1974; orig. pub. 1724 [French]).

27. J. G. A. Pocock, *Barbarism and Religion,* vol. 2 of *Narratives of Civil Government* (Cambridge, 1999), chaps. 20, 21, 25.

28. Adam Smith, *Lectures on Jurisprudence,* ed. R. L. Meek, D. D. Raphael, and P. G. Stein (Oxford, 1978), 141–99, 438–58.

29. Ibid., 181.

30. John Millar, *Observations Concerning the Distinction of Ranks in Society,* 2d ed., greatly enlarged (London, 1773; orig. pub. 1771), 144. The widely cited posthumous fourth edition came out in 1806 in Edinburgh under the title *The Origin of the Distinction of Ranks.*

31. Millar, *Observations* (1773), 143.

32. Compare chap. 1, sec. 6, in the 1773 and 1806 editions.

33. Millar, *Origin* (1806), 294–96.

34. See Richard Olson, *The Emergence of the Social Sciences 1642–1792* (New York, 1993), 178–89; and Ronald L. Meek, *Social Science and the Ignoble Savage* (Cambridge, 1976), 1–3, and chap. 5.

35. Feaver, *From Status to Contract,* 43.

36. Maine, *Ancient Law,* 181; Feaver, *From Status to Contract,* 54.

37. Peter W. Bardaglio, *Reconstructing the Household: Families, Sex, and the Law in the Nineteenth-Century South* (Chapel Hill, 1995); Laura F. Edwards, *Gendered Strife and Confusion: The Political Culture of Reconstruction* (Urbana, Ill., 1997).

38. See David R. Roediger's summary of this development (*The Wages of Whiteness: Race and the Making of the American Working Class* [London, 1991], chap. 3), which has been examined closely by a number of prominent nineteenth-century historians.

39. Amy Stanley, *From Bondage to Contract: Wage Labor, Marriage, and the Market in the Age of Slave Emancipation* (Cambridge, 1998), esp. chap. 1.

40. A print illustrating the southern happy slave versus the oppressed factory worker— titled *Slavery As It Exists in America, Slavery As It Exists in England* (1850)—may be found in John Ebert and Katherine Ebert, *Old American Prints for Collectors* (New York, 1974), 77.

41. As quoted in Bardaglio, *Reconstructing the Household* (27, 138). In his book, Bardaglio argues that the southern states' commitment to slavery made them slower to accept changes to the patriarchal aspects of family law.

42. Joan Hoff, *Law, Gender, and Injustice: A Legal History of U.S. Women* (New York, 1991), 135–40.

43. Forest Chester Ensign, *Compulsory School Attendance and Child Labor* (Iowa City, 1921), 48.

44. See Pavla Miller, *Transformations of Patriarchy in the West, 1500–1900* (Bloomington, Ind., 1998).

45. Friedrich Engels, *The Origin of the Family, Private Property, and the State* (London, 1985; orig. pub. 1884), 110–11.
46. Allen, "Feminism, Social Science, and Meanings of Modernity," 1085–113.
47. Herbert Spencer, preface to *Social Statics or the Conditions Essential to Human Happiness* (New York, 1865; orig. pub. 1850), xiv. The section on women's rights is found on pages 173–217.
48. Herbert Spencer, *The Principles of Sociology* (London, 1876), 1: 737–38, 790–91, 794–95.
49. Henry Adams, "Primitive Rights of Women," in *Historical Essays* (New York, 1891), 40–41. This essay was a revision of an 1876 lecture.
50. Carl Nicolai Starcke, *The Primitive Family in Its Origin and Development*, ed. Rodney Needham (Chicago, 1976; orig. pub. 1888 [German] and 1889 [English]), 269, 271–72.
51. Howard, *History of Matrimonial Institutions.*
52. Philip J. Ethington, "Constructing the Crisis," chap. 1 in *The Metropolitan Crisis of Modernity in the United States, 1890s-1920s* (Chapel Hill, forthcoming). Ethington includes some interesting biographical information about Howard.
53. Robyn Muncy, *Creating a Female Dominion in American Reform 1890–1935* (New York, 1991).
54. This maternalist strategy has been much studied among women's historians. See, for example, Theda Skocpol, *Protecting Soldiers and Mothers: The Political Origins of Social Policy in the United States* (Cambridge, Mass., 1992); Sonya Michel and Seth Koven, eds., *Mothers of a New World: Maternalist Politics and the Origins of Welfare States* (New York, 1993); and Linda Gordon, "Putting Children First: Women, Maternalism, and Welfare in the Early Twentieth Century," in *U.S. History as Women's History: New Feminist Essays*, ed. Linda K. Kerber, Alice Kessler-Harris, and Kathryn Kish Sklar (Chapel Hill, 1995), 63–88. This environment was not one in which American women like Elizabeth Cady Stanton, who attacked the misogyny of the Christian clergy in *A Woman's Bible* (1895), flourished. See Lois W. Banner, *Elizabeth Cady Stanton: A Radical for Woman's Rights* (Boston, 1980), chap. 8.
55. New York, 1915.
56. The policy concerns in both Howard and Goodsell are expressed in the hundreds of pages of their work. Awareness of Edward Westermark and the problems with that framework also surface; see Howard, History of *Matrimonial Institutions*, 1: 9.
57. Arthur W. Calhoun, *A Social History of the American Family: From Colonial Times to Present*, 3 vols. (Cleveland, 1917–19), 1: 10. On the origins of the volumes, see Michael Gordon's introduction to the volume he edited, *The American Family in Social-Historical Perspective*, 2d ed. (New York, 1978), 2.
58. Calhoun, *Social History of the American Family*, 3: 332.
59. Marianne Weber, "Die historische Entwicklung des Eherechts" (The historical development of marriage rights) (1904), in *Frauenfragen und Frauengedanken* (Tübingen, 1919), 10, 18–19. In criticizing the "verlorenes Paradies" (paradise lost) of the "Mutterrechtsepoche" (mother-right era), Weber was following the anthropological mainstream opinion of the time. See Coward, *Patriarchal Precedents*, 52–54.

60. M. Gordon, introduction to *The American Family in Social-Historical Perspective*, 1–2. Daniel Scott Smith, in "The Curious History of Theorizing about the History of the Western Nuclear Family" (*Social Science History* 17 [1993]: 325–53), reports how relatively unimportant the supposed modernization view of the family evolving from extended to nuclear actually was in the literature of the period prior to 1960. Both of the two histories of the American family that appeared date to the second decade of the twentieth century, and both stress the role of economic factors such as the frontier, urbanization, and industrialism in familial change. See Willystyne Goodsell, *A History of the Family as a Social and Educational Institution* (New York, 1915); and Calhoun, *Social History of the American Family*. Calhoun's book is a fascinating summary of the research and concerns about American family life at the beginning of the twentieth century.

61. Richard Hofstadter, *Social Darwinism in American Thought*, rev. ed. (Boston, 1955; orig. pub. 1944); Thomas L. Haskell, *The Emergence of Professional Social Science* (Urbana, Ill., 1977); Dorothy Ross, *The Origins of Social Science in the United States* (Cambridge, 1991).

62. Steven Mintz and Susan Kellogg, *Domestic Revolutions: A Social History of American Family Life* (New York, 1988), xv; Calhoun, *Social History of the American Family*, 173, 178.

63. While this characterization of late-twentieth-century family history may be unduly crude, I believe a perusal of the *Journal of Social History*, the *Journal of Interdisciplinary History*, and the *Journal of Family History*—the main outlets for historical work on the household—will bear me out.

64. In United States history, Michael Grossberg's pioneering study, *Governing the Hearth: Law and the Family in Nineteenth-Century America* (Chapel Hill, 1985), was one of the first efforts to put the pieces together. Daniel Scott Smith—who has doubts about the enterprise of linking the household with the political order—has written several important articles on the nature of headship and the household, such as: "The Meanings of Family and Household: Change and Continuity in the Mirror of the American Census," *Population and Development Review* 18 (1992): 421–56; and "The Curious History." The works cited above by Peter Bardaglio, Amy Stanley, and Laura Edwards bring together the constituent parts, as does Christopher L. Tomlins, "Law and Authority as Subjects in Labor History," working paper no. 9312, American Bar Foundation (1993). Pavla Miller, in *Transformations of Patriarchy in the West, 1500–1900*, includes the United States in her analysis of state and household relations. On this subject, see also the forum on "Anglo-American Household Government in Comparative Perspective," with contributions by Daniel Scott Smith, Richard White, Patricia Seed, and Carole Shammas, in the *William and Mary Quarterly*, 3d ser., 52 (1995): 104–66.

65. Among the most influential of those raising these arguments are Bernard Bailyn, *Education in the Forming of American Society* (Chapel Hill, 1960); Richard Morris, *Studies in the History of American Law: With Special Reference to the Seventeenth and Eighteenth Centuries* (New York, 1930); Gordon Wood, *The Radicalism of the American Revolution* (New York, 1992); Sean Wilentz, "Society, Politics, and the Market

Revolution," in *The New American History,* rev. ed, ed. Eric Foner (Philadelphia, 1997; orig. pub. 1990), 61–84.

2. The Expansion of Household Government in the Colonial Period

1. The powers of the household head and the legal disabilities of dependents originated in customary laws and practices and show up primarily in case law rather than statute.

2. See Herlihy, *Medieval Households;* and Jack Goody, *The Development of the Family and Marriage in Europe* (Cambridge, 1983).

3. See, for example, the powers described in Gerda Lerner, *The Creation of Patriarchy* (New York, 1986), chaps. 4–5; and in Jane Gardner, *Women in Roman Law and Society* (Bloomington, Ind., 1986), chap. 2.

4. See Miller, *Transformations of Patriarchy in the West,* chap. 1, for a summary of this development and citations to the relevant research.

5. See Linda Pollock, *Forgotten Children: Parent-Child Relations from 1500 to 1900* (New York, 1983); and John R. Gillis, *For Better, For Worse: British Marriages, 1600 to the Present* (New York, 1985), 4–5.

6. Lawrence Stone, *The Family, Sex, and Marriage in England, 1500–1800* (New York, 1977).

7. Alan Macfarlane, in *The Origins of English Individualism* (New York, 1979), deals with the issue of the individualism of the English household head, but he does not connect it to the state of the lineage system.

8. Carole Shammas, Marylynn Salmon, and Michel Dahlin, *Inheritance in America: Colonial Times to the Present* (New Brunswick, N.J., 1987), 23–30.

9. Susan Staves, *Married Women's Separate Property in England, 1660–1833* (Cambridge, Mass., 1990).

10. Lewis Namier's work established the importance of kin and locality in eighteenth-century politics. Richard Grassby's *Kinship and Capitalism: Marriage, Family, and Business in the English-Speaking World, 1580–1740* (Cambridge, 2001) argues for the importance of marriage and kin in the capitalization and running of early modern London businesses, a point that I am not disputing here.

11. There are a number of studies of European conversation pieces. For the earlier pieces, see Ralph Edwards, *Early Conversation Pictures: From the Middle Ages to about 1730* (London, 1954). Arthur Devis is showcased in Ellen D'Oench, *The Conversation Piece: Arthur Devis and His Contemporaries* (New Haven, 1980). Marcia Pointon, *Hanging the Head: Portraiture and Social Formation in Eighteenth-Century England* (New Haven, 1993), 159–76. The fullest cataloging is in Mario Praz, *Conversation Pieces: A Survey of the Informal Group Portrait in Europe and America* (University Park, Pa., 1971).

12. Richard H. Saunders and Ellen G. Miles, *American Colonial Portraits, 1700–1776* ([Washington, D.C., 1987], 47), drawing on the research of Charles Coleman Sellars.

13. The colonial artist's heavy reliance on British mezzotint prints for poses, arrangements, and clothing is well known. See Waldron Phoenix Belknap Jr., *American Colonial Paintings: Materials for a History* (Cambridge, Mass., 1959).

14. Margaretta M. Lovell, "Reading American Family Portraits: Social Images and Self-Images," *Winterthur Portfolio* 22 (1987): 245–47.

15. Before 1760, the only well-known family group painting commissioned by a colonist is the 1741 picture of the family of another Massachusetts resident, Isaac Royall, his wife, daughter, her sister, and his sister, all under the age of twenty-five. There is also John Watson's circa 1725 portrait of Captain Johannes Schuyler and his wife, which looks like two individual portraits put together. *The Bermuda Group* portrait of George Berkeley's family and associates was painted by a colonial painter, but it would be hard to count Berkeley as a colonial resident. Artists' paintings of their families are also idiosyncratic. In 1747, John Greenwood painted himself and family members in what is much closer to a conversation piece than is either the Winslow or Royall family portrait. As illustrated by Benjamin West's and Charles Willson Peale's portraits of their own families, artists experimented with themes and compositions not found in the portraits of their elite clients.

16. See Carole Shammas, "A New Look at Long-Term Trends in Wealth Inequality in the United States," *American Historical Review* 98 (1993): 412–31; and Daniel Scott Smith, "Female Household in Late-Eighteenth-Century America and the Problem of Poverty," *Journal of Social History* 28 (1994): 83–107.

17. I am thinking here particularly of the work of Laurel Thatcher Ulrich on women and of David Galenson and Farley Grubb on indentured servants, the implications of which conflict with a view that the enhanced legal disabilities of dependents in America are of much importance.

18. Research on the family in the 1960s and 1970s led to a dismissal of the thumbnail sketch of the early American family appearing in Bailyn, *Education in the Forming of American Society* (15–16), but mostly the objection was to the idea that the frontier transformed an extended family into a nuclear one. For the standard textbook account of how the family became more egalitarian in America, see Mintz and Kellogg, *Domestic Revolutions*, 17–23. Even those arguing for Anglicization in the eighteenth century consider the family as having stayed "Americanized" as long as new lands were available; see John M. Murrin et al., *Liberty, Equality, Power: A History of the American People* (Fort Worth, Tex., 1996), 121–24.

19. Allan Kulikoff, in *From British Peasants to Colonial American Farmers* (Chapel Hill, 2000), has produced an impressive synthesis of the research on rural communities and colonial agriculture in the thirteen colonies, pointing out the importance of British markets and the serious impact of the American Revolution on farmer prosperity. The description in the text is consistent with his portraits of farming economies.

20. U.S. Bureau of the Census, *Statistical Abstract of the United States: 2000* (Washington, D.C., 2001), table 870.

21. For example, the "masters" of the families where Virginia freemen resided had the power to detain their share of crops or profit to make sure that taxes were paid (Fischer, *Albion's Seed,* 280).

22. Daniel Scott Smith, "The Demography of Widowhood in Preindustrial New Hampshire," in *Aging in the Past: Demography, Society, and Old Age,* ed. David I. Kertzer and Peter Laslett (Berkeley, Calif., 1995), 253; and Daniel Scott Smith,

"Female Householding in Late-Eighteenth-Century America and the Problem of Poverty," in *Aging in the Past: Demography, Society, and Old Age,* ed. David I. Kertzer and Peter Laslett (Berkeley, 1995), 90.

23. Amy Louise Erickson, in "Common Law versus Common Practice: The Use of Marriage Settlements in Early Modern England" (*Economic History Review,* 2d ser., 43, no. 1 [1990]: 28–29), estimates that approximately 2 percent of chancery cases from 1558 to 1714 fell in the category of what she refers to as marriage settlements. These were not necessarily separate estates, but they did at least secure a certain amount for the wife's jointure upon widowhood and thus protected her against testator fickleness.

24. Staves, *Married Women's Separate Property,* chaps. 5–6; Erickson, "Marriage Settlements," 21–39. The development of equity proceedings to protect the feme covert is traced in Maria L. Cioni, *Women and Law in Elizabethan England with Particular Reference to the Court of Chancery* (New York, 1985).

25. Erickson, in "Marriage Settlements" (31–35), argues that 10 percent of the probate documents she examined include some type of marriage settlement, by which she means either a provision requiring husbands to give certain amounts to their wives or stepchildren at death or provisions for women to have separate estates. Only four cases, or one-ninth of the sample, fell into the "separate estate" category, one-ninth of 10 percent therefore being the 1 to 2 percent that I cite. My own experience with wills in which women with separate property are testators would also back up this 1 to 2 percent figure, as that is their usual incidence in will samples. Over half of the cases Erickson cites are bonds that were taken out after a widowed executrix married a second husband to ensure that he pay the portions due to the children that she had by her first husband. They do not in anyway safeguard a woman's estate; rather, they safeguard the patrilineage of her first husband. That is why the figure I give for marriage settlements differs from hers.

26. Carole Shammas, "Re-assessing the Married Women's Property Acts," *Journal of Women's History* 6 (1994): 9–30.

27. This number is the estimate in 1774; see Jones, *American Colonial Wealth* (New York, 1977), 3: 1787.

28. Richard Starke, *The Office and Authority of a Justice of the Peace* (Williamsburg, Va., 1774), 318–20.

29. Deborah Gray White, "Female Slaves: Sex Roles and Status in the Antebellum Plantation South," in *Unequal Sisters: A Multi-Cultural Reader in U.S. Women's History,* ed. Ellen Carol DuBois and Vicki L. Ruiz (New York, 1990), 22–33.

30. Joan Lane, *Apprenticeship in England, 1600–1914* (Boulder, Colo., 1996), 3. By law, apprenticeship could extend to age twenty-four for males and twenty-one for females, until 1768 when the ages were lowered to twenty-one and eighteen, respectively. Indentures seldom show the term lasting to age twenty-four, however.

31. Lane, *Apprenticeship in England,* 18–19; W. Newman Brown, "The Receipt of Poor Relief and Family Situation, Aldenham, Hertfordshire, 1630–1690," in *Land, Kinship, and Life Cycle,* ed. Richard M. Smith (Cambridge, 1984), 416–19; Ruth Wallis Herndon, "Governing the Affairs of the Town: Continuity and Change in Rhode

Island, 1750–1800," (Ph.D. diss., American University, 1992), 400; Lawrence W. Towner, "The Indenture of Boston's Poor Apprentices 1734–1805," *Publications of the Colonial Society of Massachusetts* 43 *Transactions 1956–1963* (Boston, 1966), 425; Holly Brewer, *Constructing Consent: The Legal Status of Children and Anglo-American Revolutionary Ideology* (Chapel Hill, forthcoming), 229–58.

32. Harford County, Maryland, Census 1776; dataset kindly supplied by Steven Ruggles, University of Minnesota.

33. See Peter Karsten, "'Bottomed on Justice': A Reappraisal of Critical Legal Studies Scholarship Concerning Breaches of Labor Contracts by Quitting or Firing in Britain and the U.S., 1630–1880," *American Journal of Legal History* 34 (1990): 213–61; Robert J. Steinfeld, *Invention of Free Labor*; Karen Orren, *Belated Feudalism: Labor, the Law, and Liberal Development in the United States* (Cambridge, 1991); and Christopher L. Tomlins, *Law, Labor, and Ideology in the Early American Republic* (New York, 1992).

34. Steinfeld, *Invention of Free Labor*, 44–46.

35. Ibid. Steinfeld states (121) that from the mid-eighteenth century, hired servants gained the right to depart without criminal action, but Karsten, in "Bottomed on Justice" (218), argues that agricultural laborers in England were still being convicted and imprisoned for threatening or leaving their employers in the third quarter of the nineteenth century.

36. Peter J. Coleman, *Debtors and Creditors in America: Insolvency, Imprisonment for Debt, and Bankruptcy, 1607–1900* (Madison, Wis., 1974), 142, 144, 147. This law was modified in 1730, but involuntary servitude for debt was not abolished in Pennsylvania until 1810.

37. Petty debtors in colonies with imprisonment for debt could make an oath of poverty and gain release.

38. See James Davis, *The Office and Authority of a Justice of the Peace* (New Bern, N.C., 1774), 248, 310–12; and Starke, *Office and Authority of a Justice of the Peace*, 318–20. Chapter 6 in Terri Snyder, "'Rich Widows are the Best Commodity this Country Affords'": Gender Relations and the Rehabilitation of Patriarchy in Virginia, 1660–1700" (Ph.D. diss., University of Iowa, 1992) deals with the development of these laws in late-seventeenth-century Virginia.

39. *Vestry Book of St. Paul's Parish, Hanover County, Virginia, 1706–1786*, transcribed and edited by C. G. Chamberlayne (1940; reprint, Richmond, Va., 1989), 567.

40. Michael Dalton, *The Country Justice* (London, 1655; orig. pub. 1618), 102, 112; Blackstone, *Commentaries*, bk. 1, 458; bk. 4, 65.

41. New York, 1981.

42. Axtell, *Indian Peoples of Eastern America*, 110, 119, 113–14, 86, 92, 161. The comments of Champlain can be found in Karen Anderson, *Chain Her by One Foot* (New York, 1991), 131.

43. Helen Rountree, *Pocahontas's People* (Norman, Okla., 1990), 8; Peter C. Mancall, *Valley of Opportunity: Economic Culture along the Upper Susquehanna, 1700–1800* (Ithaca, N.Y., 1991), 40; Kathryn E. Holland Braund, "Guardians of Tradition and Handmaidens to Change: Women's Roles in Creek Economic and Social Life

during the Eighteenth Century," *American Indian Quarterly* 14 (1990): 252; Joan M. Jensen, "Native American Women and Agriculture: A Seneca Case Study," in *Unequal Sisters*, ed. Ellen Carol DuBois and Vicki L. Ruiz (New York, 1990), 62; Ramon A. Gutierrez, *When Jesus Came, the Corn Mothers Went Away: Marriage, Sexuality, and Power in New Mexico, 1500–1846* (Stanford, Calif., 1991), 76.

44. Axtell, *Indian Peoples of Eastern America*, 103–4.

45. Ibid., 110, 134.

46. Richard White, *The Middle Ground: Indians, Empires, and Republics in the Great Lakes Region, 1650–1815* (Cambridge, 1991), 61.

47. Braund, "Guardians of Tradition," 241–43; Anderson, *Chain Her by One Foot*, 107; Gutierrez, *When Jesus Came*, 15; Daniel K. Richter, *The Ordeal of the Longhouse: The Peoples of the Iroquois League in the Era of European Colonization* (Chapel Hill, 1992), 20.

48. Axtell, *Indian Peoples of Eastern America*, 82.

49. Axtell, *Indian Peoples of Eastern America*, 7, 12, 24, 33–34, 39, 42, 82; Rountree, *Pocahontas's People*, 69; Braund, "Guardians of Tradition," 241; Patrick Frazier, *The Mohicans of Stockbridge* (Lincoln, Neb., 1992), 97–99.

50. Axtell, *Indian Peoples of Eastern America*, 36, 74, 76–77, 80, 86–87, 90, 94, 134–35; Gutierrez, *When Jesus Came*, 72–73.

51. Axtell, *Indian Peoples of Eastern America*, 107, 7, 90, 10.

52. Marcia Guttentag and Paul F. Secord, *Too Many Women? The Sex Ratio Question* (Beverley Hills, Calif., 1983), 115, 118.

53. John Demos, *The Unredeemed Captive: A Family Story from Early America* (New York, 1994); Axtell, *Indian Peoples of Eastern America*, 138–39.

54. Rountree, *Pocahontas's People*, 141–42. Terri Snyder discusses the provisions of this miscegenation law in chapter 6 of "'Rich Widows.'"

55. John Cushing, ed., *The Earliest Printed Laws of North Carolina, 1669–1751* (Wilmington, Del., 1977), 1: 130. Kirsten Fischer, in "Contesting the Boundaries: Servant Women and Sexual Regulation in Colonial North Carolina"—a paper delivered at the 1994 American Historical Association Meeting, San Francisco—discusses the harsh penalties associated with interracial mixing in the colony.

56. David D. Smits, "'We Are Not to Grow Wild': Seventeenth-Century New England's Repudiation of Anglo-Indian Intermarriage," *American Indian Culture and Research Journal* 11 (1987): 3, 16, 21–22.

57. Nancy Oestreich Lurie, "Indian Cultural Adjustment to European Civilization," in *Seventeenth-Century America*, ed. James Morton Smith (Chapel Hill, 1959), 59.

58. Braund, "Guardians of Tradition," 251.

59. Russell Thornton, drawing on the work of Sheila Johansson, has made the point that populations devastated by epidemic diseases have the ability to recover a good part of their population size within a few generations if conditions are favorable. The problem in those areas that became the United States is that wars, conquests, and subjection accompanied the epidemics. See Russell Thornton, "North American Indians and the Demography of Contact: Population Dynamics and Epidemic Disease following 1492" (paper presented at the History of Health and Nutrition in the

Western Hemisphere Conference, Ohio State University, Columbus, 17 September 1993). See also Sheila Ryan Johansson, "The Demographic History of the Native Peoples of North America: A Selected Bibliography," *Yearbook of Physical Anthropology* 25 (1982): 133–52. Ann Marie Plane discusses the effects of British colonial insistence on applying their marriage rules to Indian unions and the disruptive results in "Legitimacies, Indian Identities, and the Law: The Politics of Sex and the Creation of History in Colonial New England," *Law and Social Inquiry* 23 (1998): 55–74.

60. White, *Middle Ground*, 508.

61. See Gutierrez, *When Jesus Came;* and Patricia Seed, *To Love, Honor, and Obey in Colonial Mexico* (Stanford, 1988). Of course, societies such as the Iroquois that managed to maintain some separate space and land also retained some aspects of their kinship and household organization. See Richter, *Ordeal of the Longhouse,* 261–62; Jensen, "Native American Women," 51–65; and Nancy Shoemaker, "The Rise or Fall of Iroquois Women," *Journal of Women's History* 2 (1991): 39–57.

62. Robert E. McCaa, "Introduction: Female and Family in Nineteenth-Century Latin America," *Journal of Family History* 16 (1991): 211–14.

63. Lewis Morgan, *League of the Iroquois* (New York: Corinth Books, 1962); Lewis Morgan, *Ancient Society* (New York, 1877); Friedrich Engels, *The Origin of the Family, Private Property, and the State* (New York, 1942).

64. See particularly, Russell R. Menard, "Immigrants and Their Increase: The Process of Population Growth in Early Colonial Maryland," in *Law, Society, and Politics in Early Maryland,* ed. Aubrey C. Land et al. (Baltimore, 1977), 88–102; Lois Green Carr and Lorena S. Walsh, "The Planter's Wife: The Experience of White Women in Seventeenth-Century Maryland," *William and Mary Quarterly,* 3d ser., 34 (1977): 542–57; Lorena S. Walsh, "'Till Death Us Do Part': Marriage and Family in Seventeenth-Century Maryland," in *The Chesapeake in the Seventeenth Century: Essays on Anglo-American Society,* ed. Thad W. Tate and David L. Ammerman (Chapel Hill, 1979), 126–52; Darrett B. Rutman and Anita H. Rutman, "'Now-Wives and Sons-in-Law': Parental Death in a Seventeenth-Century Virginia County," in *The Chesapeake in the Seventeenth Century: Essays on Anglo-American Society,* ed. Thad W. Tate and David L. Ammerman (Chapel Hill, 1979), 153–82; Lois Green Carr, "Inheritance in the Colonial Chesapeake," in *Women in the Age of the American Revolution,* ed. Ronald Hoffman and Peter J. Albert (Charlottesville, 1989), 155–210; T. H. Breen, "A Changing Labor Force and Race Relations in Virginia 1660–1710," *Journal of Social History* 7 (1973): 3–25; Edmund S. Morgan, *American Slavery, American Freedom: The Ordeal of Colonial Virginia* (New York, 1975); Allan Kulikoff, *Tobacco and Slaves: The Development of Southern Cultures in the Chesapeake, 1680–1800* (Chapel Hill, 1986), chaps. 1, 2, 5; Gloria L. Main, *Tobacco Colony: Life in Early Maryland, 1650–1720* (Princeton, 1982), chaps. 2, 3; and Terri L. Snyder, "'Rich Widows'" chaps. 1, 2.

65. For a good description of this process in late-seventeenth-century Virginia, see Snyder, "'Rich Widows,'" esp. chap. 6.

66. Daniel Scott Smith, "Meanings of Family and Household," 432.

67. Norton, *Founding Mothers and Fathers,* 7–10.

68. Morgan, *Puritan Family*, 45; Elizabeth Pleck, *Domestic Tyranny* (New York, 1987), 17–18; Kelly D. Weisberg, "'Under Great Temptations Heer': Women and Divorce Law in Puritan Massachusetts," in *Women and the Law: The Social Historical Perspective*, ed. Kelly D. Weisberg (Cambridge, Mass., 1982), 2: 117–31.

69. Morgan, *Puritan Family*, 87–88; Fischer, *Albion's Seed*, 130–32.

70. Lyle Koehler, *A Search for Power: The "Weaker Sex" in Seventeenth-Century New England* (Urbana, Ill., 1980). Appendix 1 of Koehler's work lists all the petitions for divorce appearing in the legislative and judicial records of the New England colonies during the seventeenth century. An amended version of these petitions for the colonies of New Haven and Connecticut appears in Cornelia Hughes Dayton's *Women Before the Bar: Gender, Law, and Society in Connecticut, 1640–1790* (Chapel Hill, 1994). Out of 118 petitions, the authorities granted 98. Of the 98, twenty-seven were granted on grounds such as impotence that would have merited an annulment in England. By 1700, the Euro-American population of New England amounted to about ninety thousand (John J. McCusker and Russell R. Menard, *The Economy of British America 1607–1789* [Chapel Hill, 1985], 103).

71. Koehler, in *A Search for Power* (137), finds that between 1630 and 1699, 128 men and 57 women were accused of abusing their spouses. Out of the 27 wife abusers sentenced in Essex County, 2 got lashings, 20 got fines ranging from 10s. to £2, and 5 received only admonitions (140–41). Martha Porter Saxton, *Being Good: Moral Standards for Puritan Women, Boston: 1630–1730* (Ph.D. diss., Columbia University, 1989), 175–77. She also notes that 20 percent of the victims of male killers were wives, while only one wife faced charges of killing her husband. Dayton, in *Women Before the Bar* (chap. 3), argues that prosecution of husbands for wife beating had been more frequent in seventeenth-century Massachusetts and Connecticut, but she found only nine wife abuse complaints in the county she studied between 1710 and 1780. Roger Thompson, in *Sex in Middlesex: Popular Mores in a Massachusetts County, 1649–1699* ([Amherst, Mass., 1986], 10–11), finds eleven convictions over the fifty-year period in the County of Middlesex, where the population went from three thousand to ten thousand. Almost all the cases, moreover, were prior to 1663.

72. Morgan, *Puritan Family*, 148–49; David H. Flaherty, *Privacy in Colonial New England* (Charlottesville, 1976), 196; Daniel Scott Smith, "Meanings of Family and Household," 40.

73. Thompson, in *Sex in Middlesex* (31–33), details the activities of this army of officials enforcing the mores of the community.

74. William Frost, *The Quaker Family in Colonial America* (New York, 1973), 56, 79, 181; Barry Levy, *Quakers and the American Family: British Settlement in the Delaware Valley* (New York, 1988), 80–82, 139, 212–13; Jean R. Soderlund, "Women's Authority in Pennsylvania and New Jersey Quaker Meetings, 1680–1760," *William and Mary Quarterly*, 3d ser., 44 (1987): 722–49.

75. Fischer, in *Albion's Seed* (89–91), summarizes this work, drawing on the research of Daniel Scott Smith and Michael S. Hindus, Robert V. Wells, Roger Thompson, and particularly essays in Peter Laslett et al., *Bastardy and Its Comparative History* (Cambridge, 1980). Besides the phalanx of enforcers, the harsh penalties for being a "stubborn child" (see John Sutton, *Stubborn Children: Controlling Delinquency in the*

United States, 1640–1981 [Berkeley, 1988], 10–28), an adulterer, or sodomizer might not have only discouraged prosecution by the enforcers but discouraged the activity on the part of potential offenders.

76. Dayton, *Women Before the Bar,* chap. 4.

77. Daniel Scott Smith and Michael S. Hindus, in "Premarital Pregnancy in America 1640–1971: An Overview and Interpretation" (*Journal of Interdisciplinary History* 5 [1975]: 554), estimate for the decade of the 1670s a conviction rate of 61 percent of all the married couples likely to have conceived a child outside of marriage.

78. Dayton, *Women Before the Bar,* chap. 4. In New Haven it became the most common crime by the 1690s, replacing drunkenness and theft. Thompson, in *Sex in Middlesex,* does not provide a breakdown of sex crimes versus other types of offenses, but it does appear that fornication was increasing over the course of the seventeenth century. Hendrick Hartog, in "The Public Law of a County Court: Judicial Government in Eighteenth Century Massachusetts" (*American Journal of Legal History* 20 [1976]: 282–329), shows it had become the most common crime by the 1720s. William E. Nelson, in *Americanization of the Common Law: The Impact of Legal Change on Massachusetts Society, 1760–1830* ([Cambridge, Mass., 1975], 37), finds that it had that status in all of Massachusetts in the mid-eighteenth century.

79. Martin Ingram, *Church Courts, Sex, and Marriage in England, 1570–1640* (Cambridge, 1987), chap. 7.

80. Koehler, *Search for Power,* charts 12.1, 12.3, 12.4.

81. N. E. H. Hull, *Female Felons: Women and Serious Crime in Colonial Massachusetts* (Urbana, Ill., 1987), 61, 67, 129.

82. Hartog, "The Public Law of a County Court," 301; Dayton, *Women Before the Bar,* 152; Daniel Scott Smith and Michael S. Hindus, "Premarital Pregnancy," appendix 1.

83. Recent work on the strict family settlement—sometimes referred to as the "marriage settlement" because it normally was drawn up at the time of the marriage of the male heir—has been done by Eileen Spring. See her "The Family Strict Settlement and Historians," *Canadian Journal of History* 18 (1983): 379–98; her "The Strict Settlement: Its Role in Family History," *Economic History Review,* 2d ser., 41 (1988): 454–60, and her "The Heiress-at-Law: English Real Property Law from a New Point of View," *Law and History Review* 8 (fall 1990): 273–96. Also, Spring's *Law, Land, and Family: Aristocratic Inheritance in England, 1300–1800* (Chapel Hill, 1993) provides a full bibliography of the research of on the strict family settlement.

84. Shammas, Salmon, and Dahlin, *Inheritance in America,* 56.

85. Daniel Scott Smith, "American Family and Demographic Patterns and the Northwest European Model," *Continuity and Change* 8 (1993): 402.

86. Philip J. Greven Jr., *Four Generations: Population, Land, and Family in Colonial Andover, Massachusetts* (Ithaca, N.Y., 1970).

3. The American Revolution and the Household

1. Wood, *The Radicalism of the American Revolution,* 3–6.

2. Ibid., 3.

3. See Jack P. Greene, *The Intellectual Construction of America: Exceptionalism and Identity from 1492 to 1800* (Chapel Hill, 1993), 130–61.

4. Wood, *Radicalism of the American Revolution,* 6.

5. Bernard Bailyn, *The Origins of American Politics* (New York, 1968); Jack P. Greene, *Understanding the American Revolution: Issues and Actors* (Charlottesville, 1995), esp. chap. 16.

6. Lee Soltow, *Distribution of Wealth and Income in the United States in 1798* (Pittsburgh, 1989), chap. 7. For an estimate of the wealth of rich colonial officials and proprietors, see Shammas, "A New Look at Long-Term Trends in Wealth Inequality in the United States," 418–19, and appendix A.

7. Patricia U. Bonomi, *Under the Cope of Heaven: Religion, Society, and Politics in Colonial America* (New York, 1986), chaps. 4, 5; Fischer, *Albion's Seed,* 423.

8. There are many examples of these encounters. Two recent ones are: "Forum: "How Revolutionary Was the Revolution? A Discussion of Gordon S. Wood's *The Radicalism of the American Revolution,*" *William and Mary Quarterly,* 3d ser., 51 (1994): 677–716; and Ronald Hoffman in *Uncommon Sense* (Winter 1998), along with the rejoinder by Carol Berkin, Richard B. Bernstein, and Pauline Maier in the summer 1998 issue (3, 5).

9. Wood, *Radicalism of the American Revolution,* 145–68.

10. Daniel Blake Smith, *Inside the Great House: Planter Family Life in Eighteenth-Century Chesapeake Society* (Ithaca, N.Y., 1980) (photographic insert of paintings between pages 125 and 126); "Power, Patriarchy, and the Heroic: The Revolution and the Transformation of American Sensibilities" (text and photo-essay), in *Liberty, Equality, Power: A History of the American People,* ed. John Murrin et al. (Fort Worth, Tex., 1996), 1: 233, 246–47.

11. Lovell, "Reading Eighteenth-Century American Family Portraits," 243–64; Sidney Hart, "Charles Willson Peale and the Theory and Practice of the Eighteenth-Century American Family," in *The Peale Family: Creation of a Legacy 1770–1870,* ed. Lillian B. Miller (New York, 1996), 101–17.

12. Stone, *The Family, Sex, and Marriage in England 1500–1800,* 411–12.

13. Holly Brewer, "Entailing Aristocracy in Colonial Virginia: 'Ancient Feudal Restraints' and Revolutionary Reform," *William and Mary Quarterly,* 3d ser., 54 (1997): 327–28.

14. Ibid., 344, quoting from William Waller Hening's version of the *Statutes at Large* (New York and Philadelphia, 1819–23), 9: 226–27.

15. See Suzanne Desan, "'War between Brothers and Sisters': Inheritance Law and Gender Politics in Revolutionary France," *French Historical Studies* 20 (1997): 597–602. Testators could dispose of only one-tenth of their property by will if they had children. The rest had to be divided equally among them. Xavier Martin, in "Fonction Paternelle et Code Napoleon" (*Annales Historiques de la Revolution Francaise* [1996]: 466–75), discusses the unhappiness with the revolutionary reforms and the support for the Napoleonic Code.

16. These were the findings from our study of Bucks County, Pennsylvania, from the late seventeenth to the late twentieth century, as reported in Shammas, Salmon, and Dahlin, *Inheritance in America,* 42–51, 108–12.

17. In the United States, grounds for divorce included such things as impotence and bigamy that in European countries under the canon law were classified as grounds for annulment. These grounds obviously were not any innovation. Two New England states where divorces had been granted in the colonial period—New Hampshire and Rhode Island—amended their laws in the 1790s to give their high courts the right to consider extreme cruelty as a ground for absolute divorce (Howard, *History of Matrimonial Institutions*, 3:11, 15). More extensive analysis of the evolution of divorce laws is presented in chapter 5 of this volume.

18. Hendrik Hartog, "Marital Exits and Marital Expectations in Nineteenth-Century America," *Georgetown Law Journal* 80 (1991): 115.

19. Roderick Phillips, *Family Breakdown in Late-Eighteenth-Century France: Divorces in Rouen 1792–1803* (Oxford, 1980).

20. See Frank L. Dewey, "Thomas Jefferson's Notes on Divorce," *William and Mary Quarterly*, 3d ser., 39 (1982): 212–23; and Norma Basch, "From the Bonds of Empire to the Bonds of Matrimony," in *Devising Liberty: Preserving and Creating Freedom in the New American Republic*, ed. David Thomas Konig (Stanford, 1995), 217–42.

21. Most recently, Aaron Fogleman, "From Slaves, Convicts, and Servants to Free Passengers: The Transformation of Immigration in the Era of the American Revolution," *Journal of American History* 85 (1998): 43–76.

22. Robert Steinfeld, "The Ambiguous Impact of the American Revolution," chap. 5 in *The Invention of Free Labor* (Chapel Hill, 1991), 124.

23. Gary B. Nash and Jean R. Soderlund, *Freedom by Degrees: Emancipation in Pennsylvania and Its Aftermath* (New York, 1991), chap. 6.

24. Farley Grubb, "The End of European Immigrant Servitude in the United States: An Economic Analysis of Market Collapse," *Journal of Economic History* 54 (1994): 794–824.

25. Nash and Soderlund, *Freedom by Degrees*, 7; Arthur Zilversmit, *The First Emancipation: The Abolition of Slavery in the North* (Chicago, 1967), 4.

26. Ira Berlin, *Slaves without Masters: The Free Negro in the Antebellum South* (New York, 1974), 29.

27. Robert William Fogel and Stanley L. Engerman, "Philanthropy at Bargain Prices: Notes on the Economics of Gradual Emancipation," *Journal of Legal Studies* 3 (1974): 377–401.

28. Zilversmit, in *The First Emancipation*, discusses the politics around the passage in all the northern states.

29. Gary B. Nash, *Race and Revolution* (Madison, Wis., 1990), chap. 2.

30. Rosemarie Zagarri, in "The Rights of Man and Woman in Post-Revolutionary America" (*William and Mary Quarterly*, 3d ser., 55 [1998]: 203–30), examines the opening that natural rights language gave to women, largely in the French revolutionary period. That women and supporters of women's citizenship used this language seem undeniable. The problem to which Pateman and others refer is that the republican revolutions, in their transformation of subjects into citizens, specifically excluded women. Later, even as women received citizenship rights such as the franchise, policies continued to assume that the entitled citizen was male (for example, in the structuring of social security).

31. Wars—the Seven Years War and the Revolution—offered indentured servants and slaves opportunities for release. The court decision interpreting the 1780 Massachusetts constitution as prohibiting slavery came about as a result of an enslaved man simply declaring his right to hire himself out. See T. H. Breen, "The Last Days of Slavery in Massachusetts," in *Through a Glass Darkly: Reflections on Personal Identity in Early America*, ed. Ronald Hoffman, Mechal Sobel, and Fredrika J. Teute (Chapel Hill, 1997).

32. John Adams to Abigail Adams, 14 April 1776, in *Adams Family Correspondence*, ser. 2 of *The Adams Papers*, ed. L. H. Butterfield et al. (Cambridge, 1963), 1: 382. John Ferling, in *John Adams, A Life* (Knoxville, 1992) discussed this episode to indicate the limits of Adams's views on women's rights (172).

33. Greene, *Intellectual Construction of America*, 154–56.

34. See James Traer, *Marriage and the Family in Eighteenth-Century France* (Ithaca, N.Y., 1980); and Margaret H. Darrow, *Revolution in the House: Family, Class, and Inheritance in Southern France, 1775–1825* (Princeton, 1989), 9–13.

35. See Greene, "The Limits of the American Revolution," chap. 15 in *Understanding the American Revolution*, 351–70.

36. Esmond Wright, *Franklin of Philadelphia* (Cambridge, Mass., 1986), 34–41; Leonard Labaree et al., eds., *The Papers of Benjamin Franklin* (New Haven, 1959), 1: 362–67; Sheila L. Skemp, *Benjamin Franklin and William Franklin* (Boston, 1994), chap. 1. All treatments of Franklin's early years lean heavily on his own *Autobiography*, which does not dwell much on his marriage but does reveal his ambitions to marry for money. See Russsel B. Nye, ed., *"Autobiography" and Other Writings* (Boston, 1958), 62.

37. Douglas Southall Freeman's first three volumes of *George Washington: A Biography* (New York, 1948–51) deal extensively with the estates left by Augustine Washington, Lawrence Washington, and especially Daniel Parke Custis. He also describes the steps Washington took to manage the properties under his control.

38. *Diary and Autobiography of John Adams*, ser. 1 of *The Adams Papers*, ed. L. H. Butterfield et al. (Cambridge, 1960), 1: 108.

39. Peter Shaw, *The Character of John Adams* (Chapel Hill, 1976), 3, 41, 45; Lynne Withey, *Dearest Friend: A Life of Abigail Adams* (New York, 1981), 15; Edith B. Gelles, *Portia: The World of Abigail Adams* (Bloomington, Ind., 1992), 24–25.

40. "Will of Reverend William Smith, September 12, 1783," in *Adams Family Correspondence*, ser. 2 of *The Adams Papers*, ed. Richard Alan Ryerson et al. (Cambridge, 1993), 5: 245–49.

41. Withey, *Dearest Friend*, 286.

42. *Diary* (1759).

43. *Jefferson Himself: The Personal Narrative of a Many-Sided American*, ed. Bernard Mayo (Charlottesville, 1942), 26.

44. Dumas Malone, *Jefferson the Virginian* (Boston, 1948), 430.

45. Dumas Malone put together the inheritance information about the Jefferson and Wayles estates. See Malone, *Jefferson the Virginian*, appendix 2.

46. T. H. Breen, *Tobacco Culture: The Mentality of the Great Tidewater Planters on the Eve of Revolution* (Princeton, 1985), 144.

47. Jacob Ernst Cooke, *Alexander Hamilton* (New York, 1982), 19

48. Larry E. Tise, in the introduction to the volume he edited—*Benjamin Franklin and Women* ([University Park, Md., 2000], 13–14)—discusses Franklin's many relationships with women and the debate over the sexual nature of them. Cooke, *Hamilton*, 177ff.

49. Harold C. Syrett, ed. *Papers of Alexander Hamilton* (New York, 1979), 26: 305.

50. *The Last Will and Testament of George Washington*, ed. John C. Fitzpatrick (Mount Vernon, Va., 1939), 2–3.

51. Philip J. Schwarz, *Slave Laws in Virginia* (Athens, Ga., 1996), 52–53.

52. On Virginia slave and manumission laws, see ibid.; and Luther Porter Jackson, *Free Negro Labor and Property Holding in Virginia, 1830–1860* (1942; reprint, New York, 1969).

53. Almost all early American historians now accept that Jefferson had a second group of sons and daughters with Sally Hemings, his slave and the half sister of his first wife. See "Forum: Thomas Jefferson and Sally Hemings Redux," *William and Mary Quarterly*, 3d ser., 57 (2000): 121–209.

54. Gary B. Nash and Jean R. Soderlund document Franklin's views and ownership of slaves in *Freedom by Degrees*, ix-xiv.

55. Quoted in Zilversmit, *First Emancipation*, 46.

56. L. H. Butterfield et al., eds., *The Adams Family Correspondence* (Cambridge, Mass., 1963), 1: 416.

57. Syrett, *Papers of Hamilton*, 11: 640.

58. Carl Van Doren, ed. *Benjamin Franklin's Autobiographical Writings* (New York, 1945), 688.

59. Family tradition had it that Dolley "never meant to marry" but wed John Todd to please her father (*Memoirs and Letters of Dolly Madison* [Port Washington, N.Y., 1971], 10–11). These family memoirs, however, lack candor. For example, there is no mention of her problems with the Todd family after her husband's death and her decision to leave the Quakers.

60. I thank John Stagg, editor of the Madison Papers, for the information that Dolley is almost always described as taller than Madison, although estimates of his height vary from 5′2″ to 5′6″.

61. Catherine Allgor, *Parlor Politics: In Which the Ladies of Washington Help Build a City and a Government* (Charlottesville, 2000).

62. On the adventures of Dolley Madison, see Irving Brant, *James Madison: Father of the Constitution 1787–1800* (Indianapolis, 1950), 408–11; Ralph Ketcham, *James Madison: A Biography* (New York, 1971), chap. 15; Maud Wilder Goodwin, *Dolly Madison* (New York, 1897), 42–46; Virginia Moore, *The Madisons: A Biography* (New York, 1979), 15; and Paul Sifton, "'What a Dread Prospect . . .': Dolley Madison's Plague Year," *Pennsylvania Magazine of History and Biography* 87 (1963): 182–88.

63. Ryerson, *Adams Family Correspondence*, ser. 2, 5: 245–49, 304–5.

64. Wood, *Radicalism of the American Revolution*, 147.

65. Traer, *Marriage and the Family in Eighteenth-Century France*, chap. 6; Blackburn, *Overthrow of Colonial Slavery*, 248–53.

66. Carrie Rebora et al. *John Singleton Copley in America* (New York, 1995), 184.

67. Hart, in "Peale and the Theory and Practice of the Eighteenth-Century American Family" (109), corrects Lovell on this point.
68. Levy, *Quakers and the American Family: British Settlement in the Delaware Valley* (insert of paintings and text between pages 148 and 149).
69. G. J. Barker-Benfield, *The Culture of Sensibility: Sex and Society in Eighteenth-Century Britain* (Chicago, 1992); John Brewer, *Pleasures of the Imagination: English Culture in the Eighteenth Century* (New York, 1997), 113–22.
70. See Mintz and Kellogg, *Domestic Revolutions,* 54; and the photo-essay in Murrin et al. *Liberty, Equality, Power,* 1:247–51.

4. Marriage and the Early American Household

1. Philip Alexander Bruce, *Social Life of Virginia in the Seventeenth Century* (1907; reprint, Williamstown, Mass., 1968), 230–31; Daniel Blake Smith, *Inside the Great House,* 140; Kulikoff, *Tobacco and Slaves,* 174; Fischer, *Albion's Seed,* 284.
2. Morgan, *Puritan Family,* 79–80.
3. Ibid., 82, and cited in Mintz and Kellogg, *Domestic Revolutions,* 11.
4. Greven, *Four Generations,* 74.
5. Mintz and Kellogg, *Domestic Revolutions,* 19, 41. On New England, they write, "Up to the mid-eighteenth century, family considerations continued to play an important role in determining marital circumstances"; and on the Chesapeake, "during the second half of the eighteenth century . . . [p]lanters' children became more likely to select marriage partners without parental interference." Karen Lystra, in *Searching the Heart: Women, Men, and Romantic Love in Nineteenth-Century America* ([New York, 1990], 158–59), links romantic courtship with the power of participants to decide marriage on their own and considers that situation to be in place for the white middle and upper-middle classes "by the 1830s at least."
6. Daniel Scott Smith, "Parental Power and Marriage Patterns: An Analysis of Historical Trends in Hingham, Massachusetts," in *The American Family in Social-Historical Perspective,* ed. Michael Gordon, 2d ed. (New York, 1978), 87–100; originally published in *Journal of Marriage and the Family* 35 (1973): 419–28.
7. The nearest thing to a systematic examination of this issue is the work done by Toby Ditz, *Property and Kinship: Inheritance in Early Connecticut 1750–1820* (Ithaca, N.Y., 1986), chap. 6; and Daniel Vickers, *Farmers and Fishermen: Two Centuries of Work in Essex County, Massachusetts, 1630–1850* (Chapel Hill, 1994), 64–77 on lifetime transfers between fathers and children. This work is discussed in note 43 below.
8. See Robert V. Wells, "The Population of England's Colonies in America: Old English or New America?" *Population Studies* 46 (1992): 85–87.
9. Daniel Scott Smith, "American Family and Demographic Patterns and the Northwest European Model," 389–415.
10. Ibid, 396; and Michael R. Haines, "Long-Term Marriage Patterns in the United States from Colonial Times to the Present," *The History of the Family* 1 (1996): 15–40.
11. Fischer, *Albion's Seed,* 285.

12. J. Hajnal, "European Marriage Patterns in Perspective," in *Population in History: Essays in Historical Demography*, ed. D. V. Glass and D. E. C. Eversley (London, 1965), 101–43.

13. Daniel Scott Smith and Michael S. Hindus, "Premarital Pregnancy," 537–70.

14. G. S. Rowe, "Women's Crime and Criminal Administration in Pennsylvania, 1763–1790," *Pennsylvania Magazine of History and Biography* 109 (1985): 352–53, 363–65.

15. Fischer, in *Albion's Seed* (298), conveniently lists the results from a number of studies.

16. Michael W. Flinn, *The European Demographic System, 1500–1820* (Baltimore, 1981), 121–23.

17. For example, Fischer, *Albion's Seed*, 284; Daniel Blake Smith, *Inside the Great House*, 138–42. Greven, in *Four Generations*, actually uses early-twentieth-century British and Irish farming communities as a reference point (73–76).

18. Particularly influential at one point were Edward Shorter, "Illegitimacy, Sexual Revolutioin, and Social Change in Modern Europe," *Journal of Interdisciplinary History* 2 (1971): 237–72; and Stone, *The Family, Sex, and Marriage in England 1500–1800*.

19. For examples, see Julie Hardwick, *The Practice of Patriarchy: Gender and the Politics of Household Authority in Early Modern France* (University Park, Pa., 1998); and Cissie Fairchilds, *Domestic Enemies: Servants and their Masters in Old Regime France* (Baltimore, 1984), 98–99.

20. Gillian Hamilton, "Property Rights and Transaction Costs in Marriage: Evidence from Prenuptial Contracts," *Journal of Economic History* 59 (1999): 68–103. As Hamilton shows, these devices were used by more than just the elite and existed primarily to establish whether the couple would employ the community property system of Quebec and the terms of an annuity and a lifetime gift of the entire estate in place of the customary dower. These purposes were very different from the marriage settlements or prenuptial agreements found in the thirteen mainland colonies and the early United States.

21. Edith Couturier discusses the Spanish laws of Toro in "Women and the Family in Eighteenth-Century Mexico: Law and Practice," *Journal of Family History* 10 (1985): 295–96.

22. David Warren Sabean, *Property, Production, and Family in Neckarhausen, 1700–1870* (Cambridge, 1990), 187–201.

23. For a discussion about this development in English law, see Shammas, Salmon, and Dahlin, *Inheritance in America*, 26–27.

24. This is my reading of Diana O'Hara's study of sixteenth-century courtship in the diocese of Canterbury. See *Courtship and Constraint: Rethinking the Making of Marriage in Tudor England* (Manchester, Eng., 2000), esp. chap. 6, on dowries and property in courtship. O'Hara finds little evidence for prenuptial exchange of property. All data on portions given by fathers are postmortem in wills.

25. Spring, *Law, Land, and Family*, is a recent and lucid account of this system that H. J. Habakkuk first brought to scholarly attention, and about which Lawrence Stone, Lloyd Bonfield, and others have written extensively.

26. Lynne Vallone, *Disciplines of Virtue: Girls' Culture in the Eighteenth and Nineteenth Centuries* (New Haven, 1995), 57–58.

27. Lawrence Stone and Jean Fawtier Stone, *An Open Elite? England, 1540–1880* (Oxford, 1984).
28. See James Brundage, *Law, Sex, and Christian Society* (Chicago, 1987).
29. Sarah Hanley, "Family and State in Early Modern France: The Marriage Pact," in *Connect Spheres: Women in the Western World, 1500 to the Present,* ed. Marilyn J. Boxer and Jean H. Quataert (New York, 1987), 53–63; Barbara B. Diefendorf, "'Give Us Back our Children': Patriarchal Authority and Parental Consent to Religious Vocations in Early Counter-Reformation France," *Journal of Modern History* 68 (1996): 265–307.
30. Traer, *Marriage and the Family in Eighteenth-Century France,* chap. 6.
31. Patricia Seed, *To Love, Honor, and Obey in Colonial Mexico: Conflicts over Marriage Choice 1574–1821* (Stanford, Calif., 1988); Susan M. Socolow, "Acceptable Partners: Marriage Choice in Colonial Argentina, 1778–1810," in *Sexuality and Marriage in Colonial Latin America,* ed. Asuncion Lavrin (Lincoln, Neb., 1989); Silvia Marina Arrom, *The Women of Mexico City: 1790–1850* (Stanford, 1985).
32. Quoted in Thomas Robisheaux, *Rural Society and the Search for Order in Early Modern Germany* (Cambridge, 1989), 103, 99.
33. Ibid., 108–9.
34. R. B. Outhwaite, *Clandestine Marriage in England, 1500–1850* (London, 1995), chaps. 1, 4.
35. Ibid., chap. 4; and H. Brewer, "Constructing Consent," 212–23.
36. Jona Schellekens, in "Courtship, the Clandestine Marriage Act, and Illegitimate Fertility in England" (*Journal of Interdisciplinary History* 25 [1995]: 440), presents time series evidence of the link. The victims of the 1753 Marriage Act are the subjects of Eve Tavor Bannet's article, "The Marriage Act of 1753: 'A most cruel law for the Fair Sex,'" *Eighteenth-Century Studies* 30, no. 3 (1997): 233–54.
37. Ditz, *Property and Kinship,* 108.
38. John Demos, *A Little Commonwealth: Family Life in Plymouth Colony* (New York, 1970), 160–61.
39. Walsh, "'Till Death Us Do Part,'" 134.
40. Morgan, *Puritan Family,* 82; Greven, *Four Generations,* 78–80.
41. Anne King Gregorie, ed., *Records of the Court of Chancery of South Carolina, 1671–1779* (Washington, D.C, 1950).
42. Marylynn Salmon, "Women and Property in South Carolina: The Evidence from Marriage Settlements, 1730–1830," *William and Mary Quarterly,* 3d ser., 39 (1982): 655–85.
43. Vickers, in *Farmers and Fishermen* (223–24), reports that in his sample of fifty-two seventeenth-century Essex County fathers, only 2 percent deeded land to sons before death, while in his eighteenth-century sample of fifty-nine fathers (1700–1775), 39 percent deeded at least one son some paternal land inter vivosly, and that land for 58 percent of those sons came within five years of their marriage. So at best about a quarter of sons got some land not too distant from the time of their marriage. Vickers associates it with greater independence, as does Greven. Ditz's study of Connecticut, however, beginning in 1750 and going into the early nineteenth

century, seems to finds a decrease over time in inter vivos transfers to sons (III) and associates that decrease with independence. Vickers (personal communication, 16 May 2000) believes the discrepancy has to do with the difference in time periods. If I'm grasping the point here, their combined findings can be interpreted as a seventeenth-century withholding of land from children until death, meaning little independence, an eighteenth-century increase in inter vivos transfers giving marginally more independence, and then a nineteenth-century departure from agricultural pursuits.

44. Gloria Main, in "Portioning Children in Colonial New England: Origins of the Child Centered Family?" (paper presented at the All U.C. Group in Economic History Meeting, UCLA, 28–30 April 2000), gives examples of sons' wages listed in account books but argues that girls were not compensated at home except for long-term nursing.

45. Ibid. Main's examples of New England fathers giving portions at marriage are confined to the first generation from England. She reports that in later years, "women's dowries more often came to consist solely of household goods."

46. Ditz, in *Property and Kinship* (112–14), could document that in the last half of the eighteenth century between 46 and 67 percent of married daughters in two Connecticut communities had received some lifetime transfer of personalty (goods) prior to the death of their fathers. In the 1820s, the proportion that could be documented as receiving some lifetime transfer fell below 40 percent.

47. William Brigham, ed., *The Compact with the Charter and Laws of the Colony of New Plymouth* (Boston, 1836), 61; William Whitmore, ed., *The Colonial Laws of Massachusetts* (Boston, 1887), 101; John D. Cushing, ed., *The Earliest Laws of the New Haven and Connecticut Colonies, 1639–1673* (Wilmington, Del., 1978), 42; John D. Cushing, ed., *The Earliest Acts and Laws of the Colony of Rhode Island and Providence Plantations, 1647–1719* (Wilmington, Del., 1977), 30.

48. Howard, *History of Matrimonial Institutions,* 2:162–69.

49. Cushing, *Acts of Rhode Island, 1647–1719,* 41 (in 1647), and 70 (in 1663); Howard, *History of Matrimonial Institutions,* 2: 229–30, and 2: 240–44 in Virginia (1662) and Maryland (1658) voiding marriages for incorrect procedure.

50. Howard, *History of Matrimonial Institutions,* 2: 121–327, 388–497, 3: 161–259; Grossberg, *Governing the Hearth,* chaps. 3, 4; Nancy Cott, *Public Vows: A History of Marriage and the Nation* (Cambridge, Mass., 2000), 30–33. As Grossberg notes and Howard himself indicates (3: 191), much of the impetus for Howard's landmark study was in the end to argue for a tightening of United States marriage laws and better registration and policing of the legality of these unions. Also see H. Brewer, "Constructing Consent," 203–37.

51. *United States v. McCormick,* 26 F. Cas. 1059; 1802 U.S. App. Lexis 358 and 26 F. Cas. 1060; 1810 U.S. App. Lexis 224.

52. Grossberg, *Governing the Hearth,* 65.

53. Cushing, *Acts of Rhode Island 1647–1719,* 102. Howard, in *History of Matrimonial Institutions* (2: 228–44), discusses the imposition of the Virginia and Maryland laws voiding marriages circa 1660 and then the revocation of the acts at the end of

the century. Walsh, in "'Till Death Us Do Part'" (129–40), discusses the legal informality of marriage in seventeenth-century Maryland.

54. Pennsylvania. *Laws of the Commonwealth of Pennsylvania* (Philadelphia, 1810), 2: 180.

55. See Howard, *History of Matrimonial Institutions,* vol. 2, chaps. 12–14; and 2: 129 n. 8.

56. "English Statutes Made of Force"[1712], in *Earliest Laws of South Carolina, 1682–1716,* ed. John Cushing (Wilmington, Del., 1978).

57. H. Brewer, in "Constructing Consent" (229–30), found only one Virginia case in 1784, and in that instance—where a schoolmaster had raped a twelve-year-old girl and then married her without her father's permission—the marriage was upheld and the person officiating settled out of court with the father. The examples of court cases in the Chesapeake for marriages without parental consent under the age of twelve are from the seventeenth century. See Fischer, *Albion's Seed* (281 n. 3) for cases in Maryland (1688) and Northampton County, Virginia (1662).

58. Byron Curti Martyn, "Racism in the United States: A History of the Anti-Miscegenation Legislation and Litigation" (Ph.D. diss., University of Southern California, 1979).

59. Rhode Island. *The Public Laws of the State of Rhode Island and Providence Plantations . . . Revised . . . 1798* (Providence, 1798), 481–86.

60. See for example, the provisions in Vermont in *Laws of Vermont,* vol. 13 of *State Papers of Vermont,* edited by John A Williams (Montpelier, 1965), 266–67.

61. Laurel Thatcher Ulrich, *A Midwife's Tale: The Life of Martha Ballard, Based on Her Diary, 1785–1812* (New York, 1990), chap. 4.

62. Church figures in Fischer, *Albion's Seed* (423 n. 8), and population figures of 50,000 in 1650; 1,170,000 in 1750; and 2,500,000 in 1775.

63. Carville Earle and Changyong Cao, "The Rate of Frontier Expansion in American History, 1650–1890" (paper presented at "GIS in the Social Sciences," National Center for Geographic Information and Analysis, 21–24 March 1991). Peter Kolchin, *Unfree Labor: American Slavery and Russian Serfdom* (Cambridge, Mass., 1987).

64. Philip D. Morgan, *Slave Counterpoint: Black Culture in the Eighteenth-Century Chesapeake and Lowcountry* (Chapel Hill, 1998), 504–6.

65. Fischer, in *Albion's Seed* (481–90), reviews the work on marriage practices and summarizes the research findings on demographic patterns done by Robert V. Wells, Louise Kantrow, and others. On the reformation, see Jack Marrietta, *The Reformation of American Quakerism, 1748–1783* (Philadelphia, 1984); and Barry Levy, *Quakers and the American Family* (New York, 1988), introd., chap. 7, appendix.

66. On the colonial link, see Karin A. Wulf, "'My Dear Liberty': Quaker Spinsterhood and Female Autonomy in Eighteenth-Century Pennsylvania," in *Women and Freedom in Early America,* ed. Larry D. Eldridge (New York, 1997), 83–108.

67. Ann Twinam, in *Public Lives, Private Secrets: Gender, Honor, Sexuality, and Illegitimacy in Colonial Spanish America* ([Stanford, 1999], 8–12), points out the high illegitimacy rate, especially prior to the eighteenth century among the mixed race, or non-Spanish, populations. She studies the petitions filed for legitimization, but interestingly, for over a hundred-year period in all of the jurisdictions of the Spanish Crown in America, only 244 cases appear.

68. Auguste Carlier, *Marriage in the United States,* trans. Joy Jeffries (Boston, 1867), vii–viii, 32.

69. At least this was the case in 1996. See Michael R. Haines, "Long-Term Marriage Patterns in the United States from Colonial Times to the Present," *The History of the Family* 1 (1996): 18.

5. The Household's Civil War in the Era of Domestic Bliss

1. Lee M. Edwards, *Domestic Bliss: Family Life in American Painting, 1840–1910* (Yonkers, N.Y., 1986) is the catalog from that exhibit organized by the Hudson River Museum. The text argues that the strong impulse to memorialize the family comes from tension about its continuation.

2. Theda Skocpol, "Soldiers, Workers, and Mothers: Gendered Identities in Early U.S. Social Policy," *Contention* 2 (1993): 176.

3. David J. Rothman, *The Discovery of the Asylum: Social Order and Disorder in the New Republic* (Boston, 1971), xiv. For an example of how this view continued among historians, see Marcus Wilson Jernegan, "The Development of Poor Relief in Colonial Virginia," *The Social Service Review* 3 (1929): 1: "It is well known, that the humanitarian movement in the second quarter of the nineteenth-century was one of the important social effects of the industrial revolution. That great out-pouring of human sympathy for the unfortunate elements of society . . . continues to bear fruit on an ever increasing scale." Two years later, Jernegan published *Laboring and Dependent Classes in Colonial America, 1607–1783* (Chicago, 1931).

4. Gary B. Nash, "Poverty and Poor Relief in Pre-Revolutionary Philadelphia," *William and Mary Quarterly,* 3d ser., 33 (1976): 3–30; Steven J. Ross, "'Objects of Charity': Poor Relief, Poverty, and the Rise of the Almshouse in Early-Eighteenth-Century New York City," in *Authority and Resistance in Early New York,* ed. William Pencak and Conrad Edick Wright (New York, 1988), 138–72. In Virginia and Maryland localities, about two out of three support payments went to boarding in a different family rather than to direct support to the family to keep it together (ibid., 182); Geoffrey Guest, "The Boarding of the Dependent Poor in Colonial America," *Social Service Review* 63 (1989): 92–112; *Vestry Book of St Paul's Parish, Hanover Co. Virginia 1706–1786,* transcribed and ed. C. G. Chamberlayne (1940; reprint, Richmond, Va., 1989).

5. Joan Lane, *Apprenticeship in England, 1600–1914* (Boulder, Colo., 1996), 14–18; Benjamin Joseph Klebaner, *Public Poor Relief in America, 1790–1860* (New York, 1976), 395–411; Lawrence W. Towner, "The Indenture of Boston's Poor Apprentices: 1734–1805," *Transactions of the Colonial Society of Massachusetts* 43 (1956–63): 417–68; Ruth Wallis Herndon, "Governing the Affairs of the Town: Continuity and Change in Rhode Island, 1750–1800" (Ph.D. diss., American University, 1992), chap. 7; H. Brewer, "Constructing Consent," chap. 6.

6. "Report of the Committee Appointed by the Board of Guardians of the Poor . . . Philadelphia," in H. Brewer, "Constructing Consent," 26.

7. Ibid., 29.

8. [Yates Report] "Report of the Secretary of State in 1824 on the Relief and Settlement of the Poor," reprinted in *Thirty-fourth Annual Report of the New York State Board of*

Charities (1901), in *The Almshouse Experience: Collected Reports*, ed. David J. Rothman (New York, 1971), 1058–59.

9. "Guardians of Poor Philadelphia," 28.

10. Rothman, *Discovery of the Asylum*, 65.

11. [Josiah Quincy Report] "Report of the Committee on the Pauper Laws of this Commonwealth" [1821], in *The Almshouse Experience: Collected Reports*, ed. David J. Rothman (New York, 1971), 7.

12. Yates Report, 952.

13 Ibid.

14. Carole Shammas, "The Space Problem in Early United States Cities," *William and Mary Quarterly*, 3d ser., 57 (2000): 530–34.

15. Yates Report, 942, 1093–94; Margaret Creech, *Three Centuries of Poor Law Administration: A Study of Legislation in Rhode Island* (College Park, Md., 1969), 197.

16. These numbers are based on an analysis of the 197,736 observations in the Minnesota Project's Public Use Sample (hereafter IPUMS) of the 1850 census. The public use sample for the 1850 census shows 0.4 percent of the population as inmates of institutions like poorhouses, prisons, orphanages, and mental institutions, with another 1.8 percent in more voluntary group housing such as boardinghouses, schools, and the military. By 1880, inmates had risen to 0.6 percent, with further increases during the course of the twentieth century taking the number to 1.1 percent. The sampling procedure of these census samples, however, was set up primarily to portray the demographics of private families correctly, so just how well it represents people in group quarters, including inmates, is not clear.

17. Being identified as a pauper and being poor were of course two different things. Also, those in institutions were much more likely to be reported than those on outrelief or being boarded.

18. Joan Underhill Hannon, "Poverty in the Antebellum Northeast: The View from New York State's Poor Relief Rolls," *Journal of Economic History* 44 (1984): 1007–32; L. Lynne Kiesling and Robert A Margo, "Explaining the Rise in Antebellum Pauperism, 1850–1860: New Evidence," *Quarterly Journal of Economics and Finance* 37 (1997): 405–17. A more extensive discussion of institutions appears in chapter 6 of this volume.

19. In 1850, 11 percent of the population was foreign-born, but the foreign-born comprised 32 percent of inmates.

20. Patricia Cline Cohen, *The Murder of Helen Jewett* (New York, 1998).

21. John O'Grady, *Catholic Charities in the United States* (Washington, D.C., 1930), chap. 5.

22. Farley Grubb, "The End of European Immigrant Servitude in the United States: An Economic Analysis of Market Collapse," *Journal of Economic History* 54 (1994): 794–824.

23. Peter J. Coleman, *Debtors and Creditors in America: Insolvency, Imprisonment for Debt, and Bankruptcy, 1607–1900* (Madison, Wis., 1974).

24. Harford County, Maryland, 1776 survey (data set supplied by Steven Ruggles, University of Minnesota); 1850 IPUMS, individual level data, University of Minnesota Census Project.

25. Steinfeld, *Invention of Free Labor,* 180–84.
26. Robert J. Steinfeld, *Coercion, Contract, and Free Labor in the Nineteenth Century* (New York, 2001), chap. 8.
27. Nancy F. Cott, in *Public Vows: A History of Marriage and the Nation* (Cambridge, Mass., 2000), has drawn attention to the way marriage surfaced in national debates. It is also apparent, however, that for changes in power relationships in the nineteenth and early twentieth century, it is to the states rather than to the federal government that one should look.
28. The term *absolute divorce* identifies the type of divorce that today is commonly termed simply *divorce,* as distinguished from *bed and board,* or *limited,* or *mensa et thoro* divorce, terms that describe what today would be called a *legal separation.*
29. Norma Basch, *Framing American Divorce* (Berkeley, 1999); and Hendrik Hartog, *Man and Wife in America: A History* (Cambridge, Mass., 2000), discuss some of these cases.
30. U. S. Commissioner of Labor. *A Report on Marriage and Divorce in the Untied States 1867 to 1886* (Washington, D.C., 1891), 169.
31. Randolph A. Roth, "Spousal Murder in Northern New England, 1776–1865," in *Over the Threshold: Intimate Violence in Early America,* ed. Christine Daniels and Michael V. Kennedy (New York, 1999), 68–69.
32. Martin Schultz, "Two Hundred Years of Divorce in Pennsylvania: Past Trends and Implications for the Future," in *Sociology toward the Year 2000,* ed. Charles Babbitt (Harrisburg, Pa., 1983), 314; Martin Schultz, "Divorce in Early America: Origins and Patterns in Three North Central States," *Sociological Quarterly* 25 (1984): 520; Martin Schultz, "Divorce Patterns in Nineteenth-Century New England," *Journal of Family History* 15 (1990): 105–8.
33. Elizabeth Pleck, *Domestic Tyranny: The Making of American Social Policy against Family Violence from Colonial Times to the Present* (New York, 1987), 55.
34. Schultz, "Divorce in Pennsylvania", 317; Schultz, "Divorce in Early America," 518; Schultz, "Divorce in Nineteenth-Century New England," 106.
35. Carroll D. Wright, *A Report on Marriage and Divorce in the United States, 1867 to 1886,* rev. ed. (Washington, D.C., 1891)), table 3. Divorces between 1867 and 1886 increased 257 percent. The increase in divorces granted to women on the grounds of cruelty, drunkenness, or both increased 395 percent, or almost fourfold. These national statistics include limited divorce decrees as well as absolute. Not included were multiple-grounds divorces that included, along with cruelty and/or drunkenness, also desertion, adultery or some other factor.
36. I have analyzed these acts in detail. See Shammas, "Re-assessing the Married Women's Property Acts," 9–30.
37. Michael Grossberg, in *A Judgment for Solomon: The d'Hauteville Case and Legal Experience in Antebellum America* ([New York, 1996], 52–54), discusses the mixed messages being conveyed in various judgments coming out of the British courts.
38. Grossberg, *Governing the Hearth,* 240–41. Mary Ann Mason, in *From Father's Property to Chidren's Rights: The History of Child Custody in the United States* ([New York, 1994], 60–61), points out that even in this case there was considerable waffling around the issue. In 1830, New York passed a statute allowing mothers to apply for

a writ of habeas corpus to have the court settle custody (*Ahrenfeldt v. Ahrenfeldt; Mercein v. People;* and *People v. Mercein,* the latter case reversing the ruling of the earlier one).

39. Grossberg, *Governing the Hearth,* 244–47, 290–91.

40. "Annual Report of the Board of Education of the State of Connecticut, 1872," in *Children and Youth in America,* ed. Robert H. Bremner et al. (Cambridge, Mass., 1971), 2: 1421.

41. Commissioner of Education, *Report made to the Secretary of the Interior for the Year 1870* (Washington, D.C., 1875), 153.

42. Bremner et al., in *Children and Youth* (2: 1422), excerpt a case in Indiana in 1901 that involves the state ordering a parent to send his child to school. On the truancy, custody, and injury, see *Dumain v. Gwynne,* 92 Mass. 270, (1865); *O'Malia v. Wentworth,* 65 Me. 129 (1876); *Van Heck v. New York Catholic Protectory,* 101 N.Y. 195 (1885); *Reynolds v. Board of Education,* 53 N.Y. 75; and *Rhall v. Board of Education,* 57 N.Y. 977, (1899).

43. The main exception is North Carolina, which established free public education for whites only in 1852.

44. Maris Vinovskis, *The Origins of Public High Schools: A Re-examiniation of the Beverly High School Controversy* (Madison, Wis., 1985); Ward M. McAfee, *Religion, Race, and Reconstruction: The Public School in the Politics of the 1870s* (Albany, 1998). On African American school funding, see J. Morgan Kousser, *Dead End: The Development of Nineteenth-Century Litigation on Racial Discrimination in Schools* (Oxford, 1986).

45. Amy Dru Stanley, *From Bondage to Contract: Wage Labor, Marriage, and the Market in the Age of Slave Emancipation* (New York, 1998); Elizabeth B. Clark, "Matrimonial Bonds: Slavery and Divorce in Nineteenth-Century America," *Law and History Review* 8 (1990).

46 Bardaglio, *Reconstructing the Household,* 117, 120.

47. Nina Baym, *Feminism and American Literary History* (New Brunswick, N.J., 1992), chap. 11.

48. Currier and Ives, *Age of Iron: Man As He Expects to Be . . . after Wife's Emancipation,* and *The Age of Brass or the Triumphs of Woman's Rights* (1869); Edward Clay, *The Fruits of Amalgamation* (1839); E. C. Kellogg and Co., *Seven States of Matrimony* (ca. 1850); David Gilmore Blythe, *The Firecracker* (1859), Duquesne Club, Pittsburgh.

49. Raymond Lee Muncy, *Sex and Marriage in Utopian Communities, Nineteenth-Century America* (Bloomington, Ind., 1973), 127–28.

50. *An American Prophet's Record: The Diaries and Journals of Joseph Smith,* ed. Scott H. Faulring (Salt Lake City, 1989), 4.

51. John L. Brooke, *The Refiner's Fire: The Making of Mormon Cosmology, 1644–1844* (New York, 1994).

52. *George Fox's Journal,* on-line Street Corner Society version of Rufus M. Jones's 1908 edition, chap. 1, paragraph 25, www.strecorsoc.org/gfox/cho7/html.

53. Lawrence Foster, *Religion and Sexuality: Three American Communal Experiments of the Nineteenth Century* (New York, 1981), 174–77.

54. Demographic information from the IPUMS sample of the 1880 Census, Minnesota Project.

55. Robert L. Lively Jr., "Some Sociological Reflections on the Nineteenth-Century British Mission," in *Mormons in Early Victorian Britain*, ed. Richard L. Jensen and Malcolm R. Thorp (Salt Lake City, 1989), 25; Ray Jay Davis, "Law and the Nineteenth-Century British Mormon Migration," in *Mormons in Early Victorian Britain*, ed. Jensen and Thorp, 243–57. The British mission plunged in terms of membership numbers in the mid-1850s, and that affected the numbers available for migration out.

56. Sarah Barringer Gordon, "'The Liberty of Self-Degradation': Polygamy, Woman Suffrage, and Consent in Nineteenth-Century America," *Journal of American History* 83 (1996): 815–47.

57. Foster, *Religion and Sexuality*, 81.

58. John H. Noyes, *The Berean* (1847; reprint, New York, 1969), 17.

59. Foster, *Religion and Sexuality*, 75–122.

60. Albert Brisbane, *The Social Destiny of Man; or, Association and Reorganization of Industry* (1840; reprint, New York, 1968), 5.

61. Raymond Muncy, *Sex and Marriage in Utopian Communities*, 70.

62. Carl J. Guarneri, *The Utopian Alternative: Fourierism in Nineteenth-Century America* (Ithaca, N.Y., 1991), 17–20, 407–12.

63. See for example, how Raymond Muncy, in *Sex and Marriage in Utopian Communities*, explains the place of innovative marriage arrangements in his introduction (1–15).

64. Ann Douglas, *The Feminization of American Culture* (New York, 1977).

65. Nina Baym, *Woman's Fiction: A Guide to Novels by and about Women in America 1820–70*, 2d ed. (Urbana, Ill., 1993; orig. pub. 1978). See also Mary Kelley, *Private Woman, Public Stage: Literary Domesticity in Nineteenth-Century America* (New York, 1984).

66. Gillian Brown, *Domestic Individualism: Imagining Self in Nineteenth-Century America* (Berkeley, 1990).

67. Susanna Rowson, *"Charlotte Temple" and "Lucy Temple"* (New York, 1991; orig. pub. in the United States in 1794 and 1828, respectively).

68. Baym, *Feminism and American Literary History*, 173–75, 183–96.

69. This point was made years ago by William R. Taylor, *Cavalier and Yankee: The Old South and American National Character* (New York, 1961), 162–65.

70. Maria Susanna Cummins, *The Lamplighter*, rev. ed., ed. Nina Baym (New Brunswick, N.J., 1988; orig. pub. 1854). The quotation from Hawthorne appears on page ix.

71. Baym, *Woman's Fiction*, xi.

72. Perhaps the best one-sentence description of the conversation piece is by Sacheverell Sitwell in *Conversation Pieces: A Survey of English Domestic Portraits and their Painters* (London, 1936), 1. He defines it as a picture portraying "definite personalities in their intimate surroundings." Another great lover of material life, Mario Praz, produced an even more impressive collection of conversation pieces in *Conversation Pieces: A Survey of the Informal Group Portrait in Europe and America* (University Park, Pa.,

1971). Another important collection is in Ralph Edwards, *Early Conversation Pictures from the Middle Ages to about 1730: A Study in Origins* (London, 1954).

73. Lovell, in "Reading Eighteenth-Century American Family Portraits," points out that there are very few group portraits in eighteenth-century America; she estimates that there are no more than fifty.

74. In the 130 English domestic conversation pieces collected by Sacheverell Sitwell, mostly from the eighteenth century, only Queen Charlotte (the wife of George the III) appeared in the family domicile surrounded by her children and without her husband. Men appear slightly more often with their children in their own household, despite the fact that they spent less time in the household caring for children.

75. For example, see in Praz, *Conversation Pieces*, plate 46, Frederick Spencer, *Family Group* (1840); and plate 49, Henry F. Darby, *Reverend John Atwood and His Family* (1845, not 1870, as indicated by Praz). See also James Cameron, *Colonel Whiteside's Family*, Hunter Museum of American Art, Chattanooga. This form continued in other parts of the Americas, as can be seen in Antonio Becerra Diaz's 1896 painting of a northern Mexican hacienda owner's family and estate, *Hacendados*, in Metropolitan Museum of Art, *Mexico: Splendors of Thirty Centuries* (New York, 1990), plate 273.

76. *The Blodgett Family* hangs in the Metropolitan Museum of Art, New York, and the other three appear in Praz, *Conversation Pieces*, plates 246, 53, 54.

77. More men portrayed in sumptuous surroundings with a newspaper are Edward Lamson Henry, *Mr. and Mrs. John Bullard* (1872), Hirschl and Adler Galleries; *American Genre Painting in the Victorian Era: Winslow Homer, Eastman Johnson, and their Contemporaries* (New York, 1978), front cover; and Walter Launt Palmer, *Olcott Interior* (1878), in Edwards, *Domestic Bliss*, 40.

78. Other examples are Praz, *Conversation Pieces*, plates 51, 52; George Hollingsworth, *Hollingsworth Family* (ca. 1840), where the artist himself is the miserable head of household; and American School, *Family Group* (ca. 1875). Possibly Johnson's *Warren Family* is a mourning picture, a portrait done in memory of a dead family member.

79. John Koch, *The Edgar W. Garbisch Family* (1955) in Praz, *Conversation Pieces*, plate 249.

80. Edwards, in *Domestic Bliss* (87, 99–100, 139), shows Thomas Hovenden, *Bringing Home the Bride* (1893); William Henry Lippincott, *Infantry in Arms* (1887); and Lippincott's *A Private Rehearsal* (1896). David M. Lubin, *Picturing a Nation* ([New Haven, 1994], 309) contains Hovenden's *Breaking Home Ties* (1890). The Lippincott pictures appear to be actual conversation pieces sans father recycled as genre paintings.

81. The Currier and Ives prints *Home to Thanksgiving* (1867) and *Pioneer's Home* (1867) may be found in Ebert and Ebert, *Old American Prints*, 149–50.

82. Stephen Frank, *Life with Father* (Baltimore, 1998), 39–41.

83. As Barbara Sicherman has indicated in "Reading *Little Women:* The Many Lives of a Text," (in *U.S. History as Women's History*, ed. Linda K. Kerber, Alice Kessler-Harris, and Kathryn Kish Sklar [Chapel Hill, 1995], 255), Alcott and Martha

Finley—the author of the Elsie Dinsmore books—present very different role models to their young female readers. Both role models, though, are strong characters. Sicherman discusses the strict obedience demanded of Elsie, but that is less the point of the series than is Elsie's Christian martyrdom. In these very popular postbellum and early-twentieth-century books, Elsie is the only child of a rich Virginia gentleman who—despite his indulging in behavior that today would bring charges of child abuse—is nevertheless referred to by his daughter as "her own dear sweet Papa." Her mother is dead. Elsie's devotion to her temporal father is only exceeded by her attachment to her Father in heaven. As a good Christian, she is compelled above all to obey God, and this creates constant conflict with her agnostic Papa and with most of the rest of her fashionable extended family. Because she follows the teachings of the Bible, little Elsie is always right and always her father's moral superior. The sadistic treatment meted out to Elsie repels today's reader, but she is meant to be a strong character who upholds the Christian lifestyle in a sinful world.

84. Christopher Reed, *Not at Home: The Suppression of Domesticity in Modern Art and Architecture* (London, 1996).

6. After the War

1. Eric Foner, "Slavery, the Civil War, and Reconstruction," in *The New American History,* rev. ed., ed. Eric Foner (Philadelphia, 1997), 85–106.

2. Claudia Goldin, *Understanding the Gender Gap: An Economic History of American Women* (New York, 1990), chaps. 6, 7; Susan Lehrer, *Origins of Protective Labor Legislation for Women: 1905–1925* (Albany, 1987); Alice Kessler-Harris, *Out To Work: A History of Wage-earning Women in the United States* (New York, 1982); Alice Kessler-Harris, "Designing Women and Old Fools: The Construction of the Social Security Amendments of 1939," in *U.S. History as Women's History: New Feminist Essays,* ed. Linda K. Kerber, Alice Kessler-Harris, and Kathryn Kish Sklar (Chapel Hill, 1995), 87–106; L. Gordon, "Putting Children First," 63–86; Lee J. Alston and Joseph P. Ferrie, *Southern Paternalism and the American Welfare State: Economics, Politics, and Institutions in the South, 1865–1965* (Cambridge, 1999); Alex Lichtenstein, *Twice the Work of Free Labor: The Political Economy of Convict Labor in the New South* (London, 1996); Matthew J. Mancini, *One Dies, Get Another: Convict Leasing in the American South 1866–1928* (Columbia, S.C., 1996); Martha A. Myers, *Race, Labor, and Punishment in the New South* (Columbus, Ohio, 1998); William E. Forbath, *Law and the Shaping of an American Labor Movement* (Cambridge, Mass., 1991).

3. These views are most associated with Peter Laslett and his work with the Cambridge Group, but many family historians and historical sociologists have contributed to this kind of research in the 1970s and 1980s, including Tamara Hareven, Michael Anderson, John Modell, Frank Furstenberg, and Elizabeth Pleck.

4. Steven Ruggles, "The Transformation of American Family Structure," *American Historical Review* 99 (1994): 103–28. Daniel Scott Smith early on identified the changing residential patterns of the elderly in the United States; see his "Life Course, Norms, and the Family System of Older Americans in 1900," *Journal of Family History* 4 (1979): 285–98; and his "Historical Change in the Household

Structure of the Elderly in Economically Developed Countries," in *Aging: Stability and Change in the Family*, ed. Robert W. Fogel, S. B. Keisler, and Ethel Shanas (New York, 1981).

5. Robert V. Wells, in "The Population of England's Colonies in America: Old English or New Americans?" (*Population Studies* 46 [1992]: 85–102), makes transatlantic comparisons but only of the demographic factors of fertility, mortality, and immigration, not of household composition. Information about household size and composition in early America can be found in chapter 8 of his *The Population of the British Colonies in America before 1776* (Princeton, 1975).

6. U.S. Bureau of the Census, *Century of Population Growth: 1790–1900* ([Washington, D.C., 1909], 996–98) shows 7.04 mean household size in 1790, 5.74 if only free persons are counted. Also Harford County, Maryland, 1776 data derived from the two volumes edited by Gaius Marcus Brumbaugh, *Maryland Records: Colonial, Revolutionary, County, and Church* (Baltimore, 1967) and generously supplied in machine readable form by Steven Ruggles, University of Minnesota Project. Maryland data show mean household size of 7.28 persons and 4.93 when restricted to free persons.

7. Steven Ruggles, "The Demography of the Unrelated Individual: 1900–1950" (*Demography* 25 [1988]: 521–36), is an exception, although the analysis is geared toward explaining the rise of single-person households (primary individuals) and showing that it was largely due to an increase of elderly living alone and younger persons postponing marriage. It was not an analysis of those living in group quarters. The article does have valuable information about changes in how the census dealt with college students' place of residence in different years.

8. Daniel Scott Smith, "The Meanings of Family and Household: Change and Continuity in the Mirror of the American Census," *Population and Development Review* 18 (1992): 430, 436–37. Smith discusses the changes. The quotation he cites comes from an article by David Herlihy.

9. Margo Anderson, *A Social History of the Census* (New Haven, 1988), chap. 2.

10. Stem families are those with a parent or parents and a married child. Consequently I added all those whose relation to the head of household was parent or parent-in-law and doubled the proportion indicated by child-in-law to get the percentage of people in a household as part of stem arrangements.

11. Edward Leo Lyman, *Political Deliverance: Utah's Quest for Statehood* (Urbana, Ill., 1986); S. Gordon, "'The Liberty of Self-Degradation,'" 815–47; Joan Smyth Iversen, *The Anti-Polygamy Controversy in U.S. Women's Movements, 1880–1925* (New York, 1997).

12. The 1850 census shows a big decline from the colonial period in the proportion of native-born youth from ages seventeen to twenty-six in the households of nonrelatives. See chapter five in this volume.

13. U.S. Bureau of the Census, *Benevolent Institutions 1904* (Washington, D.C., 1905), 56–305; Timothy A. Hacsi, *Second Home: Orphan Asylums and Poor Families in America* (Cambridge, Mass., 1997), 52; Matthew Crenson, *Building the Invisible Orphanage: A Prehistory of the American Welfare System* (Cambridge, Mass, 1998), 42.

14. Joan Hannon, "Shutting Down Welfare: Two Cases from America's Past," *Quarterly Review of Economics and Finance* (1997): 424

15. Quoted in Michael B. Katz, *In the Shadow of the Poorhouse: A Social History of Welfare in America*, rev. ed. (New York, 1996), 111.

16. IPUMS data sets, 1850, 1880, 1910 general samples, University of Minnesota Project.

17. Inmates include those residing in correctional facilities, mental asylums, hospitals, old age homes, orphanages, and poorhouses. The "other group quarter" category includes those living in military barracks, school dormitories, rooming houses, religious orders, and worksites. The latter also includes in some surveys those congregations of over twenty people living together without a reason being apparent. Most of these appear also to be in large rooming-house situations.

18. The 1990 rise can be attributed to a rekindling of enthusiasm for imprisoning drug offenders and the increase in the survival rates of the very elderly.

19. Katz, *Shadow of the Poorhouse*, 109–11; Susan Tiffin, *In Whose Best Interest? Child Welfare Reform in the Progressive Era* (Westport, Conn., 1982), chap. 4; Walter I. Trattner, *From Poor Law to Welfare State: A History of Social Welfare in America*, 6th ed. (New York, 1999), chap. 6.

20. (1872; reprint, Washington D.C., National Association of Social Workers, 1973), 225. His orphan trains are studied in Miriam Z. Langsam, *Children West: A History of the Placing-Out System of the New York Children's Aid Society, 1853–1890* (Madison, Wis., 1964). He is discussed in David J. Rothman, *The Discovery of the Asylum: Social Order and Disorder in the New Republic* (Boston, 1971), 259–60; Thomas Bender, *Toward an Urban Vision: Ideas and Institutions in Nineteenth-Century America* (Lexington, Ky., 1975), chap. 6; Tiffin, *In Whose Best Interest?*, 88–92, 190; Katz, *Shadow of the Poorhouse*, 110–11, Crenson, *Invisible Orphanage*, 63.

21. Lori D. Ginzberg, *Women and the Work of Benevolence* (New Haven, 1990). Crenson, *Invisible Orphanage*, 32–33, and chap. 7.

22. Crenson, *Invisible Orphanage*, 95

23. E. Wayne Carp, *Family Matters: Secrecy and Disclosure in the History of Adoption* (Cambridge, Mass., 1998), 11.

24. Katz, *Shadow of Poorhouse*, 117.

25. (New York, 1894), 174–75, 223–24.

26. Folks, *Care of Destitute, Neglected and Delinquent Children*, 120–21, 189.

27. Robyn Muncy, *Creating a Female Dominion in American Reform.*

28. Crenson, *Invisible Orphanage*, has a full account of this conference in chaps. 1 and 10.

29. Theda Skocpol, *Protecting Soldiers and Mothers* (Cambridge, Mass., 1992), chap. 8; Kathryn Kish Sklar, "The Historical Foundations of Women's Power in the Creation of the American Welfare State, 1830–1930," in *Mothers of a New World: Maternalist Politics and the Origins of Welfare States*, ed. Seth Koven and Sonya Michel (New York, 1993), 43–93; Molly Ladd-Taylor, *Mother-Work: Women, Child Welfare and the State, 1890–1930* (Urbana, Ill., 1994); Linda Gordon, *Pitied But Not Entitled: Single Mothers and the History of Welfare 1890–1935* (New York, 1994); Kessler-Harris, "Designing Women and Old Fools," 87–106.

30. Hyman Bogen, *The Luckiest Orphans: A History of the Hebrew Orphan Asylum of New York* (Urbana, Ill., 1992); Marilyn Irvin Holt, *The Orphan Trains: Placing Out in America* (Lincoln, Nebr., 1992); Nurith Zmora, *Orphanages Reconsidered: Child Care Institutions in Progressive Era Baltimore* (Philadelphia, 1994); Kenneth Cmiel, *A*

Home of Another Kind: One Chicago Orphanage and the Tangle of Child Welfare (Chicago, 1995); Dorothy M. Brown and Elizabeth Mckeown, *The Poor Belong to Us: Catholic Charities and American Welfare* (Cambridge, Mass., 1997); Hacsi, *Second Home;* Crenson, *Invisible Orphanage;* Linda Gordon, *The Great Arizona Orphan Abduction* (Cambridge, Mass., 1999); Maureen Fitzgerald, "Irish-Catholic Nuns and the Development of New York City's Welfare System, 1840–1900" (Ph.D. diss., University of Wisconsin–Madison, 1992).

31. Hacsi, in *Second Home* (53), had collected the numbers and sizes from the census reports.

32. See chapter 2 of this volume.

33. In *Invisible Orphanage* (313–17), an otherwise very valuable book on child welfare agencies and asylums, Crenson takes the reformers' analysis at face value and assumes the placing-out system and the payment for young children unable to work was an innovation of the period.

34. Brown and Mckeown, *Poor Belong to Us*, 5, 23, 87; Fitzgerald, "Irish-Catholic Nuns"; Crenson, *Invisible Orphanage*, 73–93, 100–12; Bogen, *Luckiest Orphans*.

35. Reprinted in Brace, *Dangerous Classes*, 90–93.

36. Ibid., 28. See Brown and McKeown, *Catholic Charities*, on the link between political change, anti-Catholicism, and anti-institutionalism.

37. Brace, *Dangerous Classes*, 76.

38. J. G. A. Pocock, in *Barbarism and Religion* (vol. 2 of *Narratives of Civil Government* [Cambridge, 1999]), defines the "enlightened" narratives; see esp. 370–71.

39. Warner, in *American Charities* (338), quotes her on the irony of New York giving support to private institutions while public ones are crumbling.

40. State Board member Elizabeth Glendower Evans used the phrase "downing R.C. aggression" in recalling in 1904 some battles waged by Elizabeth Cabot Putnam twenty years earlier. Quoted in Crenson, *Invisible Orphanage*, 192.

41. David Wallace Adams, *Education for Extinction: American Indians and the Boarding School Experience, 1875–1928* (Lawrence, Kans., 1995), 66–72, 164–73, 320. Indian population was at a nadir in 1900, about 250,000. If roughly a quarter, or 62,500, were of boarding-school age—roughly six to sixteen—then 33.8 percent were in these boarding schools. Many fewer were in reservation or public school day schools in this period.

42. Ward M. McAfee, in *Religion, Race, and Reconstruction: The Public School in the Politics of the 1870s* (Albany, 1998), has argued that public schooling became a national crusade of the Republican Party.

43. McAfee, in *Religion, Race, Reconstruction,* reprints many of these, although not the one featured in figure 17.

44. David P. Baker, "Schooling All the Masses: Reconsidering the Origins of American Schooling in the Post-bellum Era," *Sociology of Education* 72 (1999): 197–215, table 1.

45. U.S. Bureau of the Census, *Benevolent Institutions: 1904* (Washington, D.C., 1905), 15–18.

46. From IPUMS data 1880: 2.6 percent with employer or boarding with family versus 0.4 percent in an institution, while in 1910 the comparable numbers were 1.5 and 0.7 percent.

47. Roosevelt, using the 1904 report, claimed that 93,000 were in orphanages/children's homes, 25,000 were in reformatories, and an estimated 50,000 were placed in homes as foster children or adoptees (U.S. Senate, *Proceedings of the Conference on the Care of Dependent Children,* 60th Cong., 2d sess., Doc. 271 [Washington, D.C., 1909], 5).

48. Herbert G. Gutman, *The Black Family in Slavery and Freedom, 1750–1925* (New York, 1976), 403–10; Donald G. Nieman, *To Set the Law in Motion: The Freedmen's Bureau and the Legal Rights of Blacks, 1865–1868* (New York, 1979), 76–81, 92–94; Laura F. Edwards, *Gendered Strife and Confusion: The Political Culture of Reconstruction* (Ithaca, N.Y., 1992), chap. 1; Mary J. Farmer, "Because They are Women: Gender and the Virginia Freedmen's Bureau's 'War on Dependency,'" in *The Freedmen's Bureau and Reconstruction,* ed. Paul A. Cimbala and Randall M. Miller (New York, 1999), 174–77; Carolyn M. Moehling, "Family Structure, School Attendance, and Child Labor in the American South in 1910" (paper presented at the All-U.C. Group in Economic History Meeting, UCLA, 29 April 2000, table 1).

49. Linda Gordon, "Black and White Visions of Welfare: Women's Welfare Activism, 1890–1945," *Journal of American History* 78 (1991).

50. U.S. Senate, *Proceedings, Care of Dependent Children,* 20–31.

7. The Troublesome Alternatives

1. James Axtell, *Indian Peoples of Eastern America* (New York, 1981), 7.

2. The English version appears as Father Joseph-François Lafitau, *Customs of the American Indians Compared with the Customs of Primitive Times,* 2 vols., ed. and trans. William N. Fenton and Elizabeth L. Moore (Toronto, 1974).

3. Ibid., 335–36; A. R. Radcliffe-Brown and Daryll Forde, eds., *African Systems of Kinship and Marriage* (London, 1950), 8.

4. John Millar, *Observations Concerning the Distinction of Ranks in Society,* 2d ed. (London, 1773), chap. 1.

5. Ibid., 41. In the 1806 edition, which appeared under the title *The Origin of the Distinction of Ranks,* Millar associates this family prominence with the Amazon stories (51).

6. Trautmann, *Morgan and the Invention of Kinship.*

7. David F. Aberle, "Matrilineal Descent in Cross-cultural Perspective," in *Matrilineal Kinship,* ed. David M. Schneider and Kathleen Gough (Berkeley, 1961), 663. The Murdock *World Ethnographic Sample* was used. Out of 565 cultures, 248 were patrilineal, 84 matrilineal, 28 duolineal, and 204 bilateral. One was unclassifiable.

8. I am basing this statement on the bibliography contained in E. Franklin Frazier's 1957 edition of *The Negro in the United States* ([New York, 1957], 718–52) and on the discussion in Donna L. Franklin's recent *Ensuring Inequality: The Structural Transformation of the African-American Family* (New York, 1997), chap. 1.

9. W. E. Burghardt Du Bois, *The Negro American Family* (Atlanta, 1909), and E. Franklin Frazier, *The Negro Family in the United States* (Chicago, 1939). More recently on the Africa versus slavery explanations, see Claire Robertson, "Africa into the Americas? Slavery and Women, the Family, and the Gender Division of Labor," in *More than Chattel: Black Women and Slavery in the Americas,* ed. David Barry Gaspar and Darlene Clark Hine (Bloomington, Ind.,), 1–40; and Steven Ruggles, "The Origins

of African-American Family Structure," *American Sociological Review* 59 (1994): 136–37. Ruggles's article concisely summarizes the various positions in the public policy literature since Daniel P. Moynihan's *The Negro Family: The Case for National Action* (Washington, D.C., 1965).

10. United Nations, *The World's Women, 1970–1990* (New York, 1991).

11. Ann Varley, "Women Heading Households: Some More Equal than Others?" *World Development* 24 (1996): 505–20; Marida Hollos, "Why is It Difficult to Take a Census in Nigeria? The Problem of Indigenous Conceptions of Households," *Historical Methods* 25 (1992): 12–19. The United States census has also had problems with accommodating American Indian lineage arrangements into its concept of household census. See Nancy Shoemaker, "The Census as Civilizer: American Indian Household Structure in the 1900 and 1910 U.S. Censuses," *Historical Methods* 25 (1992): 4–11. On undercounting single mothers in Latin America, see Nancy Folbre, *Who Pays for the Kids? Gender and the Structures of Constraint* (London, 1994), chap. 6.

12. United Nations, *World's Women, 1970–1990*, 17–18; Varley, "Women Heading Households," 308.

13. For an economic analysis of the broader issues involved in family policy, see Folbre, *Who Pays for the Kids?*, chap. 7.

14. Ibid., 140–43.

15. Franklin, *Ensuring Inequality*, chaps. 2–8.

16. U.S. Bureau of the Census, *Statistical Abstract of the United States: 1999* (Washington, D.C., 1999), 222.

17. See appendix 2. In that table the mean household size for 1890 is shown as slightly higher than the 4.86 for 1880, but that rise is due to the use of public use samples in 1880 and the full census numbers for 1890. Using the full census count produces a mean household size of 5.04 (U.S. Bureau of the Census, *Historical Statistics of the United States: Colonial Times to 1970* [Washington, D.C., 1975], 41).

18. Three of the most consulted comprehensive histories of the American family are Calhoun, *Social History of the American Family;* Carl N. Degler, *At Odds: Women and the Family in America from the Revolution to the Present* (New York, 1980); and Mintz and Kellogg, *Domestic Revolutions.*

19. Shammas, Salmon, and Dahlin, *Inheritance in America.*

INDEX